A TRAILS BOOKS GUIDE

# BIKING ILLINOIS

## 60 GREAT ROAD AND TRAIL RIDES

DAVID JOHNSEN

Trails Books
Madison, Wisconsin

Library of Congress Control Number: 2005908955
ISBN: 1-931599-64-5

Editor: Mark Knickelbine
Photos: David Johnsen
Designer: Kathie Campbell
Maps: Magellan Mapping Company

Printed in the United States of America by Sheridan Books

11 10 09 08 07 06     6 5 4 3 2 1

Trails Books, a division of Big Earth Publishing
923 Williamson Street
Madison, WI 53703
www.trailsbooks.com

# BIKING ILLINOIS

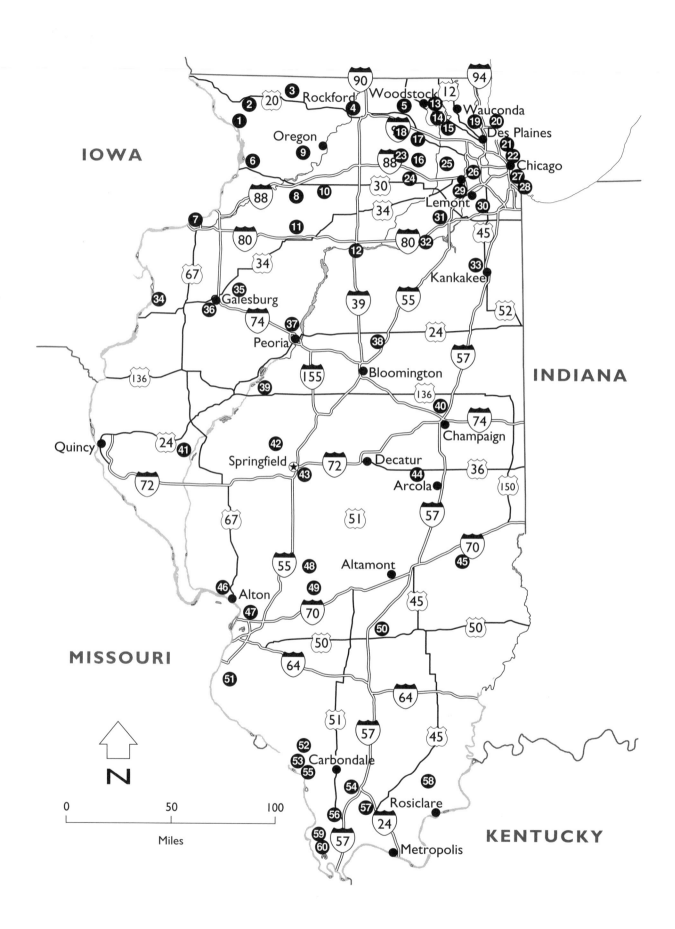

# CONTENTS

## CENTRAL

## SOUTH

# PREFACE

As a lifelong Illinoisan, I thought I knew my home state well. After all, I had visited every county at least once, and I had bicycled through a quarter of them. I had driven Route 66 and the Lincoln Highway, and I had pedaled the entire Grand Illinois Trail. Once I began scouting rides for this book, however, I discovered how little I knew about some regions of the state, especially southernmost Illinois. I had never hiked the awesome Observation Trail at the Garden of the Gods nor squeezed between the Makanda sandstone walls of Giant City State Park.

In contrast to the rapidly changing Chicago area, parts of rural Illinois seem lost in a time warp. Villages like Maeystown appear untouched by the 20th century, much less the 21st. The Moonshine Store not only serves great burgers, but the owners trust you to take your food outside to eat and come back inside to pay afterward.

Even as I returned to areas I had visited before, I found new things. I explored the reconstructed Apple River Fort in Elizabeth. In Fulton I discovered Heritage Canyon, the fruit of one couple's dedication to preserving our pioneer past. Closer to home there were surprises too, such as Kline Creek Farm. Some favorite places proved to be better seen by bike. At a cycling pace, I could fully appreciate the majestic bluffs along the Mississippi River between Alton and Grafton. Along Sheridan Road in the tony North Shore suburbs of Chicago, I could stop to look at fabulous homes without fretting over where to park.

Due in part to the stealth of cycling, I had unexpected wildlife encounters. On the Hickory Creek Trail in southwest suburban Chicago, I watched a doe and her fawn pause to drink from the creek. Near Stephen A. Forbes State Park, I yielded to a flock of wild turkeys walking across the road. The beauty and diversity of Illinois' vegetation was evident as well. On the Great Western Trail between Saint Charles and Sycamore, I saw lush blooms of spring wildflowers. At Horseshoe Lake Conservation Area, I could have sworn I was in a Louisiana bayou among the tupelo and cypress trees.

Biking has always given me cherished memories, and these rides were no exception. I watched an exciting bike race in Hillsboro. Having ridden the course earlier, I could feel their suffering as they climbed Major Hill. At Lincoln's New Salem, I enjoyed the warmth of a fire with volunteers in 1830s dress in a reconstructed tavern. Near Giant City State Park, I felt the exhilarating rush of a 40-mph descent—until my notepad fluttered out of my handlebar bag and I had to stop to retrieve it.

From friendly historians to quirky trail runners, I met great people everywhere. Some wondered why I was riding a bike in the December cold, while others looked at me with a mix of pity and disbelief as I strapped on my helmet in 95-degree heat. All offered encouragement and advice about the road or trail ahead. Restaurants served up tasty surprises along the way too. To fuel my rides, I had exceptional calzones in Moline, milkshakes in Fulton, blueberry pancakes in West Frankfort, and barbecue in Marion.

Though great biking was obviously my first criterion for including a ride in this book, I sought interesting locales as well. Each ride is an invitation to explore, absorb, and remember the sights, history, and people of an area or town. As a mode of travel, bicycling has much to offer. The scenery isn't blurred as when viewed from a car. You can easily pull off the road or trail to look around, take pictures, or listen to songbirds in the woods. And maybe best of all, you get some exercise so you won't feel so guilty about those milkshakes.

That's enough about my memories. Now it's time to make your own. Let's go for a ride.

# ACKNOWLEDGEMENTS

At first blush, this sounded like an easy assignment: Ride your bike and write about it. Of course, it was more complicated than that. I could handle the pedaling by myself, but I needed some help for the rest.

Thank you to everyone who visited Dave's Bicycling Pages (www.djrider.com) over the years. You gave me the inspiration and confidence to write this book. Thanks also to the Illinois Department of Natural Resources for launching the GIT Trail Blazer program. Completing the Grand Illinois Trail was a great introduction to exploring this state by bicycle.

The Illinois Department of Transportation provided maps that were invaluable in scouting potential routes. Thanks to Chris Strout for giving me directions for Ride 13 and half of Ride 42, as well as telling me about the Hillsboro-Roubaix race (Ride 48). The staffs of countless tourism bureaus, state parks, and historic sites merit thanks for giving me the background information that makes these rides not just fun but interesting and educational.

Thanks to the people at Trails Books for shepherding me and my work through the publication process. My editor, Mark Knickelbine, answered lots of questions and improved the consistency and quality of this book. Former editor Stan Stoga recruited me to write this book at precisely the moment when I was changing careers to become a freelance writer.

And of course, thanks to my wife, Judy, for holding down the fort during the weeks I was away and putting up with me in general. By the way, Ride 27 goes past the place where we met (incidentally, neither of us was on a bike). Finally, thanks to Teddy and Rosco for always greeting me with wagging tails when I returned from my two-wheeled adventures. We'll miss you, Teddy.

Before we get into the rides themselves, here's a little background information about Illinois and some tips about the diverse conditions it can throw at bicyclists. I hope the information will deepen your appreciation of this richly endowed state and of the rides you'll find yourself enjoying throughout its length and breadth.

**Visit the Chicago Botanic Garden by bike to save the parking fee.**

The first thing you will learn by riding a bicycle in Illinois: It's not all flat. A lot of people have an impression of our state as a big pancake with nary a pat of butter to enliven its profile. Maybe it's because they only experience Chicago, where a highway overpass qualifies as a hill. Or perhaps it's because of our nickname, the Prairie State, which evokes the image of grasslands stretching to the horizon. Or maybe it is because any state that grows so much corn and soybeans must be flat, right?

There is no easier way to find a hill than to ride a bike. The road doesn't have to turn very far upward before you begin to feel it in your legs and your lungs.

Obviously, Illinois doesn't have any mountains. In fact, the difference between the highest point in the state (Charles Mound) and the lowest point (Fort Defiance Point) is less than one thousand feet. There are, however, plenty of hills. You won't find a climb of several thousand feet here, but you can do several thousand feet of climbing a couple hundred feet at a time. In fact, one could argue that a series of steep, rolling hills presents a different challenge than the long inclines of the Rockies because you can't settle into one steady rhythm.

At this point, some readers may wonder if I crashed my bike and landed on my head before I wrote this. Allow me to remind them of a few geological factors:

• **The Driftless Area** – When the glaciers were reshaping the landscape of Illinois, they missed a spot. Northwestern Illinois, particularly Jo Daviess County, is one of the most rugged and beautiful areas in the state. Not surprisingly, it makes for some challenging cycling.

• **Rivers** – Illinois is a land of many rivers, and those waterways have carved some impressive valleys over the millennia. It might get boring after a while, but you could get quite a workout just going up and down a road out of a deep river valley.

• **Ancient mountains** – Southernmost Illinois has plenty of hills, including the Illinois Ozarks in the far southwest and the Shawnee Hills in the rest of the south. The glaciers stopped short of these ranges. They are very old—the Shawnee Hills are twice the age of the Rocky Mountains—and they used to be much taller.

Of course, there is plenty of flat riding in Illinois. The glaciers smoothed out the vast majority of the state. There are a few rides in this book where you might measure elevation change in inches. However, flatness has its benefits, and one is that the lack of natural obstacles makes it easier to develop a good road network. Most of Illinois was surveyed into townships made up of square-mile sections. Most areas outside northwestern and southernmost Illinois have a system of "section roads." This means there is a straight road every mile, creating a full grid of cycling opportunities. Except where rivers interfere, you can usually avoid busy highways by finding a parallel, low-traffic road just a mile or two away. Some counties are better than

others regarding how those roads are surfaced, though. For any long ride in unfamiliar territory, the Illinois state bicycling maps are a good resource, and best of all, they are free for the asking. Write to:

Illinois Department of Transportation
Map Sales – Room 121
2300 South Dirksen Parkway
Springfield, IL 62764

You can also view and order them online at www.dot.state.il.us/bikemap/bikehome.htm.

**Racers dig deep while climbing Major Hill in Hillsboro.**

Illinois ranks second in railroad miles to Texas, and Chicago is still a major hub in the national rail system. With so many tracks in the state, it comes as no surprise that hundreds of miles have been abandoned and converted into trails over the last forty years. The Illinois Prairie Path was one of the first rails-to-trails conversions in the country, and it inspired many others. Northern Illinois also has two long, defunct canals, the Illinois & Michigan and the Hennepin, whose towpaths have been remade into trails that stretch almost from the Mississippi River to Lake Michigan.

The Grand Illinois Trail (GIT) is a collection of trails forming a giant loop around the northern quarter of the state. This route of more than 500 miles is well represented in this book, albeit in bite-sized portions. If you like what you see, you may be inspired to tour the entire trail. If you do, either piecemeal or all at once, you can earn a certificate and a T-shirt as a GIT Trail Blazer. Call the Illinois Department of Natural Resources at (217) 782-3715 or e-mail greenway@dnrmail.state.il.us for details about this program. For GIT cue sheets, visit www. bikegit.org.

Illinois is nearly 400 miles from top to bottom, and

**Don't let the scenery distract you from potential hazards.**

the climate difference is noticeable. Northern cyclists who are getting cabin fever (or stationary bike fever) in late winter should consider a weekend getaway to southern-most Illinois.

Outside of northeastern Illinois, the low-traffic roads preferred by cyclists are often paved with a technique called chip seal. First a coat of tar is sprayed on the roadbed. Then rock chips are spread across the road, making it similar to gravel. The weight of traffic eventually forces the chips into the tar, which holds them in place. Chip seal presents many challenges to cyclists. The rural road rides in this book could be great or miserable depending on how recently the county or township applied a fresh surface to the road. Fresh chip seal is hardly better than a gravel road. Middle-aged chip seal, on the other hand, can be as smooth as as-phalt, giving you no trouble at all. Old chip seal is black with tar on its surface. This is fine in cooler months, but in the summer heat, the tar makes a crackling sound as it sticks to your tires. Riding over loose chips can even form a chip-seal surface on your tire. Regardless of the age of the surface, chip-seal roads tend to have loose chips at inter-sections, so be attentive.

## GETTING READY TO RIDE

### Riding Safely

Entire books have been written about how to ride and interact with traffic, but here are a few general tips for safe cycling:
• **Pay attention.** Whether you are on road or trail, be aware of what is going on around you.
• **Obey traffic laws.** Some cyclists think laws and traffic controls don't apply to them. Running stop signs and stoplights is a good way to get into an accident, and it doesn't exactly endear us to motorists.
• **Always ride with traffic.** This means you should be on the right side of the road. Statistics show that the argu-ment that it is safer to see cars coming toward you does-n't hold water.
• **Be predictable.** Give motorists time to react to what you are going to do. Don't suddenly dart across traffic.
• **When railroad tracks cross the road or path**

diagonally, turn to cross them perpendicularly to avoid getting a tire stuck. Similarly, watch out for sewer grates that can swallow a bike tire.
• **On streets with parallel parking,** ride far enough from the parked cars so that you won't be struck by an opening door. Also, ride in a straight line rather than weaving around parked cars.

About half of the rides in this book use recreational trails. While they keep you away from auto traffic, there is still potential for accidents. Here are some additional recommendations for trails:
• **Respect other trail users.** Most "bike trails" are really "multiuse paths." Yield to horses and pedestrians.
• **Ride to the right and pass on the left.** Announce your intention by calling out, "On your left," but be prepared for a surprised trail user to move the wrong way.
• **Watch your speed.** The trail is no place for hard training. If you want to ride fast, stay on the roads.
• **At street crossings,** keep an eye out for barricades intended to stop motor vehicles from using the path. Although taller posts are now standard, some older trails have short blocks that are not as easily seen.
• **If you want to take a break,** pull over to the side before stopping, just like you would on the road.
• **Keep in mind that most trails close after sunset.** Sometimes parking lot gates are locked then too. Plan accordingly.
• **Trails are a great place to introduce kids to longer rides once they have mastered riding around the block.** Be sure to teach them to follow laws and trail etiquette. Lead by example—wear a helmet, keep to the right, and obey traffic signs.

### Equipment

Almost any bike can handle the rides in this book. A triple chain ring is recommended for rides with a high sweat factor, if only for the sake of your knees. Generally you will be more comfortable with tires slightly wider than the 700 x 23s that come with most road bikes, especially on rougher stone paths and recently chip-sealed roads.

Always carry a mini-pump, a patch kit, and a spare tube. Pushing a bike home with a flat tire is no fun. A compact multitool with Allen wrenches can come in handy too. There are many ways to carry these things, ranging from a tiny bag that hides under your bike seat to a larger pack that sits atop a rear rack. Racers tend to go for the littlest bags, while the former Boy Scouts among us who like to be prepared favor a pack that can hold a jacket, tools, snacks, and an extra bottle of water.

Speaking of water, make sure you have enough. Outside of cities and suburbs, finding a place to replen-ish can be difficult, especially since cyclists tend to eschew the busier highways. Most of the rides in this book men-tion if and where stores and restaurants are available.

If you might be out after dark, remember that Illinois law requires a headlight visible for at least 500 feet and a red rear reflector visible for up to 600 feet. Brightly colored, reflective clothing is recommended, as is a taillight.

Equipment to leave at home: earphones. Whether you are on the trail or the road, you need to hear what is going on around you.

Give your bike a quick once-over at the start of your ride. It's better to discover a problem in the parking lot than in the middle of a 40-mph descent. Check your tires for air, test your brakes, and make sure your chain is lubricated.

## Clothing

You can wear almost anything to ride. Some people favor the expensive jerseys and shorts that their favorite pro riders wear, but others prefer a cotton T-shirt and a pair of blue jeans or cutoffs. Wool and synthetic fabrics wick moisture away from your skin, keeping you warmer and drier than cotton.

Cycling shorts can make riding easier on your sensitive parts. Creams such as Chamois Butt'r can help prevent chafing too. On the other hand, spandex shorts stand out in a crowd. If you plan to blend in with the regulars at restaurants and stores, you might want to try baggy shorts. Popular with mountain bikers, these shorts look more like ordinary attire on the outside, but with a chamois inside.

If it is chilly, dress in multiple layers. You may be cold when you start, but you could be sweating after 10 minutes. Then you can just peel away a layer and keep going.

Illinois law does not require you to wear a helmet, but it is a good idea. Whether you are on road or trail, accidents happen, and a cracked helmet is far better than a cracked skull. Also, make sure your helmet fits properly, and don't tilt it back on your head.

## USING THIS BOOK

Rides are grouped by region starting in the northwest and ending at the southern tip of the state. The distance given is always round-trip. Many of these rides are out-and-back, so you can make them any length you desire. If you want to do longer rides, many of the loops are much different when ridden in the opposite direction. Pedaling time is just a guess for a casual rider; a fit rider can certainly go faster, while someone who stops to smell the roses could take longer. With experience you'll be able to make your own estimate based on distance, terrain, and sweat factor. For terrain, keep in mind that this is judged by Illinois standards. A hilly ride here is not like a hilly ride in Colorado or West Virginia. Likewise, what is described as a "long climb" may only be half a mile, which is long in Illinois. When using this book's maps, keep in mind that some counties are better about posting route shields on county highways than others. It is safer to look for road names than county highway numbers.

Finally, visit www.bikingillinois.com to get updates and share your experiences.

**Adventure awaits on the state trails of Illinois.**

# RIDE 1
## Hellacious Hills of Hanover

**Location:** Jo Daviess County between Hanover and Galena
**Distance:** 28.5 miles
**Pedaling time:** 2.5–3.5 hours
**Surface:** Paved and chip-seal roads
**Terrain:** Very hilly
**Sweat factor:** High
**Trailhead:** Corner of Jefferson Street and Washington Street, Hanover

Hanover bills itself as the "Mallard Capital of the World" (no pun intended) thanks to its Whistling Wings Duck Hatchery. Whistling Wings started with a backyard incubator in 1954 and now raises more than 200,000 mallard ducks every year. Most go into the wild, but some are sold to restaurants. The town's big celebration is Mallardfest in the fall, which features the usual combination of food, games, entertainment, and fireworks. Far less touristy than Galena up the road, Hanover offers the same challenging riding without the crowds.

Park your car on a side street in downtown Hanover. The spaces on State Highway 84 have a two-hour time limit, and you are unlikely to finish this ride so quickly. Begin at the west end of downtown where Highway 84 turns north. This highway has some traffic, but the shoulders are paved and you won't be on it for long. The large Invensys factory to the west was built in the 1920s as a woolen mill. Cross the Apple River, then go over a hill. Angle left on Blackjack Road at 0.3 mile following the "ski area" sign. Don't take the 90-degree left at this intersection—you are on the right road if you pass a mini-storage facility. Blackjack Road goes generally uphill from town, getting steeper at 1.4 miles. Go past Rodden Road, which is gravel here. Every time you think you have reached the crest, there is still more climbing ahead. In fact, you still haven't reached the top at 3.4 miles where you turn right on Saw Mill Road. In spite of the name, you are more likely to encounter gravel trucks than lumber trucks here.

**Ouch! This climb is going to hurt!**

Go down a long hill and negotiate a couple of sharp turns.

Turn left on Rodden Road at 4.9 miles, heading uphill. At the top of the hill, you can see a road stretching far into the distance, but it is gravel so you won't be following it. Instead, curve sharply to the left at 5.4 miles, followed by a sharp right to go north again. An old steel bridge with wooden planks crosses Irish Hollow Creek at 6.7 miles. Shortly after, keep left to turn onto Irish Hollow Road. This road gives you a break from the big hills, at least for a while. At 8.4 miles on the left are the remains of Buzzard Gulch, which looks like a former "Old West"-style roadside tourist attraction. When the road crosses over Irish Hollow Creek at 9.1 miles, the easy part of your ride is over. After a half-mile climb, the road goes up and down repeatedly with some steep climbs. Keep right at the Y intersection with Cemetery Road at 11.2 miles. A steep, curvy descent of 0.6 mile follows, and then the terrain gets easier until another half-mile-long, occasionally steep climb begins at 13.6 miles. After yielding at Rocky Hill Road, curve to the right to stay on Irish Hollow Road. This road ends at 15 miles.

Turn left on Blackjack Road and follow it all the way back to Hanover. Keep left when the road forks at Pilot Knob Road (15.4 miles). The road goes mostly downhill for the next couple of miles, passing Ochs Tree Farm and Hart John Road on the way. After crossing the unlabeled and ominously named Smallpox Creek, the road goes up a bit, and then you are into rolling hills for a while. At 17.6 miles, the "No Trespassing" signs and piles of stone are evidence of a quarry or possibly a mining operation. Are you tired yet? The real fun begins at 19.8 miles as the road heads upward again. A "15% grade" sign at 20.2 miles is a forecast for pain. After reaching the crest at 20.9 miles, there is still a fair bit of climbing along the ridge. These rolling hills seem to go up more than down. There is a sign for the Iris and Jack Witkowsky State Wildlife Area at 22.7 miles, and several parking areas follow. You finally run out of climbing just before you pass Saw Mill Road at 25.2 miles. The descent begins in earnest at 26.7 miles, and you can just about coast all the way back to Hanover from here. Turn right on Highway 84 at the stop sign, go up one last hill (nothing compared to what you've been through), cross the Apple River, and finish at 28.5 miles.

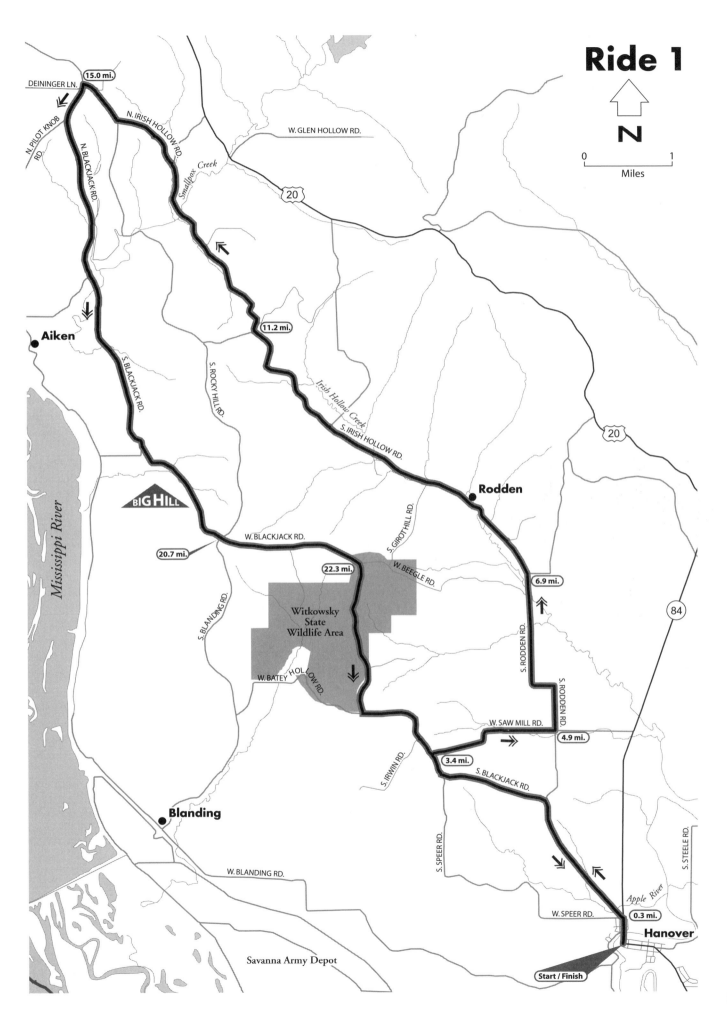

# Ride 1

N

0       1
Miles

DEININGER LN.

15.0 mi.

N. PILOT KNOB RD.

N. IRISH HOLLOW RD.

W. GLEN HOLLOW RD.

N. BLACKJACK RD.

Smallpox Creek

20

**Aiken**

S. BLACKJACK RD.

11.2 mi.

S. ROCKY HILL RD.

Irish Hollow Creek

S. IRISH HOLLOW RD.

**Rodden**

20

BIG HILL

W. BLACKJACK RD.

20.7 mi.

S. GIROT HILL RD.

W. BEEGLE RD.

22.3 mi.

6.9 mi.

84

S. BLANDING RD.

Witkowsky State Wildlife Area

S. RODDEN RD.

S. RODDEN RD.

W. BATEY HOLLOW RD.

W. SAW MILL RD.

4.9 mi.

3.4 mi.

S. IRWIN RD.

S. BLACKJACK RD.

Mississippi River

**Blanding**

S. SPEER RD.

S. STEELE RD.

W. BLANDING RD.

Apple River

W. SPEER RD.

0.3 mi.

**Hanover**

Savanna Army Depot

**Start / Finish**

5

# RIDE 2
## Are You in Shape for Schapville?

**Location:** Jo Daviess County north of Elizabeth
**Distance:** 30.2 miles
**Pedaling time:** 2.5–3.5 hours
**Surface:** Paved and chip-seal roads
**Terrain:** Very hilly
**Sweat factor:** High
**Trailhead:** Apple River Fort Interpretive Center, Elizabeth

### Apple River Fort

**The interpretive center features displays about the history of the fort and the Black Hawk War, including a 15-minute video. Perhaps more important to cyclists, it has indoor restrooms and water, plus a pop machine outside in back. You can bicycle up to the fort, which makes a nice little warm-up or cool-down. The fort contains several authentically rebuilt and furnished buildings. The site is open Wednesday–Sunday from 9 to 5 in the summer and 9 to 4 in the winter. Throughout the year, special events at the fort make history come alive. Visit www.appleriverfort.org or call (815) 858-2028 for more details.**

The Black Hawk War only lasted 16 weeks, but it left its mark in Illinois lore and legend. On June 24, 1832, Chief Black Hawk led an attack on Apple River Fort with some 200 Sauk and Fox warriors. Although the settlers inside were outnumbered four to one, they managed to put up enough of a fight that Black Hawk assumed they were heavily armed and called off the attack. The original fort was dismantled 15 years later, but in 1995 archeologists and historians set about locating and rebuilding the historic fort to its former glory. Apple River Fort State Historic Site also includes an interpretive center just north of U.S. Highway 20 where you can park for this ride (another parking lot is located on the south side of Highway 20). Like Galena and Hanover, Elizabeth is in the Driftless Area, a place the glaciers missed in the last ice age. Without the flattening effect of the glaciers, the area remains very hilly. You will see plenty of corn and other crops, but much of this land is better suited for grazing cattle. Although parts run through river bottomlands, this is a challenging ride.

Ride north from the interpretive center on Myrtle Street, which becomes Apple River Road outside of town. Gradually descend through rolling hills to the river valley, where you get a reprieve from the big hills. At 1.9 miles, go through the intersection with Goose Hollow Road and Becker Road, then curve sharply to the right. Two miles later, turn right on South Woodbine Road to head away from the Apple River. At 5 miles, go left on East Woodbine Road. Continue straight through Woodbine, then turn left on Scout Camp Road at the stop sign on the east end of town. This road features lots of curves with big, rolling hills including climbs half a mile long. Where

Welch Road goes off to the right at 7.9 miles, curve left and begin a long climb followed by a steep descent into the next valley. Go back up again after passing Apple River Road, then over some steep rollers. At 10.3 miles, descend through a forest to the Apple River. When you reach the bottom, you can see rocky bluffs to the left, a hint of the beauty of Apple River Canyon State Park a few miles further upstream. Cross the river and climb another steep hill. As you reach the top, turn left on Schapville Road and climb a bit more before heading back downhill.

This road repeats the pattern of descending into valleys and climbing onto ridges. The intersection with Grebner Road and Brandt Road is a little tricky; curve to the left as you ride through the intersection to stay on Schapville Road. After passing a skeet shooting range on the left at 14.9 miles, begin a steep climb through Schapville. A repair garage in town has a pop machine in front. Zion Presbyterian Church at 15.4 miles dates back to 1886. Beyond Schapville, the road heads skyward again and then runs along a ridge to Elizabeth Scales Mound Road at 18.7 miles. Less than six miles to the north is Charles Mound, the highest point in Illinois at 1,235 feet. Turn left on this relatively well-traveled road, then turn right on Rawlins Road less than a mile later. Go downhill past the Guilford Township building, and take the first left on North Morley Road. After more hills and curves, the road curves right onto Wachter Road. Ride through a residential area and turn left on Brodrecht Road at 22.6 miles. This road zigzags near the Shenandoah Riding Center and ends at Long Hollow Road. Turn left and enjoy some relatively flat terrain for a few miles. Look up on the ridge at 26.5 miles and you may glimpse an unusual sight—it appears to be a partial model of Stonehenge!

At 27.8 miles, bear left at the intersection with Georgetown Road. At Elizabeth-Scales Mound Road, jog right a bit, then turn left to continue on Georgetown Road. Begin a short, steep descent into the Apple River valley at 29.2 miles. Go very slow here—there is a sharp right turn at the bottom. Cross the river on an old steel bridge with a wooden plank deck. Climb a steep hill into Elizabeth, where this road becomes Main Street. Before you get to the top of the hill, turn right on West Street, then go left immediately onto Ash Street. Cross busy U.S. Highway 20, then ride down a hill and turn left on Myrtle Street at the bottom. The red Chicago Great Western Railway Depot Museum on the right is open on weekends 1 to 4 from May through October. Elizabeth lies on the same old right-of-way as the rail-trails in Rides 23 and 25. Cross Highway 20 again and finish at the interpretive center.

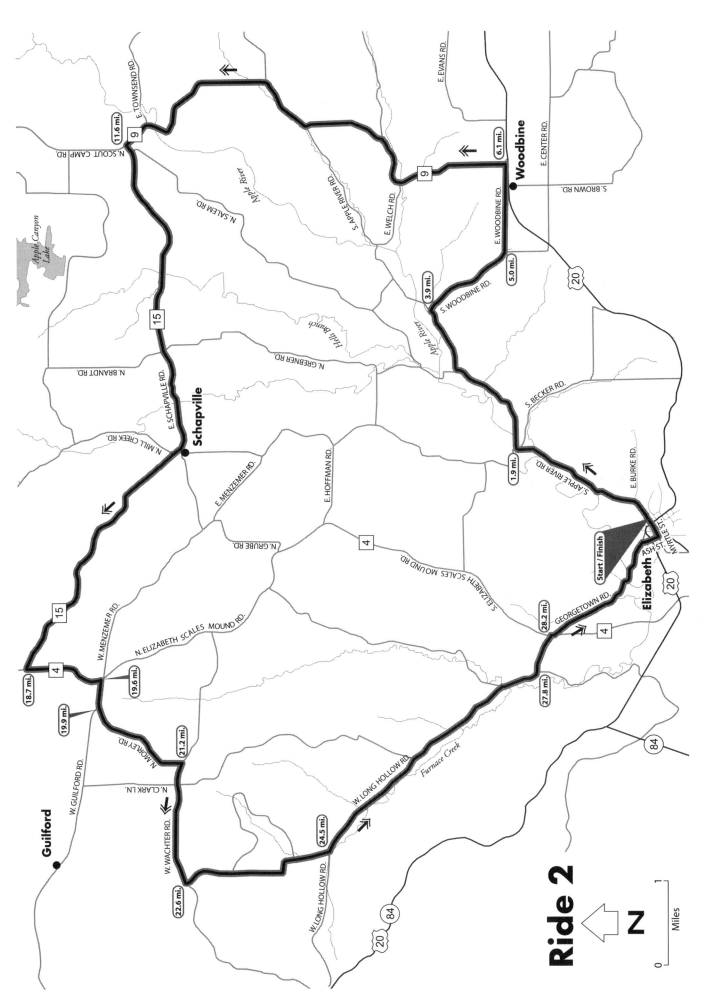

# Ride 2

N

Miles
0   1

# RIDE 3
## Jane Addams Trail

**Location:** Stephenson County north of Freeport
**Distance:** 14 miles
**Pedaling time:** 1.5 hours
**Surface:** Crushed-stone trail
**Terrain:** Flat
**Sweat factor:** Low
**Trailhead:** Wes Block Trail Access, Fairview Road off U.S. Highway 20, Freeport

### Jane Addams

A historical marker in Addams's hometown of Cedarville lists her many roles: humanitarian, feminist, social worker, reformer, educator, author, and publicist. She was born in 1860. Her mother died when she was two years old, but her father, a miller and 16-year state senator, was the wealthiest man in Stephenson County. Addams graduated from college and traveled to Europe twice. After seeing Toynbee Hall, which catered to those living in the slums of London, Addams was inspired to do something similar to help the poor, mostly immigrant population of Chicago. With Ellen Starr, she opened Hull-House in 1889. Hull-House was quite successful, eventually expanding to thirteen buildings. It evolved from a community center into an agent for social reform. Addams worked for women's suffrage and for legislation at the state and federal level to address the exploitation of women, children, and immigrants.

Addams believed in peace and strongly opposed World War I. She participated in the International Congress of Women in 1915, which evolved into the Women's International League for Peace and Freedom. Addams was that organization's first president. Her work was recognized with a Nobel Peace Prize in 1931. Addams wrote 11 books, her most famous being the autobiographical *Twenty Years at Hull-House*. She also helped to start the NAACP and the ACLU. When she died in 1935, her funeral was held at Hull-House, but she was buried at the family plot in Cedarville Cemetery. Hull-House is now a museum on the campus of the University of Illinois at Chicago.

The trail takes advantage of blasting done by the railroad.

Jane Addams is arguably the most prominent woman in Illinois history. She founded Hull-House in Chicago to help struggling immigrants, and she received the Nobel Peace Prize in 1931. It is fitting that a trail passing near her hometown of Cedarville be named in her honor. The Jane Addams Trail follows the path of the former Illinois Central Railroad from Freeport to the Wisconsin state line. From there, the Badger Trail will someday extend all the way to Madison. This ride provides a sample of the trail from Freeport to Buena Vista.

Freeport is a large town with restaurants, lodging, and a bike shop. Look for a trail sign on U.S. Highway 20 about 1.5 miles west of the State Highway 26 interchange and follow the signs to the Wes Block Trail Access. This gravel parking lot has toilets plus a picnic bench under a small shelter. Although there are a few clearings, the majority of this trail is shaded. Mile markers measured from the Wisconsin state line are posted at bridges and road intersections. The old railroad followed the bottoms of Richland Creek most of the way, but there are a few spots where blasting is evident. As with most rail-trails, elevation changes are too gradual to mention. The trail is used by cross-country skiers and snowmobilers during the winter, and you can thank the Illinois Association of Snowmobile Clubs for the warning signs approaching bridges and stop signs.

Begin at the north end of the parking lot and ride north under Highway 20 and into the woods. At 1.8 miles, cross Scioto Mills Road. The town of Scioto Mills sits on the hill to the east but has no services. Just north of this road is an old grain elevator on the right, followed by the ruins of a few other buildings. Cedarville Road, which leads to Addams's hometown 1.5 miles to the east, comes at 3.1 miles. Beaver Road is unmarked at 4.3 miles. There is a parking lot here, and the small town of Red Oak lies to the east. Shortly after passing gravel Lane Road at 5.2 miles, look to the left to see an old Illinois Central caboose through the trees. Unfortunately it sits on private property, so you will have to be content with the view from the trail. Signs at Richland Road (5.7 miles) invite the trail rider to visit a church for cold water or Fenwood for fishing, picnicking, and camping, as well as a portable toilet. McConnell Road in Buena Vista has a picnic table and a tiny parking lot. Just north of McConnell Road the trail goes through a deep cut in rock and over a long wooden bridge. Turn around here at 7 miles. If you feel like continuing, the trail is easy to follow. Orangeville is 3.5 miles further north with restaurants and stores, and it is 2.5 more miles from there to the Wisconsin state line.

Back at the parking lot, an adventurous rider may continue almost a mile south on the "snowmobile spur" to a steel truss bridge over the Pecatonica River. The problem is that this section of the trail has a rougher surface, and in the summer it is overgrown with weeds several feet tall. But if you have a mountain bike and love bridges, it's worth riding. If cycling this rail-trail makes you want to ride a real train, the Silver Creek & Stephenson Railroad at 2954 S. Walnut Road south of Freeport runs antique steam engine train rides on certain days from May through October (www.thefreeportshow.com). For more about the Jane Addams Trail, see www.janeaddamstrail.com.

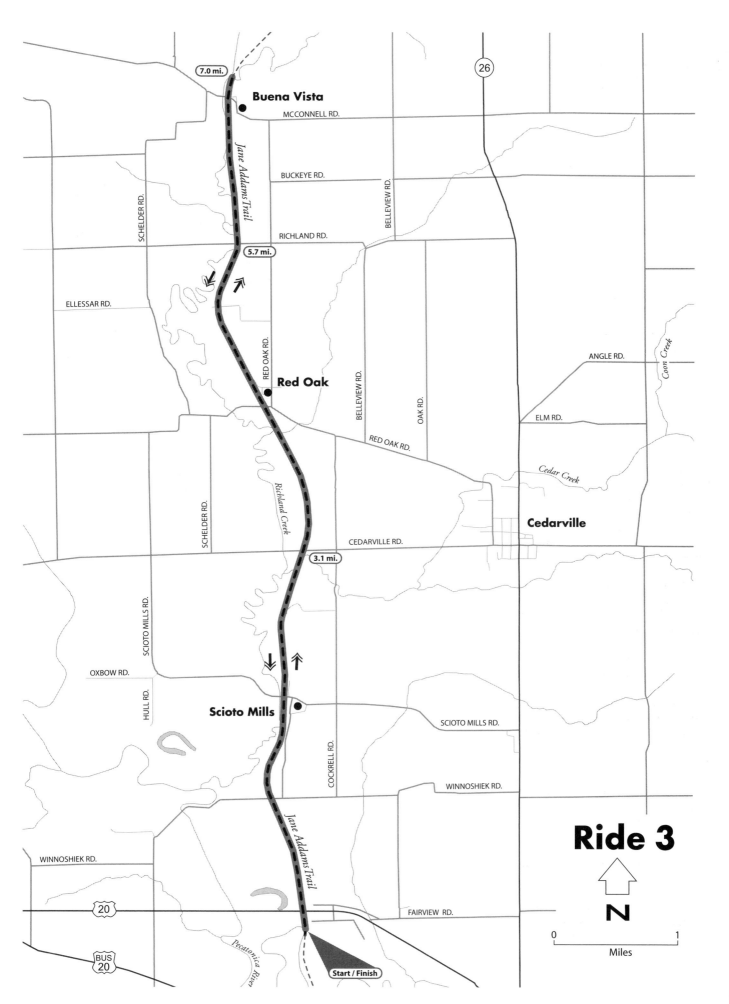

7.0 mi.

**Buena Vista**

MCCONNELL RD.

BUCKEYE RD.

*Jane Addams Trail*

BELLEVIEW RD.

RICHLAND RD.

5.7 mi.

(26)

SCHELDER RD.

ELLESSAR RD.

RED OAK RD.

**Red Oak**

BELLEVIEW RD.

OAK RD.

ANGLE RD.

*Coon Creek*

ELM RD.

RED OAK RD.

*Cedar Creek*

**Cedarville**

*Richland Creek*

SCHELDER RD.

CEDARVILLE RD.

3.1 mi.

SCIOTO MILLS RD.

OXBOW RD.

HULL RD.

**Scioto Mills**

SCIOTO MILLS RD.

COCKRELL RD.

WINNOSHIEK RD.

*Jane Addams Trail*

WINNOSHIEK RD.

(20)

FAIRVIEW RD.

**Ride 3**

**N**

BUS
20

*Pecatonica River*

**Start / Finish**

0        1

Miles

# RIDE 4
## Ride the Rock

**Location:** Along Rock River in Rockford
**Distance:** 9.6 miles
**Pedaling time:** 1 hour
**Surface:** Paved trails and residential streets
**Terrain:** Mostly flat
**Sweat factor:** Low +
**Trailhead:** Boat launch area, Sportscore One Park, north side of Rockford

It would seem natural that Rockford was named for the Rock River from the start, but that wasn't the case. Germanicus Kent called it Midway when he settled there in 1834 because it was about halfway between Galena and Chicago. Small towns grew on either side of the river, but the two joined together as Rockford in 1839. This scenic ride starts on the west side of the river, coincidentally the side where Kent founded what became Rockford. Then it crosses to the east side, passing through several parks.

Sportscore One is a large recreational complex on the north side of Rockford. It includes soccer fields, softball diamonds, sand volleyball courts, and a boat launch on the Rock River. A bike path runs through the park, but this ride starts at the south end. To get there on State Highway 2 (Main Street) from downtown, go north to Elmwood Road and turn right. Go east to Hiawatha Drive and turn right again. Just before you enter the boat launch parking lot, you'll see the trail. Park and start here, heading up a short hill to a pavilion with toilets, water, and a telephone. Enter the woods and climb another short hill to a railroad crossing. Stop, look, and listen because this is an active rail line. This section of the trail is characterized by curves and creek bridges punctuated by small, rolling hills. Ahead, you can see the high Riverside Boulevard Bridge over the river. When you get closer to the bridge, a sign warns you to walk your bike as the path climbs to the right. This is good advice since the

**The Rock Guardians of Rockford stand ready to protect trail users.**

hill is steep and visibility is limited. When the trail comes out to Riverside Boulevard, turn right onto the narrow sidewalk. Cross the busy road at the stoplight at 0.9 mile, then go downhill back toward the river. The long, steel, wood-decked trail bridge has a couple of turnouts where you can stop to look at the Rock River.

Back on solid ground, go right and follow sweeping curves to the right and left. At 1.2 miles, merge onto the southbound trail. This is Charles Martin Park. Go straight when the path ends at River Lane, and then turn right at the stop sign on wide East Drive. This street curves left onto Evelyn Avenue. Just past a chain-link fence, turn right onto the path through Shorewood Park. This park has toilets and a telephone, plus a set of bleachers facing the river. The Ski Broncs water ski show team performs here; call (815) 378-3000. The path goes toward the river, crosses a creek, and then curves away from the river. At 2.5 miles, keep right at the trail junction and continue south on Forest Grove Street. Turn left on Snow Avenue, then make a quick right on Arlington Street. After the road curves left, turn right on Arlington Street (again). This makes a sharp left curve onto Ransom Place, and you see a sign for Illinois Street Park. Turn right on Illinois Street. This road ends at a building with toilets, water, and a phone, but the path continues straight ahead. Several large pieces of public art liven up this trail; you pass the first around 3.2 miles. Soon after, go under the Auburn Street Bridge with just enough overhead clearance to ride through. A tenth of a mile later, you pass a huge sculpture of big, orange, metal tubing known as Symbol.

The beautiful Sinnissippi Gardens begin at 3.8 miles on the left. Bicycles are not allowed, but several bike racks are provided, including one at the Sinnissippi Lagoon. The most accessible (i.e., least abstract) public art on the trail is the Rock Guardians of Rockford on the right at 4.3 miles. These four stone-faced warriors have been protecting trail users for many years. Stay on the path close to the river as you approach a parking lot. Toilets, water, and pop machines are available at 4.5 miles. Shortly after, a path heads off to the left to loop around and go over the river on a bridge. Keep right instead, go under the bridge, and reach the end of the path at 4.8 miles. On the way back, you'll have to ride uphill across the river. Be careful going down the steep hill north of Riverside Boulevard. You should obey the sign and walk your bike.

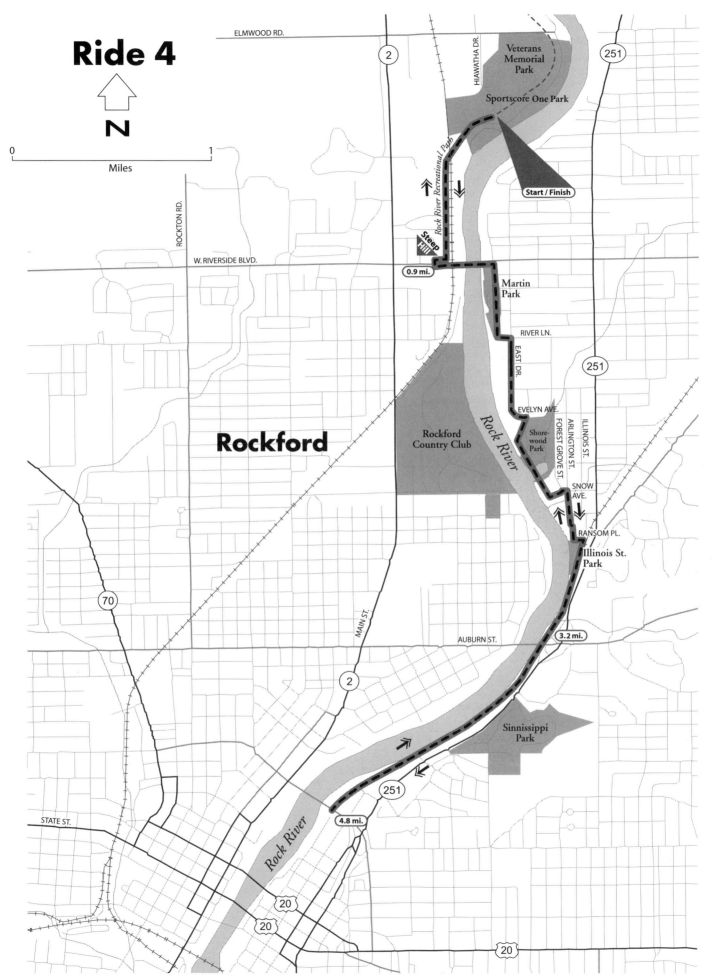

# Ride 4

N

0 — Miles — 1

ELMWOOD RD.

HIAWATHA DR.

2

251

Veterans Memorial Park

Sportscore One Park

Rock River Recreational Path

Start / Finish

Steep Hill

0.9 mi.

ROCKTON RD.

W. RIVERSIDE BLVD.

Martin Park

RIVER LN.

EAST DR.

251

**Rockford**

EVELYN AVE.

Rockford Country Club

*Rock River*

Shore-wood Park

FOREST GROVE ST.

ARLINGTON ST.

ILLINOIS ST.

SNOW AVE.

RANSOM PL.

Illinois St. Park

70

MAIN ST.

AUBURN ST.

3.2 mi.

2

Sinnissippi Park

251

STATE ST.

4.8 mi.

*Rock River*

20

20

20

11

# RIDE 5
## Long Trail on the Prairie

**Location:** Boone County, northeast of Rockford
**Distance:** 29 miles
**Pedaling time:** 2.5–3 hours
**Surface:** Paved trail
**Terrain:** Flat
**Sweat factor:** Low
**Trailhead:** County Line Road 0.5 mile north of State Highway 173

The Long Prairie Trail runs the width of Boone County from east to west. On the way, it visits three towns. The Boone County Conservation District manages the trail, and their logo promises recreation, preservation, and education. While almost every rail-trail accomplishes the first two merely by setting aside a right-of-way for a multi-use path, this trail also teaches. Interpretive signs scattered along the path describe the history and natural features of the area. The Kenosha, Rockford, and Rock Island Railroad laid tracks on this right-of-way in 1858. The Chicago & North Western Railway bought it and ran trains here for the better part of a century. A catastrophic train wreck led them to abandon the route and sell part of it to the conservation district. The railroad right-of-way preserved a bit of original prairie, which has never been plowed.

The trailhead has a toilet and a parking lot. "0.0" is stenciled on the asphalt at the start, just as the entire trail is marked every half mile. The first interpretive sign is here too. The trail is wooded until you reach Capron at 1.6 miles. There are several street crossings in town, but most are not busy. Be sure to stop, however, at 1.8 miles where the trail crosses Highway 173 on an angle. The town has restaurants and a bike shop, all of which are located a block off the trail on Highway 173. At the west end of town, Capron Road also has some traffic. Most of the Long Prairie Trail runs through farmland, so there are tractor crossings

on the trail. Many have warning signs, but some do not.

West of Capron, the path parallels Highway 173 for about two miles. There are many short bridges over creeks and ditches, but the longest goes over Beaver Creek at 4.5 miles. A mile later the trail crosses Beaverton Road. This is notable because here a train derailed and damaged the railroad bed so badly that the Chicago & North Western decided it wasn't worth fixing and stopped running trains. If that hadn't happened, you might not be pedaling on the Long Prairie Trail today.

The next town is Poplar Grove at 6.7 miles. There is a portable toilet in front of the grain elevator on the east side of town. This town has really embraced the trail; there are two restaurants and a coffee shop nearby. All have pop machines out front in case you are there outside of business hours. This town is growing, as evidenced by new home construction west of town. Highway 76 at 8.5 miles is a busy crossing. If you missed the chance to fill up in Poplar Grove, you can ride the wide shoulder of Highway 76 a short distance north to State Highway 173, where you will find a restaurant and a gas station/mini-mart. For some reason, the trail gets a painted, dashed centerline west of Highway 76.

Caledonia is the last town on the trail. Like Poplar Grove, it, too, has a toilet at the east end of town. There are pop machines in front of the fire station. After leaving town, cross Highway 173 carefully at 10.9 miles. Because most of the bridges on this trail are smooth, it is worth noting that there is a rough drop-off after the bridge at 11.1 miles. Caledonia Road is the last major crossroad at 12.4 miles. Away from Highway 173, the last few miles of the Long Prairie Trail seem more remote. Turn around when the path ends at 14.5 miles. Across the road, the Stone Bridge Trail continues northwest through Roscoe on the same right-of-way, but it is surfaced with crushed stone instead of asphalt.

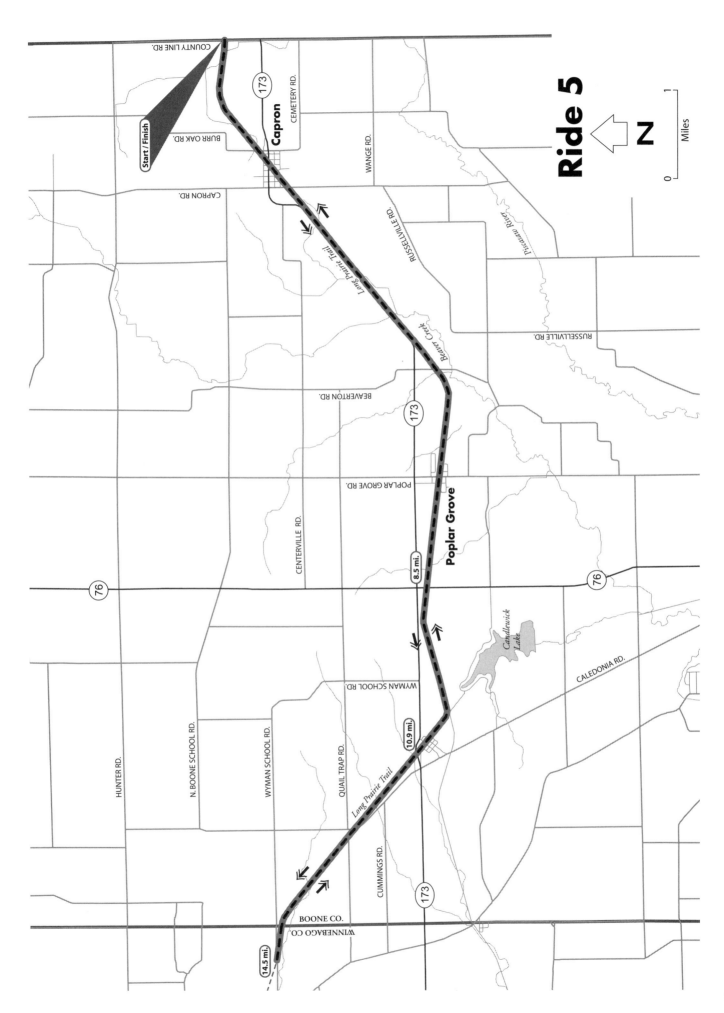

# Ride 5

N

Miles
0    1

Start / Finish

Capron

BURR OAK RD.

COUNTY LINE RD.

173

CEMETERY RD.

CAPRON RD.

WANGE RD.

Long Prairie Trail

RUSSELLVILLE RD.

Beaver Creek

BEVERTON RD.

173

RUSSELLVILLE RD.

Piscasaw River

CENTERVILLE RD.

POPLAR GROVE RD.

Poplar Grove

8.5 mi.

76

76

Candlewick Lake

CALEDONIA RD.

HUNTER RD.

N. BOONE SCHOOL RD.

WYMAN SCHOOL RD.

WYMAN SCHOOL RD.

QUAIL TRAP RD.

10.9 mi.

Long Prairie Trail

CUMMINGS RD.

173

BOONE CO.

WINNEBAGO CO.

14.5 mi.

# RIDE 6
## Windmill and Cactus

**Location:** Near Mississippi River
**Distance:** 19.9 miles
**Pedaling time:** 2–2.5 hours
**Surface:** Mixed
**Terrain:** Mostly flat
**Sweat factor:** Low +
**Trailhead:** Dutch windmill in Fulton

### What to Do with an Old Quarry?

A limestone quarry operated on the north side of Fulton for nearly a century. It closed in 1954 because blasting was causing damage on both sides of the Mississippi River. The pit lay abandoned for years.

Harold and Thelma Wieranga saw great potential in that big hole in the ground. Starting in 1967, they began to create a pioneer village of old buildings spread out along a nature trail. Some buildings were moved from farms in the area. Others were built to look like historic buildings using wood from old barns. The site covers 12 acres, but the twists of the trail make it seem larger.

The Wieranga family thoughtfully provides insect repellent at the information kiosk, and you will need it in the canyon. A small donation is requested. Heritage Canyon is located at 515 North Fourth Street. Plenty of parking is available on the other side of the street beside the river. It is open daily from 9 to 5 from April through December 15 (815-589-4545).

The river town of Fulton has a large population of Dutch descent. Each May, the town has a Dutch Days celebration. In 2000, the town finally realized its dream of erecting an authentic Dutch windmill on the Mississippi River shore. The windmill, named De Immigrant, was built in the Netherlands, dismantled, shipped to America, and reassembled in Fulton. Besides serving as a distinctive tourist information center, the windmill is used to grind wheat, corn, rye, and buckwheat into flour, which you can buy. Volunteers give tours and explain how it works (visit www.cityoffulton.us for details and hours).

The windmill is easy to find by following signs from State Highway 84 into town. There are toilets and water to the south of the windmill, and the Mississippi River Trail (MRT) runs atop the levee. In keeping with Fulton's Dutch heritage, locals refer to the levee as a dike. Take the handrail-lined sidewalk ramp up to the trail. You may need to walk your bike. Zero your odometer at the top and head north past the windmill. Follow the MRT signs on low-traffic streets through town. There are a few hills; the biggest is on Third Avenue. When Ninth Avenue dead-ends into the MRT, turn left to head north to Thomson. The asphalt trail runs parallel to State Highway 84 in a wooded former railroad right-of-way. At 4.5 miles there is a stop sign at Lock Road, which leads west to Missis-

sippi River Lock and Dam 13. The trail goes to the left, then immediately to the right on an unmarked road. A mile down the road at a sign for Mickelson's Landing, the Thomson-Fulton Sand Prairie State Nature Preserve begins on the left. Another mile later, the MRT goes left from the road onto a crushed-stone trail that becomes uncharacteristically narrow, less than half the width of the rest of the MRT. At 6.7 miles, the trail jogs to the left onto a crushed-stone road for a tenth of a mile, then curves to the north again. This little detour is not marked by MRT signs. This area is part of the Upper Mississippi River National Wildlife & Fish Refuge.

Around 7 miles, look at the vegetation near the trail. You'll see an unusual plant for Illinois—prickly pear cactus! Common in the American Southwest, prickly pear cactus is hardy enough to withstand Illinois winters. The yellow blooms are beautiful. (The cactus can also be found in Thomson-Fulton Sand Prairie, but it is easier to see here without fences.) This trail has a few spots of deeper, looser stone. Generally the northbound side is more stable, but your best bet is to keep an eye on the tracks left by other riders, especially if you have skinny tires. The trail descends toward a sharp right curve at 7.9 miles where the stone is particularly loose, so watch your speed.

The trail crosses a campground road, and then turns right onto a lovely, pine tree-lined road. There is drinking water at this intersection. Continue north to Main Street. Thomson lies to the east, but turn around to continue the ride. When you get back to Fulton, pass the intersection where you joined the north-south trail at 15.8 miles. If you have built up an appetite by now, sandwiches and ice cream are available at the trail's intersection with 10th Avenue. If you had something else in mind, there is a mini-mart on the left a bit further down the trail. The trail follows city streets briefly. At 16.3 miles, turn left at a really wide intersection, and then turn right into the woods on the asphalt trail. The trail curves west along U.S. Highway 30, ending at Fourth Street. Cross the road and head north on another trail. There is a rail yard between the path and the river. At 19 miles, the path hops onto the road briefly to go over a drainage ditch. Veer left through a gravel parking lot at 19.3 miles toward the public boat launch. As you climb the dike, follow the trail to the right. After a dip under a bridge, the ride finishes at the railed sidewalk.

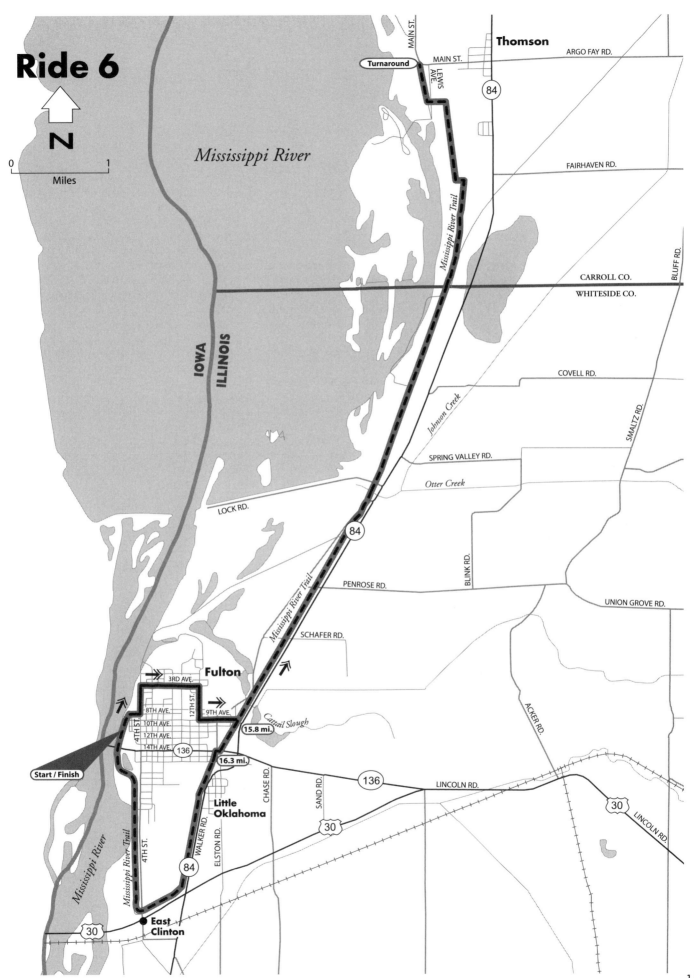

# Ride 6

**N**

0 ——————— 1
Miles

*Mississippi River*

**Thomson**

ARGO FAY RD.

Turnaround

84

MAIN ST.

MAIN ST.

LEWIS AVE.

FAIRHAVEN RD.

*Mississippi River Trail*

IOWA

ILLINOIS

CARROLL CO.

WHITESIDE CO.

BLUFF RD.

COVELL RD.

*Johnson Creek*

SMALTZ RD.

SPRING VALLEY RD.

*Otter Creek*

LOCK RD.

84

PENROSE RD.

BLINK RD.

UNION GROVE RD.

*Mississippi River Trail*

SCHAFER RD.

3RD AVE.

**Fulton**

8TH AVE.

12TH ST.

9TH AVE.

*Cattail Slough*

15.8 mi.

10TH AVE.

4TH ST.

12TH AVE.

14TH AVE.

136

16.3 mi.

ACKER RD.

CHASE RD.

**Start / Finish**

**Little
Oklahoma**

WALKER RD.

ELSTON RD.

SAND RD.

136

LINCOLN RD.

30

84

*Mississippi River Trail*

4TH ST.

30

*Mississippi River*

**East
Clinton**

30

LINCOLN RD.

# RIDE 7
## Where the River Runs West

**Location:** Quad Cities
**Distance:** 24.2 miles
**Pedaling time:** 2–2.5 hours
**Surface:** Paved trail
**Terrain:** Flat
**Sweat factor:** Low
**Trailhead:** Sunset Park in Rock Island

The Mississippi River carves a north-south path through the heart of America. But in one place it runs decidedly west rather than south: the Quad Cities region of Davenport, Bettendorf, Rock Island, and Moline. All four cities have been developing paths to revitalize the riverfront, and so far Illinois is winning the race to link contiguous trail segments. While this ride goes from Rock Island to East Moline and back, the trail continues much further upstream. Through Rock Island, Moline, and East Moline, services are plentiful on or near the trail.

Sunset Park lies north of the confluence of the Rock River and the Mississippi River. To get there, take State Highway 92 north from I-280 to the first exit, 31st Street. Go west toward the river, and park on the right at the trailhead. The RiverWay trail is generally easy to follow by staying on the painted, striped path. It begins by winding its way through a picnic area. Oddly, this part of the trail is marked in kilometers. Soon it climbs atop the levee. Short inclines like this are the most notable hills you will encounter. Industry and the river are closely linked, and much of this trail passes through industrial areas. Pass the Rock Island River Terminal. At 1.7 miles there is a rough railroad crossing. At 3 miles you'll see one of Rock Island's newest industries, a riverboat casino.

At 3.3 miles, keep right where the trail splits. The trail on the left leads to a steel bridge that goes to Arsenal Island. You won't find an island named Rock Island on the map; it was renamed Arsenal Island after the Rock Island Arsenal went into operation there. In addition to an active military facility, the island features the Military Arms Museum, the Mississippi River Visitor Center at Lock & Dam 15, and a bike path. Bicyclists are required to wear helmets and carry photo identification on the island. There is another Y at 3.6 miles. This time go left under the railroad bridge. At 5 miles, another bridge goes to the left, this one to Sylvan Island Recreational Park. The island once had a power plant and a steel mill, among other things. There are crushed-stone and single-track trails that you might want to explore on the way back. For now, turn right, pass the parking lot, and turn left on the trail.

Moline was once home to a variety of industries and a number of farm implement manufacturers. Nowadays, it seems to be all about the John Deere Company. A Deere factory stretches for nearly half a mile on the right, and this is just the beginning. The unusual, round building beside the trail at 5.8 miles is an arena called the "MARK of the Quad Cities." If you head away from the river, you can visit the John Deere Collectors Center and the John Deere Pavilion (see www.johndeereattractions.com for details). After you go under I-74, you pass the Quad Cities Convention and Visitors Bureau, which is located in an old railroad depot.

Curve toward the river at 7.1 miles. Here the River-Way is known as the Ben Butterworth Memorial Parkway, named for a former president of the park board. This area is popular with ducks and geese as well as walkers and runners. There are several parking areas with toilets along the Ben Butterworth segment of the trail, some with water or pop machines. A restaurant and marina at 8.6 miles add some congestion. Be especially careful going to the left around the restaurant. At 10.1 miles, the trail dips down off the levee and back up again as it passes the River Intake Station. Soon you will see the huge John Deere Harvester Works on the right, a facility dating back to 1913 that stretches for nearly a mile along the bike path. The workers sometimes use bicycles to get around the sprawling grounds (for factory tour info, call (800) 765-9588). Beacon Harbor at 10.6 miles has toilets and water.

The trail gets away from the riverfront a bit as it enters Henry McNeal's Reserve, a pleasant, wooded area at 11.4 miles. Turn right along the shoulder of a road at 11.5 miles. If you go toward the river instead, you can ride this road around Campbell's Island. Turn left onto the trail before the railroad tracks. This is a remote, natural area with many songbirds. The trail reaches Empire Park at the northeast corner of East Moline. This ride turns around at 12.1 miles, but the RiverWay continues across the road and to the left, eventually passing through Hampton, Rapids City, Port Byron, Cordova, Albany, Fulton, Thomson, and Savanna over the next 50 miles. On the way back, you may wish to explore Campbell's Island, Sylvan Island, or Arsenal Island. Be particularly careful of the railroad tracks near the start at 22.3 miles because you'll be descending fast from the levee. If you time it right, an afternoon ride will bring you back just in time to watch the sun set over the Mississippi River at Sunset Park.

# Ride 7

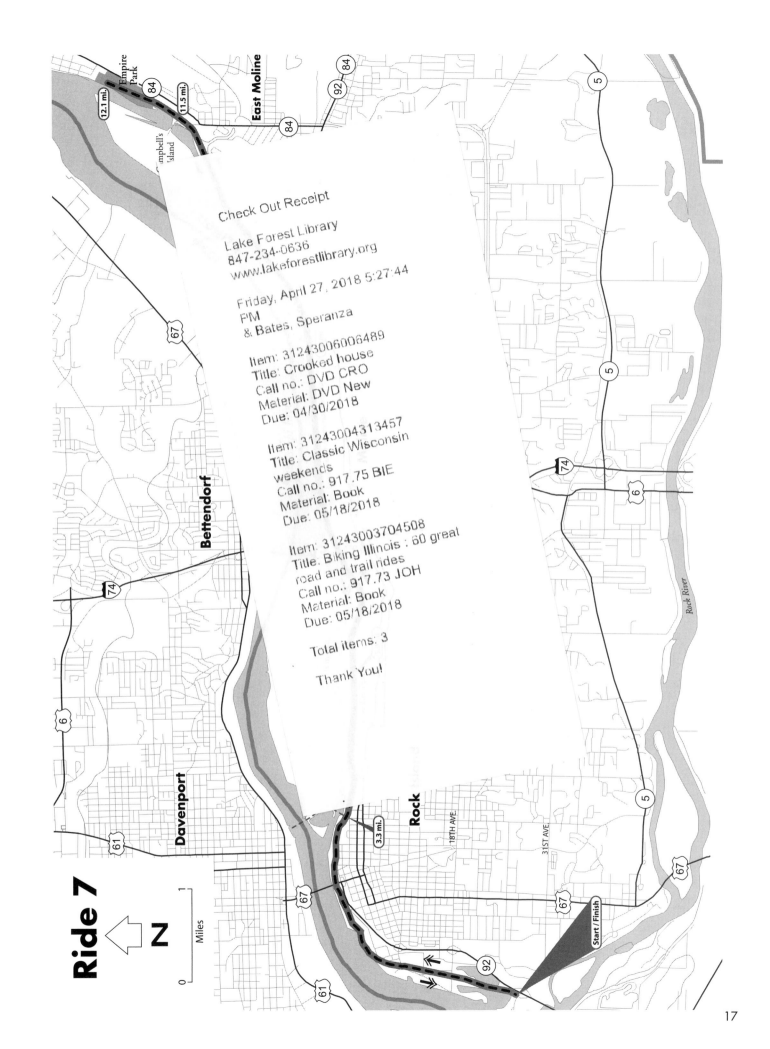

N

Miles
0      1

**East Moline**

**Bettendorf**

**Davenport**

**Rock**

84

84
92

5

5

5

74

6

67

74

6

61

67

92

67
67

67

92

61

Empire Park

Campbell's Island

Rock River

12.1 mi.

11.5 mi.

3.3 mi.

18TH AVE.

31ST AVE.

Start / Finish

Check Out Receipt

Lake Forest Library
847-234-0636
www.lakeforestlibrary.org

Friday, April 27, 2018 5:27:44
PM
& Bates, Speranza

Item: 31243006006489
Title: Crooked house
Call no.: DVD CRO
Material: DVD New
Due: 04/30/2018

Item: 31243004313457
Title: Classic Wisconsin
weekends
Call no.: 917.75 BIE
Material: Book
Due: 05/18/2018

Item: 31243003704508
Title: Biking Illinois : 60 great
road and trail rides
Call no.: 917.73 JOH
Material: Book
Due: 05/18/2018

Total items: 3

Thank You!

17

# RIDE 8
## Trail to Tampico

**Location:** Whiteside County
**Distance:** 24.4 miles
**Pedaling time:** 2–3 hours
**Surface:** Crushed-stone trail, chip-seal and asphalt roads
**Terrain:** Mostly flat
**Sweat factor:** Low
**Trailhead:** Hennepin Feeder Canal Access on State Highway 40, Rock Falls

### Why a Feeder?

A look at the topography of the region provides a quick answer. The highest point on the canal, known as Summit Pool, is 196 feet higher in elevation than the Illinois River at the east end of the canal. Summit Pool is also about 90 feet higher than the Rock River at the canal's west end. Therefore a boat moving through the canal essentially went uphill half of the way and downhill the other half. The best means to get the water necessary to work the locks needed to accomplish this feat was to build another canal to bring water from the Rock River south to the highest point on the Main Canal. To guarantee that there would be water for the Feeder Canal, a dam was constructed on the Rock River at Rock Falls to create Lake Sinnissippi. Water input to the feeder is controlled by a guard lock in Rock Falls, which is about 2.2 miles north of this ride's start.

The Hennepin Feeder Canal is a waterway leading from the Rock River to the Hennepin Canal 29.3 miles to the south. Its main purpose was to supply water to the canal rather than carry commercial boat traffic. Today fishermen and canoeists use the old Feeder Canal, which is part of Hennepin Canal Parkway State Park. It is ideal for canoeing because there are no locks or dams to portage, and the current is minimal. Paths run along both sides of the canal. The east side has a turf surface, but the west side is suitable for bicycling. The Feeder Canal passes about a mile east of Tampico, where President Ronald Reagan was born. That puts Tampico on a different trail, the auto tour route through northern Illinois known as the Reagan Trail.

The trailhead is easy to find, just a half mile north of I-88 on State Highway 40. Ride south from the end of the parking lot. The path is paved, but not for long. At 0.5 mile the trail goes under I-88.

Watch for puddles or mud on this dirt underpass. Go under Buell Road in a corrugated steel tunnel. From here to the next bridge at 2.6 miles, the trail surface is rough, crushed stone—not as fine as most crushed-stone paths but less coarse than gravel. After that, the rest of the trail surface is made of the crushed stone familiar to cyclists. There is a nice three-mile stretch of uninterrupted riding between Knief Road and Ridge Road. During this section, you may notice a few concrete telephone poles on your right. Those were poured and erected during canal construction. You have to go up and over Ridge Road rather than under it. Watch for loose stones. There are toilets on the right as you approach State Highway 172. The underpass is just above the waterline, so it may be muddy and slick. Approaching Bridge 52 at Hahnaman Road near 10.5 miles, go to the right up a rocky trail and through the parking lot. Turn right and go about 1 mile to Tampico.

In town, the road name changes to Kimball Street. Turn right at the stop sign on Main Street, which is Highway 172 again. This road carries some truck traffic, but it is very wide in town. The gas station/mini-mart on the right at 12.1 miles is your only opportunity to get water and snacks on the route. The ride turns around where Reagan was born on February 6, 1911. The Reagans lived in an apartment above the First National Bank at 111 South Main Street. You can tour the apartment, which is decorated in the style of the early 1900s. There is also a gift store and museum next door (815-438-2130).

The trail beside the Feeder Canal goes much further than Tampico, continuing another 16 miles south to the Main Canal (see Ride 11). On the way back to Rock Falls, imagine the young future president learning to swim in this canal almost 100 years ago, a skill he would put to good use as a lifeguard in Dixon.

**Trees are reflected in the placid waters of the Hennepin Feeder Canal.**

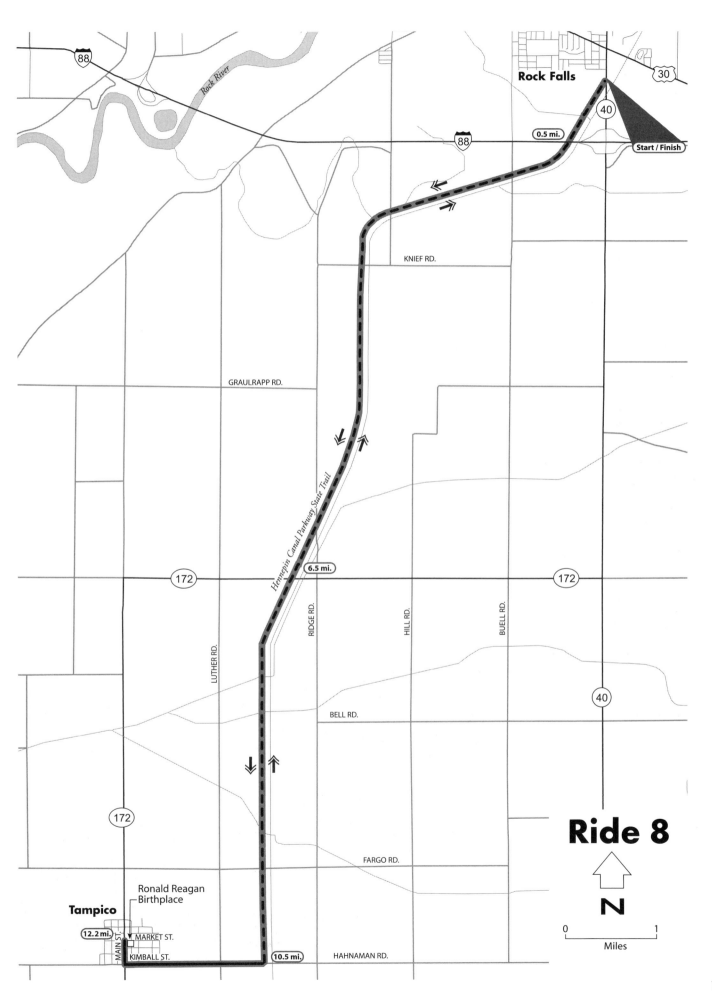

Rock Falls

88

30

88    0.5 mi.

40

Start / Finish

KNIEF RD.

GRAULRAPP RD.

*Hennepin Canal Parkway State Trail*

6.5 mi.

172                                                    172

LUTHER RD.

RIDGE RD.

HILL RD.

BUELL RD.

40

BELL RD.

**Ride 8**

FARGO RD.

N

0          1
Miles

Ronald Reagan
Birthplace

**Tampico**

12.2 mi.    MARKET ST.

KIMBALL ST.    10.5 mi.    HAHNAMAN RD.

MAIN ST.

*Rock River*

# RIDE 9
## Deere Country

**Location:** Ogle and Lee counties
**Distance:** 23.8 miles
**Pedaling time:** 2–2.5 hours
**Surface:** Paved roads, short paved trail
**Terrain:** Gently rolling hills
**Sweat factor:** Moderate
**Trailhead:** John Deere Historic Site, follow signs from State Highway 2 in Grand Detour

### Deere's Self-Polishing Plow

John Deere was born in Vermont in 1804. Like many Americans, he moved west in search of a better life. He settled in Grand Detour along with other former Vermonters. Already an accomplished blacksmith, Deere built a forge soon after he arrived in 1836. The eastern farmers struggled with their cast-iron plows because soil in the Midwest was different from the sandy soil of New England—it clung to the plows so farmers had to stop often to clean them. Deere's solution was a polished steel blade that cleaned itself. Deere's plows were popular; indeed, his ingenuity saved many a discouraged settler from returning back East in resignation.

Business grew, and in 1848 he opened a factory in Moline on the Mississippi River (see Ride 7). By the turn of the century, Deere offered a complete line of farm tools including plows, cultivators, and planters. The company started making tractors in 1918. John Deere's idea for a better plow has grown into a corporation with 46,000 employees doing business all over the world, making farm implements, lawn mowers, construction equipment, and other machinery.

The John Deere Historic Site (www.johndeerehistoricsite.com) is open daily from 9 to 5 from the beginning of April to the end of November. The home that Deere built in 1836 is authentically furnished to show how pioneer families lived in the 1830s.

One doesn't have to travel Illinois back roads for long to see the ubiquitous green tractors of the John Deere Company. Deere got his start amid the cornfields of northern Illinois near Grand Detour. Grand Detour may sound like a bad road construction experience, but the town is named for a bend in the Rock River that surrounds the town on three sides. This ride starts where Deere invented his plow, then ventures into the countryside where you may see modern Deere machinery in action. As a bonus, the ride passes Ronald Reagan's boyhood home in Dixon.

Start the ride at the John Deere Historic Site. Head north on Clinton Street to Broad Street and turn left. Follow the curve of the road onto Green Street, which becomes Ridge Road as you climb out of town. Turn left on Penn Corner Road. Oak Ridge Cemetery, which has graves dating back to the mid-1800s, sits on the southwest corner of the intersection. Turn left at the stop sign 4 miles later onto Lowell Park Road. At 11 miles, turn left into Lowell Park. This 240-acre park was established in 1907. Future president Ronald Reagan

worked as a lifeguard on the Rock River here for seven summers and by his count saved 77 lives. Follow the signs to the Lowell Parkway Trail, a paved, tree-shaded, 3.5-mile path into Dixon.

When the trail ends at Washington Street, veer to the right onto Bradshaw Street. Go left on Dixon Avenue, then right on Everett Street. Continue across busy U.S. Highway 52/State Highway 26 and turn left at the next stoplight, Peoria Avenue. Cross the Rock River and begin climbing out of the valley. The hill isn't steep, but it's harder if you don't make the stoplights. Continue south to Ninth Street and go left. At the next intersection, turn left again to see Ronald Reagan's boyhood home at 816 South Hennepin Avenue. The Reagans actually moved often and lived in several homes in Dixon, but this is the only one open to the public. The house is open for tours daily most of the year and on weekends during the winter (815-228-5176).

From the home, continue north on Hennepin back toward the river. The turreted Dixon Public Library at Third Street was built in 1900. Turn right on Second Street. This is one of several streets in Dixon labeled Petunia Boulevard; during the summer the curbs are lined with pink petunias. Dixon is the official Petunia Capital of Illinois, and volunteers plant 30,000 petunias along city streets. At 17.5 miles, the road angles to the left and becomes Ravine Avenue. Turn right on somewhat busy State Highway 2 (River Road) and go one mile. Approaching a large cement plant at 18.8 miles, bear left onto White Oak Lane and cross two diagonal railroad tracks. Turn right onto Mile Road at 20.9 miles. At 21.3 miles, be sure to obey the stop sign; crossing trucks don't have to stop. Turn right on Grand Detour Road at 22 miles, and then go left on Highway 2 to cross the Rock River again. The bridge has wide shoulders. The second left-turn lane after the bridge goes to the John Deere Historic Site via Illinois Street.

This John Deere tractor sits in front of a field of soybeans.

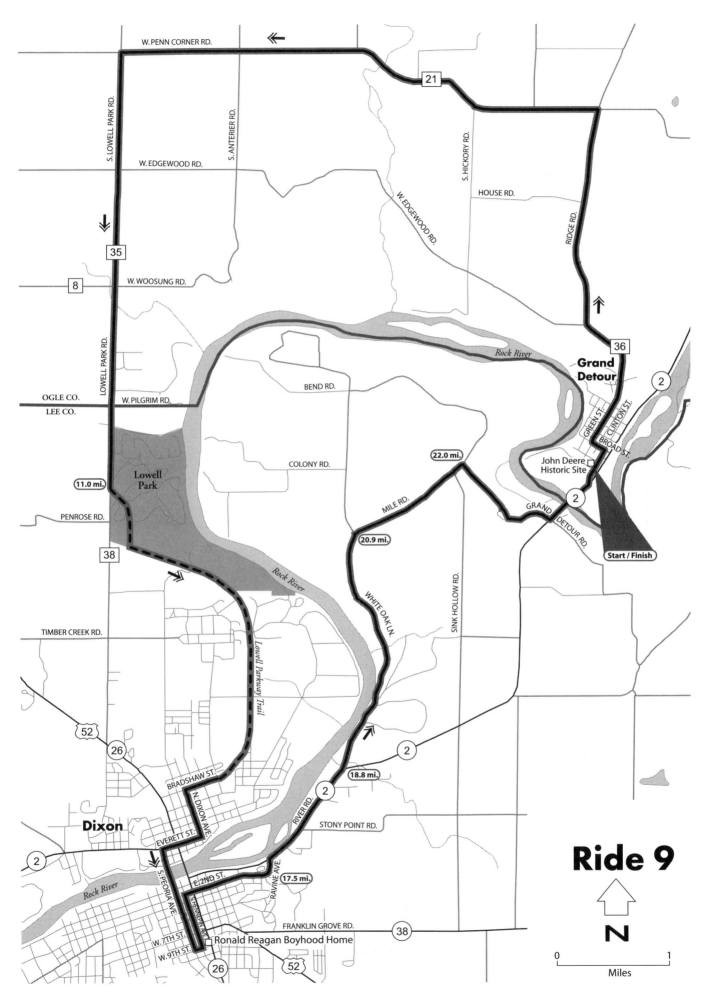

W. PENN CORNER RD.

21

S. LOWELL PARK RD.

W. EDGEWOOD RD.

S. ANTERIER RD.

S. HICKORY RD.

W. EDGEWOOD RD.

HOUSE RD.

RIDGE RD.

35

8

W. WOOSUNG RD.

LOWELL PARK RD.

*Rock River*

36

**Grand Detour**

2

OGLE CO.
LEE CO.

W. PILGRIM RD.

BEND RD.

GREEN ST.

CLINTON ST.

BROAD ST.

22.0 mi.

John Deere
Historic Site

11.0 mi.

Lowell
Park

COLONY RD.

MILE RD.

2

PENROSE RD.

20.9 mi.

GRAND DETOUR RD.

**Start / Finish**

38

*Rock River*

WHITE OAK LN.

SINK HOLLOW RD.

TIMBER CREEK RD.

*Lowell Parkway Trail*

52

26

BRADSHAW ST.

N. DIXON AVE.

2

18.8 mi.

**Dixon**

2

EVERETT ST.

RIVER RD.

2

STONY POINT RD.

S. PEORIA AVE.

E. 2ND ST.

RAVINE AVE.

17.5 mi.

*Rock River*

S. HENNEPIN AVE.

FRANKLIN GROVE RD.

38

W. 7TH ST.

W. 9TH ST.

Ronald Reagan Boyhood Home

26

52

# Ride 9

**N**

0        1

Miles

# RIDE 10
## Amboy

**Location:** Lee County
**Distance:** 21.1 miles
**Pedaling time:** 1.5–2.5 hours
**Surface:** Paved roads, chip-seal roads, some brick
**Terrain:** Gently rolling hills
**Sweat factor:** Moderate
**Trailhead:** Corner of Main Street and Mason Avenue (U.S. Highway 52)

### Making Lemonade

The woodcarvings in Amboy City Park are a classic example of taking lemons and making lemonade. On June 1, 1999, a powerful storm swept through the park, damaging many trees. Instead of just chopping up the trees for firewood and grinding the stumps into wood chips, the people of Amboy decided to have the remains of the trees carved to represent their heritage.

The subjects include famous politicians such as Illinois' three presidents, all of whom passed through Amboy (as did Zachary Taylor). More recently, Speaker of the House J. Dennis Hastert, whose district includes Amboy, was honored with a carving.

Ordinary citizens are represented as well, including a farmer, a National Guardsman, a pioneer woman, and school children. A World War II soldier serves as a memorial to Amboy's veterans of all armed conflicts, beginning with the Civil War. Other carvings represent animals, some native and some symbolic (such as the lion commissioned by the Amboy Lions Club). And of course, the railroad that brought about the town is represented as well.

All told, more than two dozen of these works of art are scattered around the park. While the trees were surely beautiful before that storm, a unique attraction has been created through their demise.

At a time when small-town America is disappearing, Amboy stands out as a success story. Main Street is still full of stores, including a pharmacy with a soda fountain and a bike shop that also sells kayaks. The First National Bank building still houses the local bank. Amboy has persevered despite losing the railroad industry that put it on the map.

Head east on Main Street from Mason Avenue (U.S. Highway 52). The first half mile is mostly brick, but it's not too rough as far as brick goes. Amboy City Park with its distinctive woodcarvings is on the right at the edge of town. Main Street heads into the small town of Binghampton at 1.1 miles. Go straight at the fork to follow Lee Center Road. Corn is king out here, and a grain elevator marks your arrival in the town of Lee Center. At the stop sign, turn right on Inlet Road, a wide street with parallel parking. Just after the road narrows, turn right on Green Wing Road. Cross Green River, which is not wide here, at 6.2 miles. At Lewis Road, turn left, then follow the curve to the right; you are still on Green Wing Road. You return to Highway 52 at 10.8 miles. Turn left, then get in the right-turn lane to continue south on Green Wing Road. Turn right on Sublette Road, then turn right again in the middle of a left-hand curve to stay on Sublette Road. Woody True Value Hardware at 13.6 miles has the only refreshments outside of Amboy on this loop. Hours are 8 to 4 Monday through Saturday and 9 to 3 on Sunday. The next mile is mostly uphill, but not steep.

Besides corn, you will see plenty of cows, pigs, soybeans, and horses along this route. Go past Dry Gulch Road at 15.3 miles and turn right at the stop sign on Rockyford Road. The Green River is wider where Rockyford Road crosses on a narrow bridge at 19.5 miles. This road turns into Main Street in town. At 20.9 miles, you see the restored, two-story Amboy Illinois Central Railroad Depot on the left. Built in 1876, this building is now a museum (815-857-4700). While cyclists think of a rail-trail as an old railroad right-of-way converted to a recreational path, the "Rail Trail" in north-central Illinois is a combination of depot museums, model train displays, and a railroad viewing park (see www.illinoisrailtrail.com) Watch for angle-parked cars backing out downtown.

After your ride, reward yourself with an old-fashioned shake or malt at the Amboy Pharmacy (815-857-2323)—the kind where they give you a glass along with a stainless steel tumbler that contains at least another glassful. Or, since you crossed it twice on this ride, order a Green River!

**The old Amboy Depot is now a museum.**

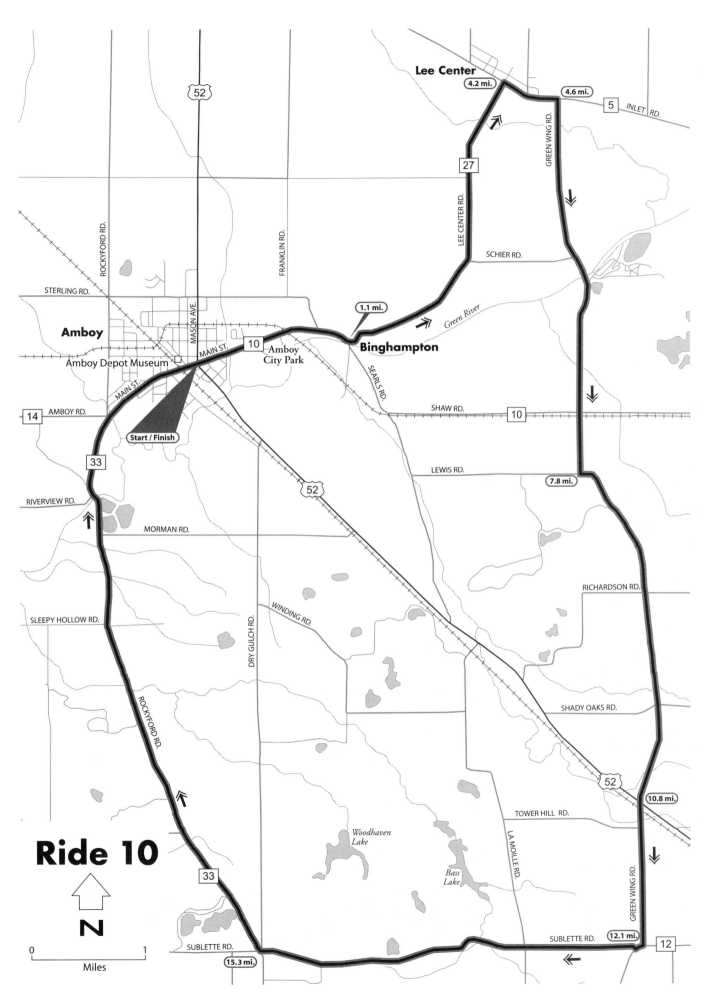

## Ride 10

**N**

0       1
Miles

**Lee Center**
4.2 mi.

4.6 mi.

52

5   INLET RD.

GREEN WNG RD.

27

LEE CENTER RD.

ROCKYFORD RD.

FRANKLIN RD.

STERLING RD.

SCHIER RD.

**Amboy**

MASON AVE.

1.1 mi.

*Green River*

10   Amboy
City Park

**Binghampton**

Amboy Depot Museum

MAIN ST.

SEARLS RD.

SHAW RD.

10

14   AMBOY RD.

**Start / Finish**

LEWIS RD.

7.8 mi.

33

RIVERVIEW RD.

52

MORMAN RD.

RICHARDSON RD.

SLEEPY HOLLOW RD.

DRY GULCH RD.

WINDING RD.

ROCKYFORD RD.

SHADY OAKS RD.

52

10.8 mi.

TOWER HILL RD.

LA MOILLE RD.

*Woodhaven
Lake*

*Bass
Lake*

GREEN WING RD.

33

SUBLETTE RD.

SUBLETTE RD.

12.1 mi.

12

15.3 mi.

# RIDE 11
## Ride the White Elephant

**Location:** Bureau County
**Distance:** 16 miles
**Pedaling time:** 1.5–2 hours
**Surface:** Paved trail
**Terrain:** Flat
**Sweat factor:** Low
**Trailhead:** Hennepin Canal Parkway State Park Visitor Center, Sheffield

These wood gates are part of the restored Lock 22.

When it was completed in 1907, the Hennepin Canal was both an engineering masterpiece and a white elephant. The idea of a water connection between the Illinois River and the Mississippi River dated back to the construction of the Illinois & Michigan Canal in the 1830s. Unfortunately, money was scarce, and construction was delayed for decades. In the meantime, railroads got cheaper and barges got bigger. In fact, while the Hennepin Canal was being constructed, the locks on the Mississippi and Illinois Rivers were being widened. Since the Hennepin's locks were narrower than those on the rivers it connected, its commercial life was short and lonely. It was not all in vain, however. The engineering and construction techniques developed and tested on the Hennepin Canal contributed to the success of the Panama Canal.

The Main Canal is 75.2 miles long, but this relatively short ride offers a good sample of its treasures. Like many decommissioned canals, the Hennepin's towpaths have been made into recreational trails. Unlike other towpaths, however, these were never actually used by animals to pull boats; by the time the canal was built, boats moved under their own power. The main path was grass for many years, but its surface was improved in the early 2000s. Unfortunately, some sections are chip seal, and trail traffic isn't heavy enough to smooth it out. At the time of publication that made for a bumpy ride on a

skinny-tired bike, but the surface should improve over time. The trail rarely strays from the canal, which has become a ribbon of wilderness amidst fertile farmland. Often, you'll have the canal on one side of the trail and fields of corn or soybeans on the other. In contrast to the shady Feeder Canal (Ride 8), there is not much tree cover on this part of the Main Canal.

Like most waterways, the Hennepin Canal is a haven for birds. In addition to the usual songbirds, there are herons and hawks. Keep an eye out for the rabbits that enjoy playing "chicken" with cyclists. You may see deer too. You will probably encounter more fishermen than cyclists along this trail.

Start at Hennepin Canal Parkway State Park, which is located off State Highway 40 just south of I-80. The park is always open. Park near the visitor center and follow the sidewalk to the building. The visitor center (open from 8 to 4 Monday–Friday) offers a great introduction to the canal plus bathrooms and water. Start the ride around the back of the building. Go to the left on the chip-seal road and then veer right on the trail. Cross Bridge 15 to the north side of the canal. The trail here is rough chip seal, but it passes under I-80 on concrete. At 2.6 miles, go left over the canal, under the road (which leads south to Sheffield), back over the canal, then left to continue west. At 5.3 miles, the path goes under a road in a tunnel, then left over the canal, but this time the path continues west on the south side. As you ride the crushed-stone trail, the Hennepin Canal Feeder flows into the Main Canal from the Rock River 29 miles to the north. This is the highest point of the canal, known as Summit Pool; the Feeder Canal provides water that goes downhill in both directions from here. Return to the north side of the canal via a road at 5.8 miles and turn left to follow the Main Canal (the trail to the right goes along the Feeder Canal to Rock Falls). The surface is rough chip seal again.

There is a special treat at 6.3 miles: Lock 22 has been restored. You can see how the gears moved the lock gates and how the adjacent lift bridge was raised and lowered. The picnic area has toilets on the south side of the canal. The next tunnel is especially low, so duck or walk your bike. This brief tour of the Hennepin Canal ends with Aqueduct 4 over Coal Creek at 8 miles. The canal and trail continue west to the Quad Cities area, but you've seen a truss bridge, a lock, a lift bridge, and an aqueduct so you can head back now with a good idea of what the Hennepin has to offer.

On the return trip, be sure to cross over the canal on Bridge 18A. Otherwise, you will head north along the Feeder Canal trail. Back at the visitor center, you can ride east to explore more of the canal. There is a steel railroad bridge just east of State Highway 40. About 5 miles further east is a designated historic area that is targeted for restoration and preservation.

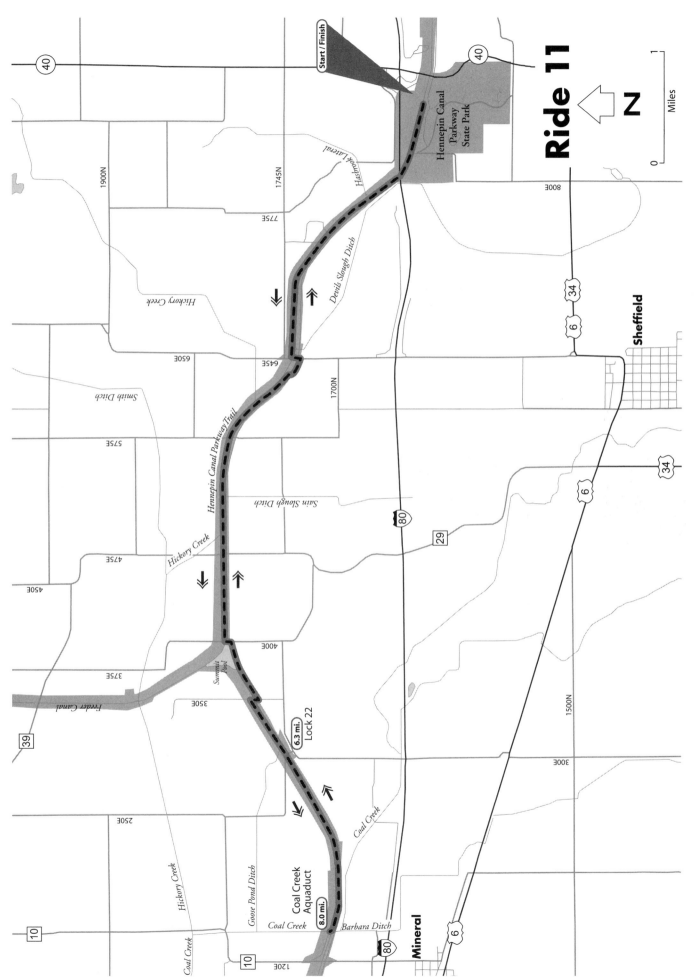

Ride 11

N

0 — 1 Miles

Start / Finish

Hennepin Canal Parkway State Park

Hennepin Canal Parkway Trail

Sheffield

Mineral

40

40

34

6

34

6

6

80

80

29

39

10

10

1900N

1745N

775E

1700N

800E

1500N

300E

659E

645E

575E

475E

450E

375E

350E

300E

250E

120E

Hickory Creek

Devils Slough Ditch

Hasbrook Lateral

Smith Ditch

Sain Slough Ditch

Hickory Creek

Feeder Canal

Summit Pool

6.3 mi.
Lock 22

Coal Creek
Aquaduct

8.0 mi.

Coal Creek

Barbara Ditch

Coal Creek

Goose Pond Ditch

Hickory Creek

Coal Creek

# RIDE 12
## End of the I & M

**Location:** LaSalle County
**Distance:** 9 miles
**Pedaling time:** 45–70 minutes
**Surface:** Crushed limestone and chip seal
**Terrain:** Flat
**Sweat factor:** Low
**Trailhead:** Utica

**Lock 14 in LaSalle has been restored.**

This ride starts in the old canal town of Utica and follows the final miles of the Illinois & Michigan Canal. Along the way you'll go through a gap blasted in bedrock and under the longest bridge in Illinois. At the end you'll see a restored lock that will give you a sense of how this whole thing worked. This is a great ride to combine with a trip to Starved Rock State Park.

To reach the trailhead, go south from I-80 on State Highway 178 toward Utica and Starved Rock State Park. Highway 178 goes through the block-long downtown area, which on summer weekends is packed with motorcycles. Turn right on the first street south of downtown,

Canal Street, before you cross the canal. By the way, the La Salle County Historical Society building on the southeast corner of this intersection is one of only two remaining canal warehouse buildings (call for hours: (815) 667-4861). It was built the same year the canal opened, 1848. There is a long, narrow, one-way parking lot on the left side of the road. The ride begins at the trail bridge on the west end of this parking lot. As you go south over the canal, you see that the water is stagnant here, as it will be for much of this ride. Follow the crushed-limestone trail to the right and go under a railroad bridge. Riding west, you can see the broad Illinois River on the left through the trees in stark contrast to the narrow canal on your right. There is also a railroad on the other side of the canal.

The canal gets narrower after 1.4 miles, and then it dries up completely for a short distance. Around 2.2 miles you can see a railroad tunnel through a mass of bedrock. Canal builders had to use black powder to blast through this wall of 550-million-year-old Saint Peter sandstone, creating what is now known as Split Rock. The trail continues on a chip-seal road at 3.3 miles. Though it is rare, you may encounter motor vehicles. The huge bridge ahead carries I-39 over the canal and the river. The concrete supports facing the canal have a limestone veneer, a stylistic nod to the cut-stone construction of the canal's locks. A plaque notes that this, the longest bridge in the state, is designated the Abraham Lincoln Memorial Bridge.

At 3.9 miles the trail crosses the Little Vermillion River beside a canal aqueduct. Then a railroad bridge soars overhead. There is a portable toilet under the next highway bridge, which carries State Highway 351. At the trail barrier beyond the bridge, turn right on the sidewalk, then right again toward Lock 14, the only restored lock on the canal. Here at 4.5 miles you can get a sense of how everything worked: how the lock tender (who was on call 24 hours a day) would push the wooden levers to open and close the gates at either end of the lock. The lock chamber measures 110 feet long by 18 feet wide. When the I & M Canal was operational, it took about fifteen minutes for a boat to pass through a lock, presuming that boat didn't have to wait in line to "lock through."

Ahead, the ruins of Lock 15, surrounded by abandoned bridge supports, mark the west end of the canal. This is a good place to turn around. If you want to follow the path to the very end, it continues for less than a mile, ending abruptly in the woods.

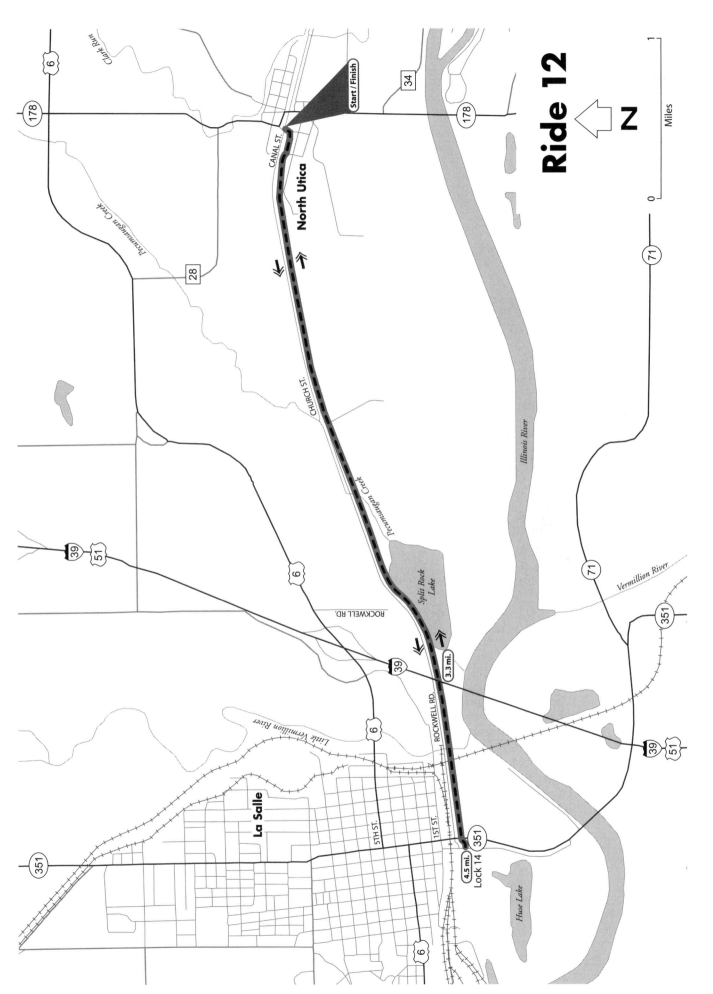

# Ride 12

La Salle

North Utica

Start / Finish

Lock 14

4.5 mi.

3.3 mi.

CANAL ST.

CHURCH ST.

ROCKWELL RD.

ROCKWELL RD.

5TH ST.

1ST ST.

Pecumsaugan Creek

Pecumsaugan Creek

Clark Run

Split Rock Lake

Illinois River

Vermillion River

Little Vermillion River

Huse Lake

N

Miles

0    1

6

178

178

34

28

6

39    51

6

6

39

71

71

351

351

39    51

351

# RIDE 13
## Hills and Valleys

**Location:** McHenry County
**Distance:** 16.6 miles
**Pedaling time:** 1.5–2 hours
**Surface:** Paved roads
**Terrain:** Rolling hills
**Sweat factor:** Moderate +
**Trailhead:** Woodstock Opera House, Van Buren and Dean streets

### Opera in Woodstock?

**Don't expect to hear arias at the Woodstock Opera House. You are much more likely to witness plays, concerts, or other performances at this beautiful venue. The Opera House was built in 1889 as a multiuse building. In fact, it was once city hall, library, and fire department. The Opera House was on the vaudeville circuit, and later Paul Newman and Orson Welles performed there at the dawn of their careers. By the 1960s, the building was showing its age, but a restoration effort over the next few decades gave it new life. For information and a schedule of performances, visit www.woodstockoperahouse.com or call (815) 338-5300.**

A glance at the road names on this ride tells you what to expect: Bull Valley, Mason Hill, Cherry Valley, Ridge, and Valley Hill. This is about as hilly as a Chicago-area ride can get. This route has more traffic than most of the rides in this book. While the village of Bull Valley is intent on preserving its character, traffic will only get worse as real estate development in surrounding cities continues. Look for a number of big barns on this ride too.

The ride starts at the south end of the brick-paved Woodstock Square. To avoid the two-hour parking limit on the Square, look for public parking in lots within a block in every direction. There are two especially prominent buildings here. The first is the Old Courthouse and Sheriff's House on the northwest corner of the Square. Built in 1857, this building now houses restaurants, shops, and the Chester Gould-Dick Tracy Museum (www.chestergould.org or 815-338-8281). Gould created the Dick Tracy comic strip in 1931. He lived in Bull Valley for the last fifty years of his life, and Woodstock celebrates Dick Tracy Days every June. The other notable building is the Woodstock Opera House, which anchors the south side of the Square.

Head south from the Square on Dean Street, riding on bricks for a block. Turn left on South Street at the second stop sign. Go straight through the next intersection, a five-way stop, and go under the railroad tracks in a narrow, 19th-century tunnel. At the stop sign just beyond the tunnel, turn right on East Lake Street (not to be confused with Lake Avenue at the aforementioned five-way stop). Turn left on Brown Street at 0.6 mile. This street ends at Washburn Street. Turn left, and then follow the sharp right curve where the road turns into South Street. It crosses busy State Highway 47 at a stoplight and becomes Country Club Road.

Gradually climb for the next mile and turn left on Bull Valley Road. Follow the curve to the right to stay on Bull Valley Road where Queen Anne Road goes north. At the four-way stop, turn right on Fleming Road. Though not named for hills or valleys, Fleming Road has its share of rolling, shady hills. At the end of the road, turn left on Country Club Road and go half a mile, and then turn left on Mason Hill Road. Another pretty, shaded road with rolling hills, Mason Hill Road is part of the McHenry County Scenic Drive. After passing Cherry Valley Road on the right, turn left on Cherry Valley Road at 6.6 miles. This road has more barns and hills. It ends at Bull Valley Road. Turn left, and then turn right at the stop sign on Ridge Road. Go up a steep hill that is interrupted briefly by a level spot at the intersection with Swathmore Road. A mile later, turn left on Valley Hill Road just before another hill gets steeper. This is yet another shaded, hilly road. Turn right on Bull Valley Road at the four-way stop and fly down a big hill. At the three-way stop at Cold Springs Road, turn left to stay on Bull Valley Road. When you reach Fleming Road, continue on Bull Valley Road and backtrack all the way to the start.

Movie buffs know Woodstock as the place where Groundhog Day, starring Bill Murray and Andie MacDowell, was filmed. In that movie, Murray had to live one day again and again. The city's Web site at www.woodstockil.gov has a map of filming locations. If you enjoy a challenging ride through shady forests and bucolic farmland, you won't mind reliving this one over and over.

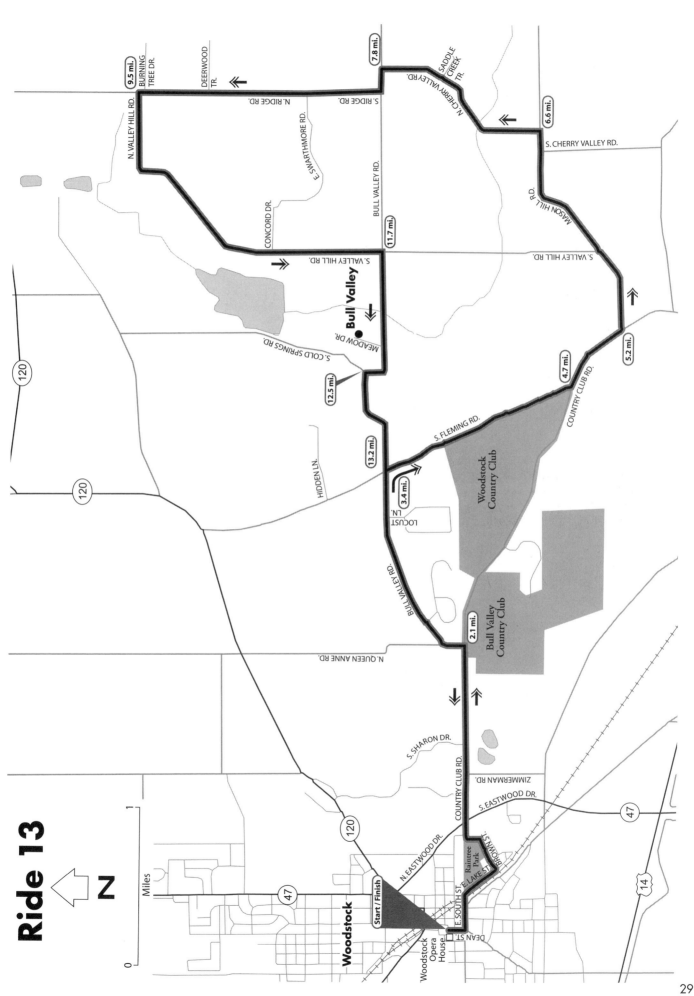

# Ride 13

N

Woodstock

Start / Finish

Woodstock Opera House

Bull Valley

Woodstock Country Club

Bull Valley Country Club

Rainttree Park

9.5 mi.

7.8 mi.

6.6 mi.

11.7 mi.

12.5 mi.

13.2 mi.

3.4 mi.

5.2 mi.

4.7 mi.

2.1 mi.

Miles

0  1

# RIDE 14
## A Gift From the Glaciers

**Location:** McHenry County
**Distance:** 9.6 miles
**Pedaling time:** 50–70 minutes
**Surface:** Crushed-limestone trails
**Terrain:** Rolling hills
**Sweat factor:** Moderate +
**Trailhead:** Kettle Woods Picnic Area

Bicycling opportunities in most Illinois state parks are limited to paved roads, but at Moraine Hills, bicycling is a primary activity. This state park is also one of the closest to Chicago, only 40 miles from the Loop. Its geological features are remnants from the withdrawal of the Wisconsin glaciation 12,000 years ago. A moraine is basically a pile of boulders and dirt left behind by a glacier, a bit like the small mass of mud and rock left behind in the springtime when a pile of plowed snow melts. The park is open from 6 AM to 9 PM (815-385-1624). This ride is pretty challenging even though it is short. The trails are mostly crushed limestone. Some of the steeper hills are paved with asphalt to prevent erosion. Others are surfaced with gravel, which makes a mountain bike preferable, though not mandatory, for this ride. There are three one-way trails in the park, and this ride covers all of them (note that these trails are one-way for bicyclists but not for hikers). The trails alternate between wooded and grassy areas. Be careful on the asphalt descents because you could hit the crushed stone at the bottom at a high speed.

Enter the park on Main Park Road and turn into Kettle Woods, the first parking area on the left. Like every picnic area in the park, Kettle Woods has drinking water and rustic toilets. The name has nothing to do with

cooking; a kettle is a depression formed by a melting block of glacial ice. The ride begins from the wooden vehicle barrier with a short, steep hill, the first of many you will encounter. This spur dead-ends at the Lake Defiance Trail, which has red markers. Bicyclists must turn left. This trail comes out to River Road and parallels the asphalt River Trail for a short distance. At Junction C (0.8 miles), veer to the left, going downhill and under the road. This two-way connector goes to Junction D. Keep right to follow the yellow-marked Fox River Trail.

At 1.8 miles, there is a wildlife viewing platform overlooking Black Tern Marsh to the left. Wetlands and lakes cover half of the park's acreage, so it is not surprising that waterfowl are abundant. Overall, more than a hundred species of birds have been identified in the park. There are also deer and smaller mammals. Shortly past the spur to the platform, the wider trail curves west toward the Fox River's McHenry Dam, but the ride continues around the loop by keeping to the left. The land around the dam was the first incarnation of the park, which was then named McHenry Dam State Park. It was acquired by the state in 1939, whereas the rest of the park was purchased and developed in the 1970s. A concession stand open from April to October is located at the dam (www.mchenrydam.com). Flush toilets are available here. Although the structure was renamed William G. Stratton Lock and Dam in 1977, the area is still known as McHenry Dam.

There is another viewing platform to the left at 2.7 miles, but it is further off the trail. When you return to Junction D, go right to retrace your path to Junction C, where cyclists must turn left on the Lake Defiance Trail. At 3.9 miles, curve to the right at Junction B. The Lake Defiance Trail and the Leatherleaf Bog Trail (blue markers) run together for the next half mile to Junction A, where you go left to follow the latter trail. Also keep left at Opossum Run Junction. The Leatherleaf Bog area has the kettle-moraine topography that is common in Wisconsin. The trail winds around and eventually returns to Junction B, where you must turn left. This time when you get to Junction A, go right. At 7.9 miles you cross the entrance to the park office. Open from 9 AM to 4 PM, the office features indoor restrooms and drinking fountains. There is a concession stand around the back that is open on weekends from April to October. The park office is a good place to get a look at Lake Defiance, one of the few glacial lakes in Illinois that is in near-natural condition.

This ride saves the toughest part for last. The trail turns away from the park road and climbs for a quarter mile. The remaining 1.5 miles are rarely flat. Be especially careful descending toward Oak Opening Junction at 8.4 miles; the crushed stone is deep and loose near the bottom. At the top of a hill near 9.5 miles, turn left at Kettle Woods Junction to return to the parking area.

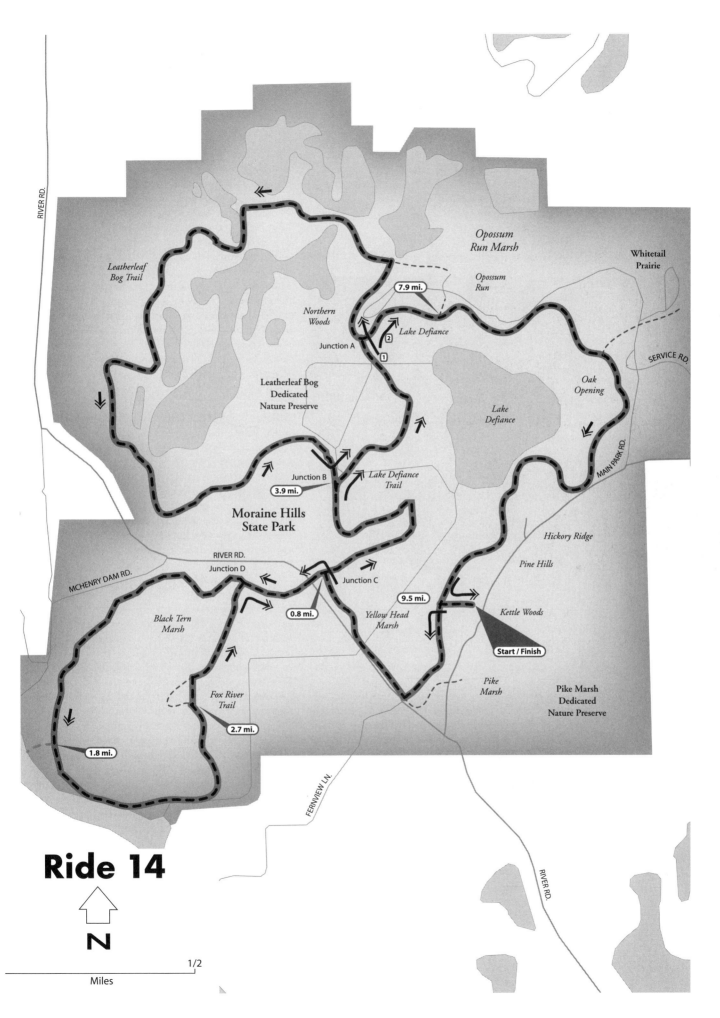

Leatherleaf
Bog Trail

*Opossum
Run Marsh*

Whitetail
Prairie

7.9 mi.

*Opossum
Run*

*Northern
Woods*

*Lake Defiance*

Junction A

SERVICE RD.

*Leatherleaf Bog
Dedicated
Nature Preserve*

*Oak
Opening*

*Lake
Defiance*

*Lake Defiance
Trail*

Junction B

3.9 mi.

**Moraine Hills
State Park**

*Hickory Ridge*

*Pine Hills*

RIVER RD.

Junction D

MCHENRY DAM RD.

Junction C

9.5 mi.

*Kettle Woods*

0.8 mi.

*Yellow Head
Marsh*

*Black Tern
Marsh*

**Start / Finish**

MAIN PARK RD.

*Fox River
Trail*

*Pike
Marsh*

**Pike Marsh
Dedicated
Nature Preserve**

2.7 mi.

1.8 mi.

FERNVIEW LN.

RIVER RD.

RIVER RD.

# Ride 14

**N**

1/2

Miles

# RIDE 15
## Frolic Along the Fox

**Location:** Kane and McHenry counties
**Distance:** 26.8 miles
**Pedaling time:** 2.5–3 hours
**Surface:** Paved trails
**Terrain:** Flat
**Sweat factor:** Low
**Trailhead:** Tyler Creek Forest Preserve, Elgin

**A bike trail crosses the Fox River in Elgin under the Northwest Tollway.**

Together, the Fox River Trail and the Prairie Trail form a recreational corridor more than 65 miles long from the Wisconsin border down to Oswego. This ride samples a 12-mile stretch of the corridor from Elgin to Crystal Lake that includes parts of both trails.

Tyler Creek Forest Preserve is just south of I-90 (Northwest Tollway) on State Highway 31. Turn west at the first stoplight and immediately angle to the left into the preserve. Keep left, pass the beginning of the bike trail on the left, and cross the narrow stone bridge to reach the parking lots. The preserve opens at 8 AM. If you want to ride earlier, there are parking areas off Duncan Avenue on the east side of the river. Zero your odometer where the trail begins along the park road. The trail quickly dives toward the creek to pass under Highway 31. Be careful here because there is no guardrail separating the trail from the creek. The next half mile is mostly uphill and you pass Judson College. On the long descent to the Fox River, you pass Providence Baptist College. At 1.3 miles, turn right onto the bridge across the Fox River. The trail bridge is directly underneath I-90 and uses the highway bridge's supports.

The wooden surface is smooth but noisy, especially with the echo from the concrete bridge overhead. On the east side of the river, the trail curves right and then left uphill to the Fox River Trail junction at 1.5 miles. Turn left toward Dundee, going back under I-90.

Between towns, much of the Fox River Trail is covered by an ample canopy of trees. East Dundee is the first town north of Elgin. Cross Main Street (State Highway 72) at the stoplight. There are many restaurants and shops near the trail, including a bike shop north of Main Street. The East Dundee Visitor Center at 3.9 miles has pop machines outside and restrooms inside. The next town is Carpentersville, where you cross another Main Street. The rest of the Fox River Trail is a pleasant, uninterrupted ride, except for a very brief crushed-limestone section of trail at 6.9 miles.

At Souwanas Trail (a street, not a bike trail) in Algonquin, enter Mc Henry County and continue north on the Prairie Trail. Following the same right-of-way formerly used by the Chicago and North Western Railroad, little changes as you pass from one trail to the other except for the painted centerline on the Mc Henry County side. The smooth, wood-surfaced bridge over the Fox River at 8.9 miles is supported by the original railroad bridge stanchions. After crossing the next street, go right on the sidewalk and then left on the trail. There is another bike shop at 9.1 miles. Around 10.4 miles, there is a large gravel processing plant on the right with long conveyors and huge piles of rock and sand. A conveyor runs beside the trail for half a mile. Later another conveyor crosses the trail. Shortly after, many railroad ties, most likely remnants from this rail-trail's conversion, are piled in the brush on the right.

Beyond the gravel mining area, the Prairie Trail lives up to its name with expanses of grassland. This includes a small tract called Larsen Prairie that is an Illinois State Nature Preserve. At 12 miles, the trail turns abruptly to the left. It curves back to the north parallel to Pyott Road. Lake in the Hills Airport is visible to the west before you cross James R. Rakow Road. At 13 miles the trail goes left onto the sidewalk past a bike shop. At the stoplight, go north across Virginia Road and west across Main Street (this Main Street is Crystal Lake's), then turn right on the trail. A park at 13.4 miles offers water and toilets. This makes an ideal turnaround point, but if you're still feeling strong you can ride at least another 12 miles north on streets and the paved trail. There are many restaurants and stores in Crystal Lake. From Ringwood north to the Wisconsin border, the trail is much rougher and best suited to mountain bikes.

In general, the trail seems a bit more uphill going north and downhill going south, so you should have an easier ride back to Elgin. Don't forget that big hill to climb from the Fox River up to Judson College near the end, though.

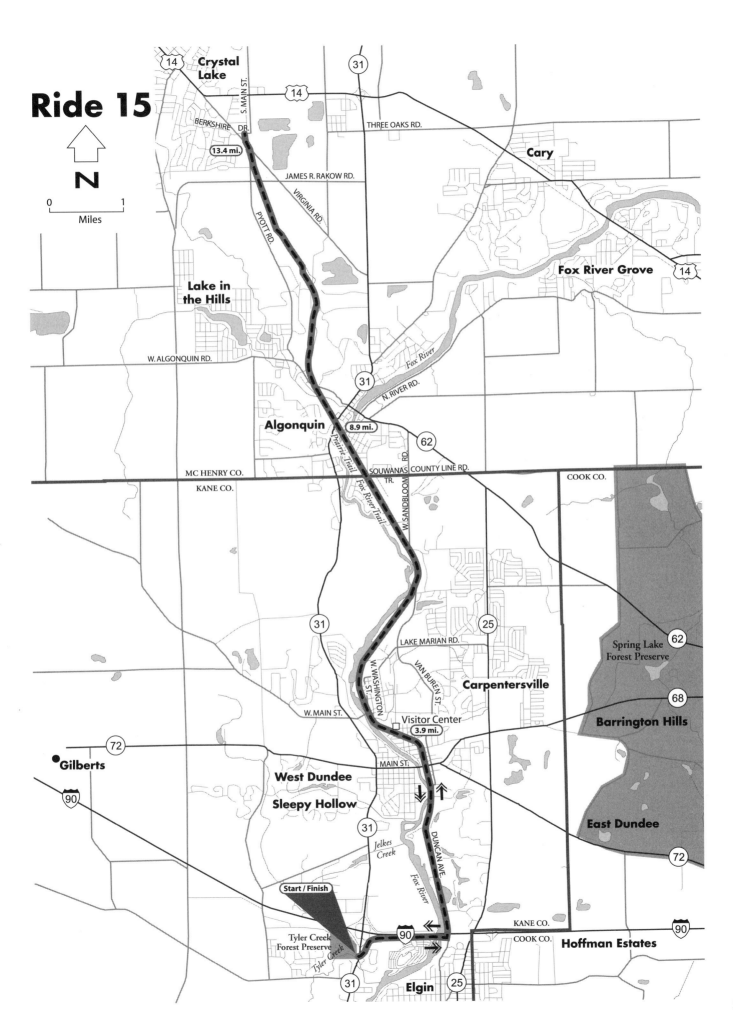

# Ride 15

**N**

0 ——— 1
Miles

# RIDE 16
## Hangin' on the Elgin Branch

**Location:** Kane and DuPage counties
**Distance:** 22.4 miles
**Pedaling time:** 2–2.5 hours
**Surface:** Crushed-limestone trail
**Terrain:** Flat with a few gentle hills
**Sweat factor:** Low
**Trailhead:** Raymond Street, Elgin

### One of America's Oldest Rail-Trails

The Illinois Prairie Path was one of the first rails-to-trails conversions in the United States. The story began with the Chicago, Aurora and Elgin Railroad, a high-speed interurban railway. For more than half a century, this electric railway brought suburbanites into Chicago. After World War II, the railroad encountered financial difficulties. Then construction of the Eisenhower Expressway severed its connection to downtown so passengers had to transfer to get to the Loop. Ridership diminished, and the final day of operation was July 3, 1957. The railroad shut down at noon, meaning everyone who rode the Chicago, Aurora and Elgin to work that morning had to find another way home in the afternoon, the day before a holiday no less!

The tracks were dismantled and sold, but the land lay unused for several years. In 1963, naturalist May Theilgaard Watts wrote a letter to the Chicago Tribune suggesting that the right-of-way be turned into a hiking trail. Public response to this idea was overwhelmingly favorable, and a group soon formed to make it a reality. The IPP Web site, www.ipp.org, details the history of this difficult process. Even before the path was completed, the movement inspired others across the country to consider the possibilities presented by the increasing number of abandoned railways in their own towns. Decades later, the IPP has proven to be one of the most popular recreational attractions in the western suburbs. The path has woven itself into the fabric of the communities it touches. Today's users can scarcely imagine a time when their favorite biking and running path carried commuters to Chicago aboard electric trains.

The Illinois Prairie Path (IPP) is the largest rail-trail system in Illinois, comprising more than 60 miles of multiuse paths. This ride samples the trail's northwestern Elgin Branch, which runs 16 miles from Elgin to Wheaton.

Parking for this ride is found at a modest gravel lot on Raymond Street south of U.S. Highway 20. A steel guardrail separates the lot from the trail. The junction with the Fox River Trail is visible to the right, but this ride goes to the left. Reset the odometer at the diagonal crossing of Raymond Street. At 0.8 mile, the trail crosses Kenyon Road and passes Clintonville Station, appropriately now home of the Valley Model Railroad Association. This building was mostly a power substation for the electric railroad with a small waiting room for passengers. After the next street, Middle Street, the trail climbs a gentle slope for 1.3 miles. The path goes over State Highway 25 and railroad tracks on bridges, but you have to cross busy Dunham Road at grade.

The path enters Du Page County and goes through Pratts Wayne Woods Forest Preserve next. This is a fairly large preserve with more than 3,400 acres, mostly wetlands. Indeed, there is a lake on the left about half a mile after Dunham Road. At 4.7 miles the IPP crosses Powis Road, followed shortly by Army Trail Road. You will find water and a portable toilet here. The trail splits briefly. Follow the sign that reads, "To avoid steep hill" and points to the wider trail on the left.

At 5 miles, make a sharp left and cross the railroad tracks, then walk your bike up a short flight of stairs. This section of the trail has gentle ups and downs. During the summer, this pleasant, wooded corridor feels somewhat remote—until you look to your right and glimpse houses through the trees. At 7.3 miles, turn sharply to the right and cross Diversey Parkway. Then begin a steep, curvy, paved climb to a bridge over State Highway 59. Watch for oncoming cyclists as you climb. The descent, on the other hand, is straight. The trail goes under State Highway 64 in a lighted tunnel. At 8.8 miles, go up a short hill and turn left at the top to follow the IPP. This is actually the

Much of the Elgin Branch of the Illinois Prairie Path is surrounded by trees.

Great Western Trail, but the two paths join to go across Prince Crossing Road. To continue on the IPP, turn right on the path parallel to the street. The path continues into Timber Ridge Forest Preserve. At 11.2 miles, enter the parking area at Geneva Road.

From here, there are several options. You can follow the Geneva Spur of the IPP west to the Fox River Trail north to the junction you saw near Raymond Street. An even more ambitious option is to continue on Ride 25, joining that 21-mile loop near its halfway point. If you want to explore a bit but not so far, head north on the Timber Ridge Trail, then west on the Great Western Trail to rejoin the IPP. Otherwise, just turn around and ride back to Elgin. At 15 miles on the return trip, you descend from the Highway 59 bridge. Stay alert, watch your speed, and keep right. Also, don't forget about the stairs before the railroad tracks at 17.3 miles, or you'll be in for a bone-rattling ride.

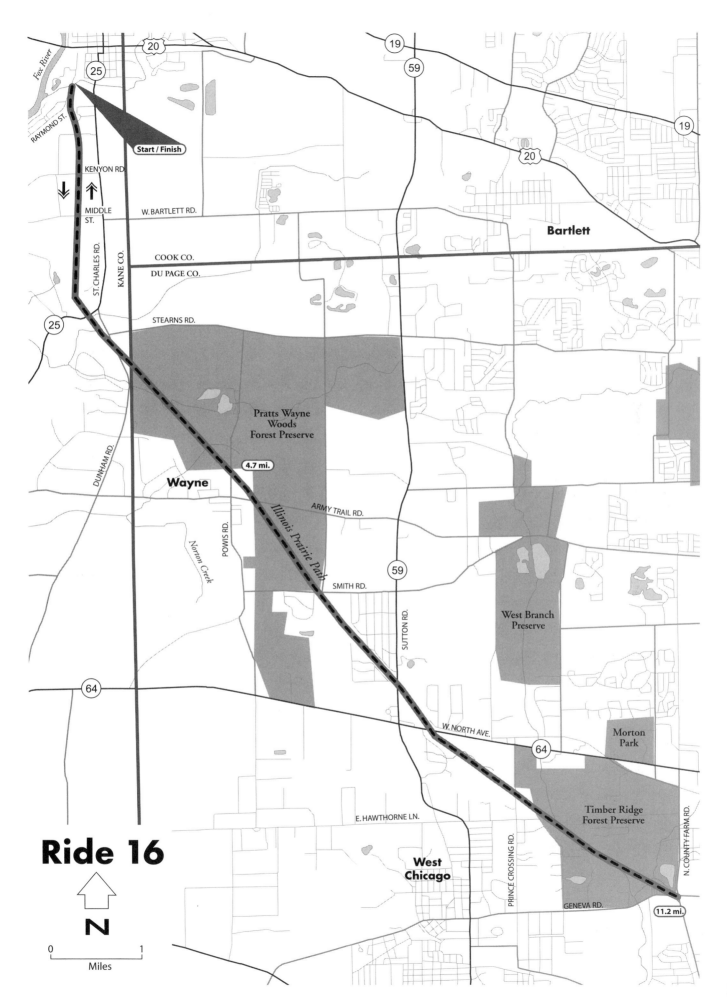

Start / Finish

Fox River

RAYMOND ST.

20

25

KENYON RD.

MIDDLE ST.

W. BARTLETT RD.

COOK CO.

DU PAGE CO.

Bartlett

19

59

20

19

STEARNS RD.

25

ST. CHARLES RD.

KANE CO.

DUNHAM RD.

Pratts Wayne Woods Forest Preserve

4.7 mi.

Wayne

POWIS RD.

Norton Creek

ARMY TRAIL RD.

*Illinois Prairie Path*

SMITH RD.

59

SUTTON RD.

West Branch Preserve

64

64

W. NORTH AVE.

Morton Park

E. HAWTHORNE LN.

West Chicago

PRINCE CROSSING RD.

GENEVA RD.

Timber Ridge Forest Preserve

N. COUNTY FARM RD.

11.2 mi.

# Ride 16

N

0        1
Miles

# RIDE 17
## Poplar Creek Trail

**Location:** Northwestern Cook County
**Distance:** : 8.9 miles
**Pedaling time:** 45–60 minutes
**Surface:** Paved trail
**Terrain:** Flat with a few gentle hills
**Sweat factor:** Low +
**Trailhead:** Shoe Factory Road Woods

This is a pleasant loop through forest preserve land in Chicago's northwest suburbs. Shoe Factory Road Woods is on the west side of State Highway 59 less than a mile south of I-90 (Northwest Tollway). You cross the trail shortly after entering the forest preserve, so park at the first opportunity. Ride to the trail sign (a big map) and reset your odometer. Head south on the path, following the counterclockwise mile markers. The noisy four-lane highway on the left contrasts with the prairie restoration area on the right. The trail curves around to the stoplight at Sutton Road (Highway 59) and Golf Road (State Highway 58). Cross both roads (either one first since there are crosswalks in all directions) to get to the southeast corner. Continuing south, the trail shares a plain bridge with Sutton Road, but to the left the equestrian trail uses a bridge with lions cast into the concrete. After the path crosses Bode Road, it heads into the woods and flows over long, rolling hills.

At 1.7 miles, keep left at the trail spur to Schaumburg Road. The trail crosses back over Bode Road and east across Bartlett Road at a stoplight. Bode Lake North is on the left after 2.4 miles, followed by Bode Lake South, which has a parking lot, water, and a portable toilet. The path goes uphill to mile marker 3. There is a field of corn on the left, an increasingly rare sight in Cook County. At 3.7 miles there is a trail spur to Barrington Road. This also leads to a parking lot with water and a portable toilet. From here, the trail turns northward and passes a mix of prairie, woods, and farmland. Cross Golf Road at the stoplight and go down a relatively steep hill. The path runs close to Barrington Road for half a mile, passing Barrington Road Pond along the way. The trail crosses Shoe Factory Road around 5.5 miles. A parking area known simply as Bike Lot is on the left. Curve sharply to the right just past the junction with the trail spur. For the next 0.4 mile, the path is paved on top of an old road. At mile 6, the path curves left. The next 1.5 miles are more open; you won't find much shade until you cross Bartlett Road again.

The generically named Family Picnic Area on the left at 8.2 miles has water and a portable toilet. Soon after, cross Highway 59. An unpaved, double-track trail continues northwest from here, so go south across Shoe Factory Road instead. The last 0.7 mile is mostly downhill, and mostly open prairie except for a small grove of trees. Return to the forest preserve road just short of 8.9 miles.

**Cyclists ride through meadows and forests on the Poplar Creek Trail.**

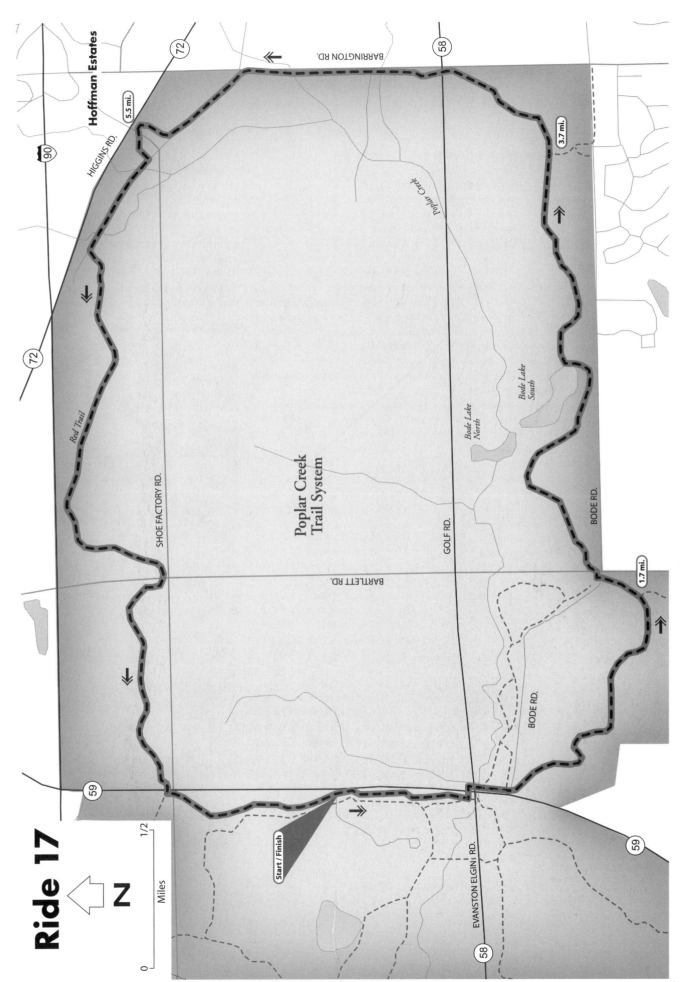

# Ride 17

N

Hoffman Estates

72

90

5.5 mi.

HIGGINS RD.

72

Red Trail

SHOE FACTORY RD.

BARTLETT RD.

59

Start / Finish

EVANSTON ELGIN RD.

58

Miles

0    1/2

BARRINGTON RD.

58

Poplar Creek

Poplar Creek
Trail System

GOLF RD.

Bode Lake
North

Bode Lake
South

BODE RD.

BODE RD.

3.7 mi.

1.7 mi.

59

# RIDE 18
## Busse Woods

**Location:** Northwestern Cook County
**Distance:** 9.1 miles
**Pedaling time:** 45–60 minutes
**Surface:** Paved trails
**Terrain:** Flat with a few gentle hills
**Sweat factor:** Low +
**Trailhead:** Ned Brown Meadow Groves 28–30

### A Bicycle Friendly Community

Schaumburg is just west of Busse Woods. One might expect a city known for a huge mall and heavy traffic to be a forbidding place for bicycling, but in 2003 Schaumburg was named as a Bicycle Friendly Community (bronze level) by the League of American Bicyclists. It was the first of only two cities in Illinois (Chicago became the other in 2005) so honored, and there are only 49 Bicycle Friendly Communities nationwide. Schaumburg has 85 miles of bike routes split evenly between on-street bike lanes and separate bike paths. To keep them tidy, the city has an "Adopt-a-Bikepath" program much like adopt-a-highway programs. You can request a bike route map by calling (847) 923-3862.

Right across the expressway from Schaumburg's massive Woodfield Mall, Busse Woods is the most popular trail in Chicago's northwest suburbs. Although it is officially Ned Brown Preserve, most people just call it Busse Woods, particularly when referring to the trail. Following the red arrows at intersections is the easiest way to stay on the main trail. It passes many picnic areas, most of which have portable toilets. The trail can get crowded on weekends, and this is not the place for fast riding. The trail has been resurfaced and has some steep drops of several inches on the edge of the asphalt, so don't ride too far to the right.

This ride starts at the north end of the Ned Brown Forest Preserve off Golf Road (State Highway 58). At the stoplight labeled "Ring Road," turn south into Ned Brown Meadow Groves 28–30. Drive past a trail crossing, continue straight ahead, and park at the south end of the lot. The ride begins where the trail crosses the "Authorized Vehicles Only" road. Heading south, the trail goes through a grassy field, then after half a mile it crosses a small creek bridge and enters the woods. There are some blind curves here, so stay on your side of the path. When the trail splits just before 0.8 mile, keep left. The trail runs along the north side of Higgins Road (State Highway 72) and passes several picnic areas before heading into the trees again. At 3.9 miles, make a sharp right to follow the trail. The fence on your left restrains a small herd of elk. Although people today associate them with Elk Grove Village, the first elk came here back when it was only Elk Grove Township. Ten were brought from Jackson Hole, Wyoming, in the 1920s. At one time the herd numbered more than 70, too many for the 15-acre pasture to sustain. Now the population is limited to eight. Veterinarians from Brookfield Zoo take care of them.

A long bridge crosses Higgins Road, and at 4.5 miles

a spur to the left leads to the intersection of Higgins and Arlington Heights Road. There are gas station/mini-marts on two corners, and a shopping center includes several restaurants and a bike shop. Just past 5.6 miles, watch out for fishermen casting from the trail as it passes over the dam on Salt Creek that created Busse Lake. When the trail reaches a T, go right and downhill. Go right again when the trail splits at 6.6 miles. At 7.1 miles, a trail map labeled "Busse Woods Boating Center" stands straight ahead. Make a sharp right, cross the road, and curve to the left.

**Busse Woods is a popular trail for bicycling.**

At 8.2 miles, the at-grade Higgins Road crossing is long and dangerous because it is near the I-290 interchange. Watch for cars turning onto Higgins Road from the ramp on your left. Push the button to get a walk signal, and then do it again in the median. After this crossing, the trail goes back into the woods. At the Y intersection, turn left to head back north toward the parking lot.

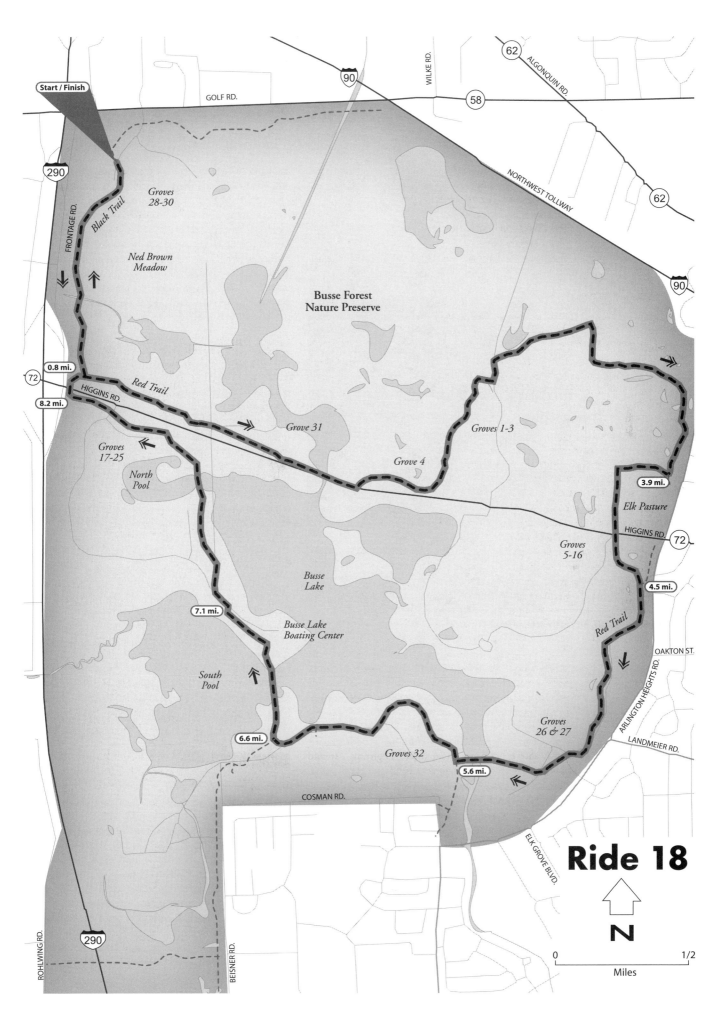

Start / Finish

290

GOLF RD.

WILKE RD.

90

62 ALGONQUIN RD.

58

62

NORTHWEST TOLLWAY

62

FRONTAGE RD.

Black Trail

*Groves
28-30*

*Ned Brown
Meadow*

**Busse Forest
Nature Preserve**

90

72

0.8 mi.

8.2 mi.

HIGGINS RD.

*Red Trail*

*Grove 31*

*Groves 1-3*

*Groves
17-25*

*North
Pool*

*Grove 4*

3.9 mi.

*Elk Pasture*

HIGGINS RD. 72

*Busse
Lake*

*Groves
5-16*

7.1 mi.

*Busse Lake
Boating Center*

4.5 mi.

*Red Trail*

OAKTON ST.

*South
Pool*

ARLINGTON HEIGHTS RD.

6.6 mi.

*Groves
26 & 27*

LANDMEIER RD.

*Groves 32*

5.6 mi.

COSMAN RD.

ELK GROVE BLVD.

**Ride 18**

N

ROHLWING RD.

290

BEISNER RD.

0                    1/2

Miles

# RIDE 19
## Des Plaines River Trail

**Location:** Lake County
**Distance:** 13.5 miles
**Pedaling time:** 1.25–1.75 hours
**Surface:** Crushed-stone trails
**Terrain:** Flat
**Sweat factor:** Low
**Trailhead:** Intersection of DPRT with spur from Shelter A and B parking area, Old School Forest Preserve

**The Des Plaines River Trail has four-legged users, too.**

The Des Plaines River Trail (DPRT) courses through a greenway stretching almost the entire length of Lake County, linking many popular forest preserves. It passes under most of the busy roads along the way, minimizing interruptions. As a sample of the DPRT, this ride goes from Old School Forest Preserve to Wright Woods Forest Preserve and back, including loop trails at both preserves. The trail surface is mostly crushed stone with a few short asphalt sections and an occasional gravel patch. Because equestrians share the trail, it can be a bit bumpy for a skinny-tired bike. Toilets and water are available at both preserves, but Old School's facilities are accessed more easily from the trail.

Old School Forest Preserve is easy to reach from I-94 (Tri-State Tollway). Take Rockland Road (State Highway 176) west to Saint Mary's Road and go south. The preserve entrance is 0.6 mile south of Rockland Road. Drive on the one-way loop road to the Shelter A and B parking area. A spur to the DPRT is located at the far end of this parking lot. Turn left onto the DPRT southbound to begin the ride. Remember to yield to horses on the trail. Fortunately, most are acclimated to bicycles and unlikely to spook. When the trail splits at 0.6 mile, go

right to head south on the DPRT. You'll get to ride the other way on the return trip. A tenth of a mile later, cross Old School Road, then go left over the railroad tracks and right onto the trail. Riding parallel to the tracks, you can see large homes on spacious lots to the left. The trail turns west, going under Saint Mary's Road at 1.4 miles. Signs warn equestrians and bicyclists to dismount. Now you are in MacArthur Woods Nature Preserve. A trail spur goes off to the left at 2.4 miles; keep right. This is a particularly curvy and shady segment of the trail.

You finally get to see the Des Plaines River after 3.1 miles of riding as the trail passes under Town Line Road (State Highway 60). This underpass may be closed due to flooding, particularly in the spring. A sign warns in advance if this is the case. As soon as you get through the underpass, climb a short hill and cross the river on a steel bridge with a smooth, wooden surface. There is a small parking lot here. Beyond the lot, turn left to continue south on the DPRT. Around 3.5 miles the trail emerges from the woods for a while. Judging from the nearby retail development on the right, this greenway was preserved just in time. The trail crosses back to the east side of the river at 4.3 miles, followed by a short, steep downhill turning to the right. This is Wright Woods Forest Preserve. At 4.7 miles, go past a trail on the left; you'll return on that trail.

At the four-way trail junction, go straight to follow the Wright Woods Trail (the DPRT goes right and crosses the river to Half Day Forest Preserve). This trail is a bit narrower than the DPRT but still plenty wide. It is a pleasant, serpentine loop through the woods. Wildflowers abound in the spring, while the trees offer cooling shade in the summer. You'll hear lots of birds, too. As you circle counterclockwise around the preserve, you pass several crushed-stone trails on your left. Simply keep going straight on the loop trail. The trail returns to the DPRT at 7.5 miles. Turn right to head back north to Old School Forest Preserve. At 9 miles, bid adieu to the Des Plaines River as you won't see it again on this ride.

At another familiar trail intersection at 11.6 miles, go right to follow the "Old School Preserve" arrow. After you cross the park road, you may glimpse a trail through the woods to the left. This is the fitness trail, which is not open to bikes. A couple of trail spurs lead to toilets and water. There is also a drinking fountain at the park entrance, which you cross at 13.3 miles. When you get back to the DPRT, there is a stop sign. Don't ignore it because riders coming uphill from the right are hard to see. Turn left onto the DPRT south, reaching the end of the ride at the first trail spur to the left a short distance later. Follow the spur back to the parking lot. You may want to explore the preserve further after your ride. The 1.5-mile, one-way, asphalt park road loop has a special lane for cyclists and inline skaters. Bikes are also allowed on the 1.5-mile, crushed-stone loop around the lake at the northeast corner of the preserve. And of course the northbound DPRT beckons, too.

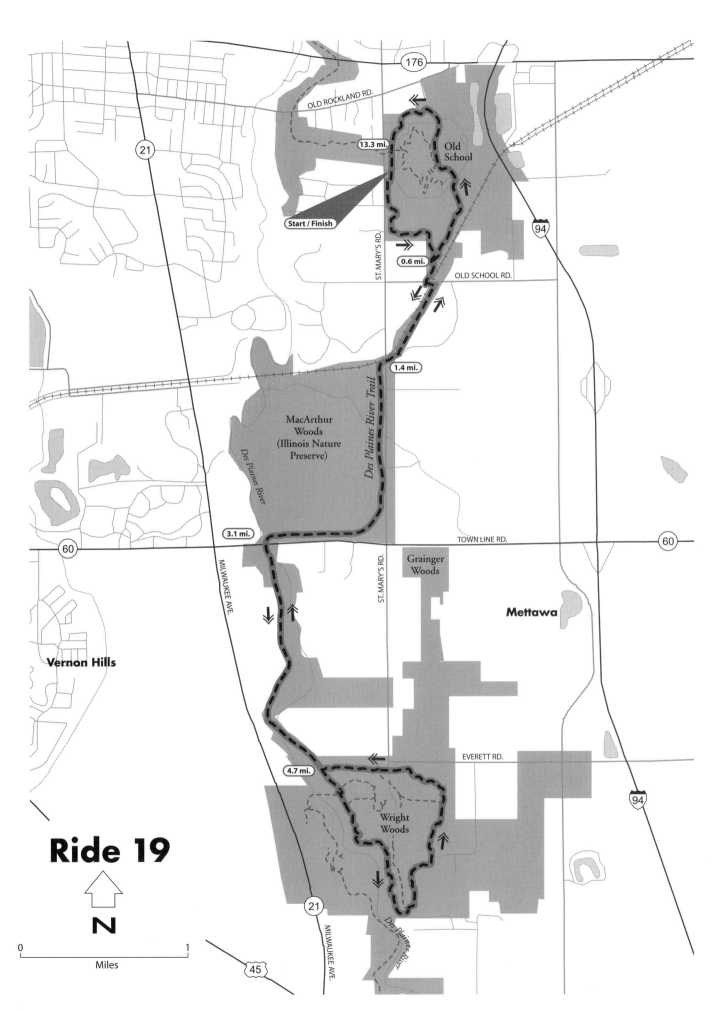

OLD ROCKLAND RD.

176

13.3 mi.

Old
School

Start / Finish

94

ST. MARY'S RD.

0.6 mi.

OLD SCHOOL RD.

1.4 mi.

MacArthur
Woods
(Illinois Nature
Preserve)

Des Plaines River

Des Plaines River Trail

3.1 mi.

60

TOWN LINE RD.

60

21

MILWAUKEE AVE.

ST. MARY'S RD.

Grainger
Woods

Mettawa

Vernon Hills

EVERETT RD.

94

4.7 mi.

Wright
Woods

21

MILWAUKEE AVE.

Des Plaines River

45

**Ride 19**

N

0                    1

Miles

# RIDE 20
## Going to the Garden

**Location:** Northern Cook County
**Distance:** 20 miles
**Pedaling time:** 2–2.5 hours
**Surface:** Asphalt trail
**Terrain:** Mostly flat, some easy hills
**Sweat factor:** Low +
**Trailhead:** Linne Woods on Dempster Street, Morton Grove

### Chicago Botanic Garden

This is a place where you can save a lot of money by biking. Cyclists get in for free, but it costs $12 to park a car. There are 23 gardens and three native-habitat areas packed into 385 acres of land. The garden opened in 1972. Nearly 800,000 people visited in 2004.

To visit by bike: Cross Dundee Road at the stoplight, which changes quickly when you press the walk button. You can go straight across and turn left on the trail, or you can go diagonally left to the service entrance. Either way, follow the service drive for a mile, passing several gardens and the Glencoe Golf Club along the way. You are coming in the back way, with the bulk of the park on your left. Approaching the stop sign, go right around the gate and turn right. Turn left where the sign points to "additional parking." Turn left at the stop sign 0.2 mile later to head toward the Gateway Visitor Center. When you reach the building, there is plenty of bike parking on the left. Bikes are not allowed on the garden paths, so you will need to lock up your bike. To leave, continue on that same road, returning to the intersection after 0.2 mile. Turn right, go around the gate, and ride back to Dundee Road. Cross and follow the trail to the right. This loop adds about 2.6 miles to your ride.

The Chicago Botanic Garden is open from 8 AM to sunset every day except December 25. Visit www.chicagobotanic.org or call (847) 835-5440 for more information.

If you ask a Chicagoan, particularly on the North Side, for a favorite bike route, odds are good that the answer will be, "Ride to the Botanic Garden." The Lakefront Bike Path may be the place to see and be seen, but for a pleasant ride through the woods, the North Branch Trail up to the Chicago Botanic Garden is hard to beat. As the name suggests, the path roughly parallels the North Branch of the Chicago River, but not as closely as other river trails follow waterways. The popular trail can be busy on weekends, but it isn't nearly as crowded as the Lakefront Bike Path.

This ride begins at Linne Woods on Dempster Street (State Highway 58) because it's easy to find from I-94 and I-294. This is 5 miles north of the trail's start at intersection of Devon Avenue and Caldwell Avenue at the north end of Chicago. Park near the first shelter off Dempster Street and ride north from the trail map sign. The path is wooded and curvy with gentle hills. After crossing Beckwith Road at 0.8 mile, the path is sandwiched between the Chick Evans Golf Course on the left and an equestrian trail and stables on the right. The path turns sharply left onto a sidewalk at Harms Road to cross Golf Road at a stoplight. Follow the concrete sidewalk to the left after crossing. At 2.5 miles the path makes another sharp left before the Harms Woods parking lot. When you cross Glenview Road, there is a convenience store nearby. The bridge over East Lake Avenue is

probably the toughest climb on the ride. Equestrians share the bridge, but a barrier separates them from cyclists.

Around this time you may be thinking, "This is a nice trail, but why is it named for a river you never get to see?" When you finally do see the river at 4.5 miles, you are near its beginning at the confluence of the Middle Fork and the Skokie River. The waterway you cross shortly after is actually the Skokie River. Keep right at the trail junction at 4.8 miles; the path to the left is just a spur. Cross an abandoned railroad, followed by Happ Road. Go left on the asphalt path after crossing. As the trail continues eastward from Happ Road, you pass a school. Go under I-94 (Edens Expressway) at 5.3 miles. The trail crosses a meadow to Winnetka Road, where cross traffic doesn't stop. The path goes back into the woods, emerging at a stoplight at Willow Road (6.2 miles). Unfortunately, you may have a long wait after you push the walk button. Once you get across, the Skokie Lagoons are straight ahead, so follow the asphalt trail to the left. This area was once the Skokie Marsh, but the Civilian Conservation Corps (CCC) redeveloped the marsh into a series of lagoons in the 1930s, mainly for flood control purposes. Another path crosses the North Branch Trail at 6.4 miles. If you go to the left over the bridge, and then go right, you can see a memorial boulder honoring the 2,000 CCC workers who made up Camp Skokie Valley. If you go right instead, there are picnic tables beside the lagoons. The North Branch Trail continues straight ahead. A mile further along, the path runs close to the expressway that the sounds are a bit distracting. At 7.5 miles, the trail passes a boat launch and a portable toilet. After you cross the park road at 7.8 miles, there is a trail junction. Go straight for now; you will return on the path to the left. Cross a bridge alongside Tower Road and go past another parking area. Make a sharp left at 8.2 miles and go north across Tower Road at the four-way stop sign with Forest Way Drive. (Note: You can connect to Ride 21 by pedaling 1.4 miles east on Tower Road.) The path between Tower Road and Dundee Road is generally hillier with less shade than most of the trail. Curve left at the trail junction at 10 miles. There is another junction just 0.1 mile ahead. Turn right to go to the Chicago Botanic Garden (see sidebar for directions), or go straight to continue the loop back toward Tower Road.

Cross a bridge next to Dundee Road, then curve left. The trail runs close to the expressway again. At 12.2 miles, cross Tower Road and turn right at the trail junction. Retrace your route back to Linne Woods.

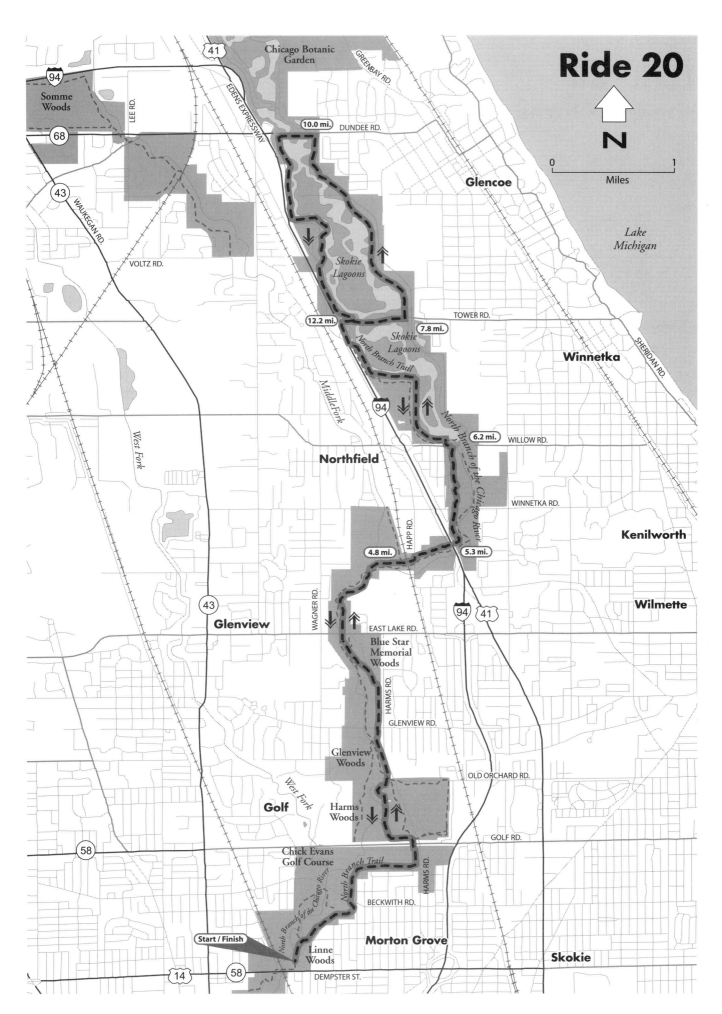

# Ride 20

**N**

0     1
Miles

Somme Woods

Chicago Botanic Garden

10.0 mi.   DUNDEE RD.

Glencoe

Lake Michigan

Skokie Lagoons

12.2 mi.

Skokie Lagoons

7.8 mi.

TOWER RD.

Winnetka

North Branch Trail

Middle Fork

West Fork

Northfield

North Branch of the Chicago River

6.2 mi.   WILLOW RD.

WINNETKA RD.

Kenilworth

4.8 mi.   HAPP RD.   5.3 mi.

Wilmette

Glenview

EAST LAKE RD.

Blue Star Memorial Woods

HARMS RD.

GLENVIEW RD.

Glenview Woods

OLD ORCHARD RD.

West Fork

Golf

Harms Woods

GOLF RD.

Chick Evans Golf Course

North Branch Trail

HARMS RD.

North Branch of the Chicago River

BECKWITH RD.

Start / Finish

Morton Grove

Linne Woods

Skokie

DEMPSTER ST.

# RIDE 21
## Sheridan Road

**Location:** North suburbs of Chicago
**Distance:** 21.2 miles
**Pedaling time:** 1.5–2.5 hours
**Surface:** Paved roads
**Terrain:** Hilly
**Sweat factor:** Moderate
**Trailhead:** Sheridan Road at Linden Avenue, Wilmette

### The Bahá'í House of Worship

**The Bahá'í Faith is relatively young, dating to the 19th century. It teaches the essential worth of all religions, plus racial unity and sexual equality.**

**There are seven Houses of Worship throughout the world. Wilmette's was the second one built, but it is the oldest one still standing. In 1903 a group of Chicago Bahá'í began planning this building. Groundbreaking was in 1912 and construction began in 1921, but limited funds made it a very slow process. The House of Worship was formally dedicated in 1953. It was placed on the National Register of Historic Places as soon as it was eligible in 1978.**

**The Bahá'í House of Worship is open to all regardless of religion, and there is no admission fee. After your ride, take a walk inside to further explore this unique building. The Bahá'í won't aggressively proselytize to you, but there is information about the faith available if you are interested. In addition to the structure, visitors can enjoy the nine surrounding gardens.**

Sheridan Road north of Chicago is a favorite training spot for cyclists. It's hard to imagine a more ideal road in a suburban setting. Because it parallels the Lake Michigan shoreline closely, there are few cross streets. Most of it is two-lane with low speed limits, which keeps traffic under control, and the lanes are often wide. Best of all, in a relatively flat area, Sheridan Road manages to serve up a series of hills. Plus, since the road is so popular with cyclists, the locals are accustomed to seeing bikes on the road. As if that weren't enough, Sheridan Road is also one of the prettiest around thanks to mature trees and large, distinctive homes in a variety of styles.

This ride begins in front of the Bahá'í House of Worship in Wilmette (colloquially known as the Bahá'í Temple), an architectural gem. Parking is available along westbound Linden, or city dwellers may take the CTA train north to the Linden stop, which is only 0.4 mile west of the trailhead. Head north on Sheridan Road and cross the North Shore Channel, with a marina on the right. Sheridan Road never runs right beside the lake, but here and in many other spots, you can catch a glimpse of it. The Wilmette part of

the ride has the worst pavement and traffic. The road is better in Kenilworth, an especially wealthy suburb with the highest median home prices in Illinois, and Winnetka. In both towns, Sheridan Road is two wide lanes. Winnetka has several lakefront parks, including Centennial, Maple Street, and Lloyd, which are good places to see Lake Michigan.

Bikes are not permitted on what would be the most challenging section of Sheridan Road, an area of steep hills and blind corners north of Tower Road known as "the ravines." Turn left on Tower Road at 4 miles. When the road heads uphill toward a bridge and a stoplight, turn right onto Old Green Bay Road before the bridge. After Old Green Bay Road makes a sharp left, you come to the intersection with Scott Avenue. Keep bearing right onto Scott. As you approach Sheridan Road heading downhill, bear left to the stop sign, and then turn left onto Sheridan. North of here, Sheridan has steeper hills and more curves than it did south of Tower Road.

You have to make several right turns to stay on Sheridan Road, which stair-steps whenever it gets close to the lakeshore. There are two homes designed by Frank Lloyd Wright along the way. The first, at 850 Sheridan Road in Glencoe, is the William A. Glasner House, built in 1905. Incidentally, Glasner was a bicycle manufacturer. The other is the Ward W. Willits House at 1445 Sheridan in Highland Park. Designed in 1901, this is considered Wright's first true Prairie Style house.

At 10.6 miles is a four-way stop sign at Saint Johns Avenue. If you need refreshments or want to explore Sheridan Road further, you can turn right toward downtown Highland Park. Otherwise, turn around here.

On the way back, be careful approaching the intersection of Old Green Bay Road and Tower Road at 16.8 miles. Cars turning from eastbound Tower onto northbound Old Green Bay tend to cut the corner. Also, eastbound traffic is coming over a bridge and has limited sight distance. (Note: You can connect to Ride 20, the North Branch Trail, by riding 1.4 miles west on Tower Road.)

Once you head east to Sheridan Road and turn right, just follow the road back to Linden Avenue at 21.2 miles. On a hot day, you may be tempted to jump into the water fountain outside the Bahá'í House of Worship!

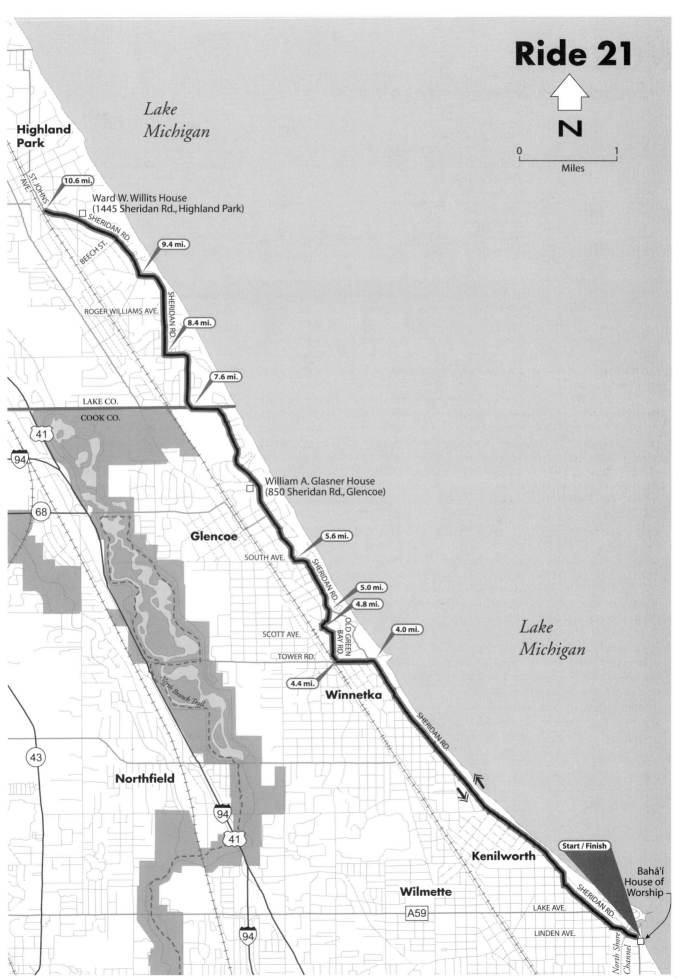

**Ride 21**

N

0 — 1 Miles

*Lake Michigan*

Highland Park

10.6 mi.

Ward W. Willits House
(1445 Sheridan Rd., Highland Park)

ST. JOHNS AVE.

SHERIDAN RD.

9.4 mi.

BEECH ST.

ROGER WILLIAMS AVE.

SHERIDAN RD.

8.4 mi.

7.6 mi.

LAKE CO.

COOK CO.

41

94

68

William A. Glasner House
(850 Sheridan Rd., Glencoe)

Glencoe

SOUTH AVE.

5.6 mi.

5.0 mi.

4.8 mi.

SHERIDAN RD.

OLD GREEN BAY RD.

4.0 mi.

SCOTT AVE.

TOWER RD.

4.4 mi.

*North Branch Trail*

Winnetka

*Lake Michigan*

43

Northfield

94

41

SHERIDAN RD.

Start / Finish

Kenilworth

Bahá'í House of Worship

Wilmette

A59

LAKE AVE.

LINDEN AVE.

*North Shore Channel*

SHERIDAN RD.

45

# RIDE 22
## Pedaling the Channel

**Location:** Evanston and Chicago
**Distance:** 13.4 miles
**Pedaling time:** 1.5 hours
**Surface:** Paved trails, some crushed-limestone trails
**Terrain:** Flat
**Sweat factor:** Low
**Trailhead:** Ladd Arboretum, Bridge Street and
    McCormick Boulevard, Evanston

Looking at the tree-lined banks and placid waters of the North Shore Channel today, you might be surprised to learn that this waterway was not built for transportation or irrigation, but for sewage. It was dug in 1910 to dilute waste in the Chicago River using Lake Michigan water. You'll be glad to know that the channel hasn't carried sewage since 1930. Instead, nature has taken over to create a habitat for birds, small mammals, and snapping turtles. Likewise, the local park districts have created an environment for urban bicyclists (note: the channel's water is still unsafe for drinking or swimming). This route starts at the Ladd Arboretum (www.laddarboretum.org) in Evanston. There is a parking lot on the south side of Bridge Street just east of McCormick Boulevard and west of the North Shore Channel. The Ecology Center (open from 9 to 5 Monday–Friday) on the north side of the street has indoor restrooms plus drinking fountains inside and out.

From the south end of the parking lot, head south on the crushed-limestone trail. Whenever the trail forks, keep to the right to follow the better cycling path. Enjoy the trees and gardens, including the International Friendship Garden shaped like the Rotary logo; Rotary International is based in Evanston. The arboretum ends at the first cross street, Golf Road. The path parallels McCormick Boulevard for the first four miles. Though it winds through parks between cross streets, the trail returns to McCormick at traffic lights so you can cross safely. Even when the signal says Walk, keep an eye out for turning traffic from McCormick Boulevard.

Continuing south into Skokie, the trail is asphalt for the rest of the ride. Skokie has made the parks along the channel into a cultural showcase. Between Church Street and Dempster Street stands a striking gold statue of Mohandas Gandhi with five of his memorable quotations. South of Dempster Street is the Skokie Northshore Sculpture Park. The gateway to the park is a circle of flags representing 14 countries along with the American, Illinois, and Skokie flags in the center. This display was inspired by the Skokie Festival of Cultures, held each May to celebrate the village's diversity. The path splits and comes back together many times over the next two miles, passing about 70 large sculptures along the way. The Skokie Northshore Sculpture Park's Web site (www.sculpturepark.org) offers self-guided tours, a family guide, and detailed information about each piece. Alas, the Web site doesn't tell you what each abstract sculpture is supposed to represent; you'll have to interpret

that for yourself.

Between Oakton Street and Howard Street, the trail is straight. A high bridge carries the Chicago Transit Authority's Yellow Line trains over the channel, the path, and McCormick Boulevard. South of Howard, there is a choice between asphalt and concrete paths. The asphalt path is smoother and more interesting. At 3.1 miles, veer left to go around a parking lot. The sculpture park ends at Touhy Avenue. Be careful crossing Touhy because there are obstructions in the sidewalk on the south side of the road. The trail runs through Lincolnwood for one uninterrupted mile.

The path continues south into Chicago as it crosses Devon Avenue, jogging left to an asphalt trail running between the channel and a shopping mall parking lot. Keep right at 5.0 miles where a path goes downhill toward the channel. Turn left onto the sidewalk at the next street, Lincoln Avenue, to cross the channel. At the first street, Kedzie Avenue, turn left again. Make a U-turn to the left where the asphalt trail starts a few hundred feet down the street. While the city's section lacks the artistic merit of the Skokie portion, it is pleasant riding because there are no street crossings for the next two miles. The path runs close to the channel as it passes under the bridge you crossed. After you go under a second bridge, Peterson Avenue, the trail heads up to Legion Park. Keep to the right; throughout Chicago, stay on the path closest to the channel. Go under Bryn Mawr Avenue at 5.8 miles and be alert for oncoming trail users. After climbing a short hill, follow the trail to the right again. The Foster Avenue underpass is similar, but with a steeper hill. This is River Park, a popular place on weekends for picnicking, swimming, and team sports. Halfway through River Park, the North Shore Channel flows into the North Branch of the Chicago River, but you can't see the confluence through the trees. In a last hurrah, the path goes down a small hill and comes back up to its end at Argyle Street. The ride turns around here at 6.7 miles.

If you want to go further, there are several options. River Park has a number of asphalt paths to wander. You can also cross the river on Argyle to explore short paths to the north and south. The path to the south on the west side of the river ends at Lawrence Avenue. If you are comfortable riding in city traffic, go east on Lawrence 0.7 mile to Lincoln Avenue, then turn right. This is the heart of the Lincoln Square neighborhood, where you will find several German shops and at least a dozen restaurants.

On the way back north toward the arboretum, be especially careful at the street crossings because cars turning right from McCormick will come up fast behind you as you cross. You may want to follow other forks in the path to see different sculptures. When you get back to the parking lot, you can visit more of the Ladd Arboretum north of Bridge Street, but the crushed-limestone path there can be muddy after a good rain.

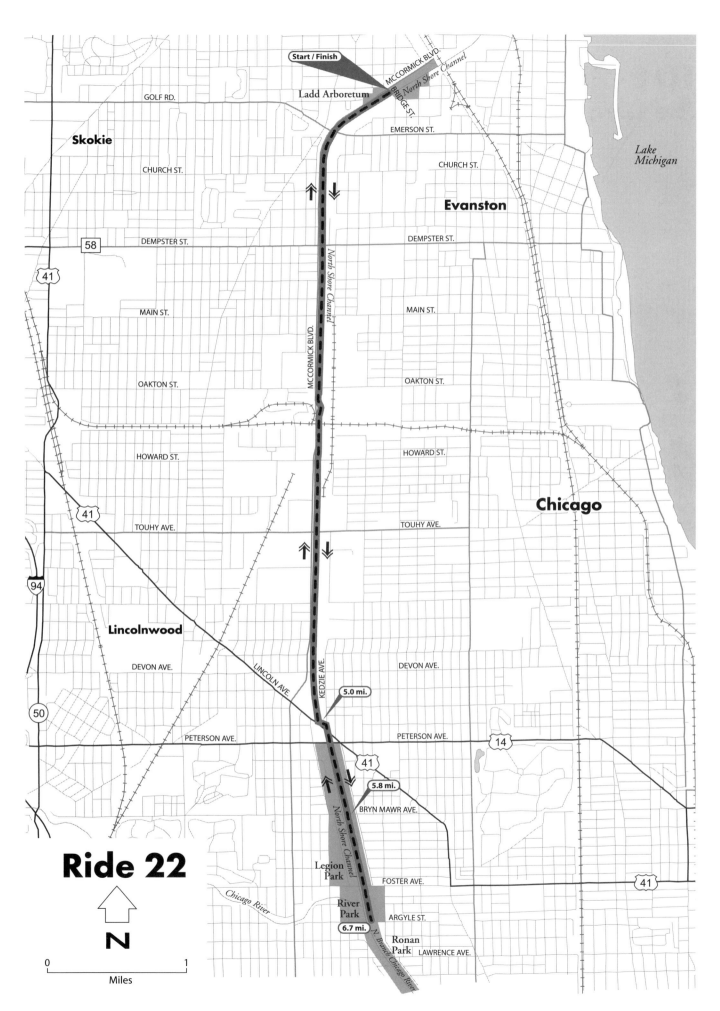

Start / Finish

MCCORMICK BLVD.

BRIDGE ST.

North Shore Channel

Ladd Arboretum

GOLF RD.

**Skokie**

CHURCH ST.

EMERSON ST.

CHURCH ST.

**Evanston**

*Lake Michigan*

58

DEMPSTER ST.

DEMPSTER ST.

41

MAIN ST.

North Shore Channel

MAIN ST.

OAKTON ST.

MCCORMICK BLVD.

OAKTON ST.

HOWARD ST.

HOWARD ST.

94

41

TOUHY AVE.

TOUHY AVE.

**Chicago**

**Lincolnwood**

DEVON AVE.

LINCOLN AVE.

KEDZIE AVE.

DEVON AVE.

50

5.0 mi.

PETERSON AVE.

PETERSON AVE.

14

41

5.8 mi.

BRYN MAWR AVE.

# Ride 22

**N**

North Shore Channel

Legion Park

FOSTER AVE.

41

*Chicago River*

River Park

6.7 mi.

ARGYLE ST.

Ronan Park

LAWRENCE AVE.

N. Branch Chicago River

0 — Miles — 1

# RIDE 23
## The Corn Belt Route

**Location:** Kane and DeKalb Counties
**Distance:** 33.4 miles
**Pedaling time:** 3–4 hours
**Surface:** Crushed-stone trail, some paved trail
**Terrain:** Flat
**Sweat factor:** Low
**Trailhead:** Dean Street in Saint Charles, just west of Randall Road and north of State Highway 64

**This sign marks the DeKalb County section of the Great Western Trail.**

The Chicago Great Western Railway was nicknamed the Corn Belt Route because it served the Midwest. The railroad merged with the Chicago and North Western in 1968 and much of it was eventually abandoned, including the entire Illinois line from Chicago to Dubuque, Iowa. The first section to be converted to a trail runs from Saint Charles to Sycamore (Ride 2 passes a museum dedicated to the railroad in Elizabeth, and Ride 25 uses another section of the old right-of-way in DuPage County).

This rail-trail is very easy to follow. Most of it is finely crushed stone, but some sections are asphalt. There are a number of street crossings, but they are not excessive, and the busier roads are crossed on bridges. Trees form a canopy over much of the trail, especially east of State Highway 47. Follow signs for the trailhead from Randall Road to Dean Street and go west 0.4 mile. When you see Leroy Oakes Forest Preserve on the right, turn left to the Great Western Trail parking area. The ride begins at the 0 mile marker (note: this trail's mile markers are not consistently accurate). The trail curves to the left from the start, and then it makes a sharp right onto the old railroad right-of-way. There are three bridges and one street crossing in the first three miles of the trail. At 3.1 miles, there are restaurants to the left across busy State Highway 64 in Wasco. A parking area for the Campton Township Community Center at 3.6 miles has baseball fields with portable toilets.

Starting around 4.2 miles, the trail is paved with asphalt and shaded by a canopy of trees. In late spring, this area is blanketed with wildflowers. The original railroad bridge carries trail users over State Highway 47 at 7.3 miles, followed by a street crossing with a parking lot. This town is Lily Lake. Though not visible from the trail, Pete's Famous Hotdogs and a gas station/mini-mart are located a short distance to the south at the intersection of Highway 47 and Highway 64. Don't expect to see the lake this town was named for, though. It was drained in the 1930s when they paved the roads.

West of Lily Lake, the character of the trail changes. The surface is crushed stone again, there is less shade for a while, and the trail more closely parallels Highway 64. There are also fewer trail users, though an occasional equestrian joins the mix. Virgil is the next town along the trail. There are a couple of street crossings. The first one, at 10.3 miles, has a pop machine to the south; the second, a tavern to the south.

After a few more crossroads, you encounter Sycamore Speedway at 13 miles. Since 1960, this clay oval has featured short-track auto racing on summer weekend nights. Events include stock car, spectator, and figure eight racing plus demolition derbies. Visit www.sycamore-speedway.com or call (815) 895-5454 for more information. The motorcycle shop north of the trail has a pop machine. The Winners Circle Bar and Grill marks the west end of this commercial area. Half a mile later, things get a bit confusing as the trail passes from Kane County into DeKalb County. There are two markers for mile 14, which are separated by more than a tenth of a mile (the second is more accurate but still only 13.9 miles).

The trail in DeKalb County isn't maintained as well; weeds grow in the middle of the trail bed in places and larger pebbles sometimes rough up the crushed stone. On the bright side, the old railroad markers are better preserved here than back east. You may see more people as the trail approaches Sycamore. The parking area at 16.7 miles marks the end of the Great Western Trail and the turn-around point for this ride. If you wish to continue, follow the bike route signs half a mile to Sycamore Community Park (portable toilets) and eventually into town (all services). Sycamore's big celebration is the Pumpkin Festival at the end of October. The return trip is pretty straightforward. As you have seen, there are no tricky turns, confusing intersections, or notable elevation changes along the way.

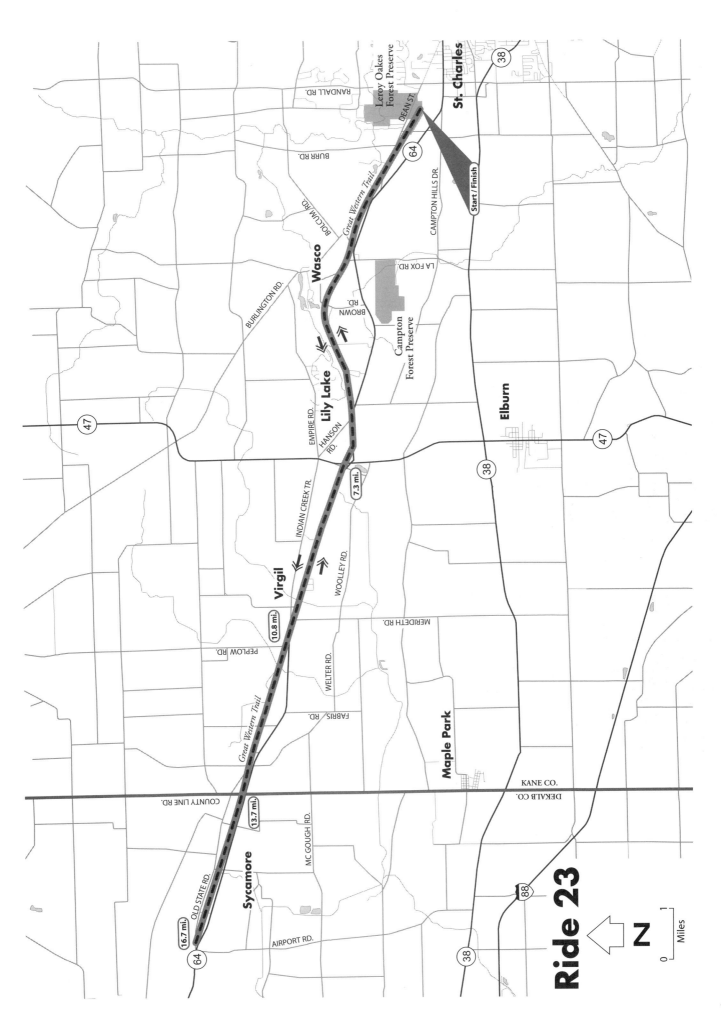

Ride 23

N

Miles
0 1

49

# RIDE 24
## Virgil Gilman Trail

**Location:** Far western suburbs of Chicago
**Distance:** 14.8 miles
**Pedaling time:** 1.5–2 hours
**Surface:** Crushed-limestone and asphalt trails
**Terrain:** Flat
**Sweat factor:** Low
**Trailhead:** South parking lot, Waubonsee Community College, Sugar Grove

**These stone barriers are unique to the Virgil Gilman Trail.**

The Virgil Gilman Trail is one of Illinois' oldest rails-to-trails projects. The original trail through Aurora used distinctive barriers of cut stone to block motor vehicle access. It has been extended over the years out to the Sugar Grove main campus of Waubonsee Community College. The college is located on State Highway 47 north of Sugar Grove. Campus hours are 7 AM to 11 PM daily. Use the south entrance, go north to the stop sign, turn right, and go to the far end of the parking lot. There is a sign marking the start of the Virgil Gilman Trail (not to be confused with the WCC Nature Trail). Parking may be hard to find during peak school hours, and campus police write plenty of tickets for cars parked in spots without painted lines. You may have to go back to the overflow lot that you passed on the way in. You can use the bathrooms and drinking fountains inside before or after your trip.

The beginning of the trail crosses open grassland. The first five miles could be called the "Blackberry Creek Trail" because the path crosses it several times. After the

first crossing at 0.6 mile, a crushed-limestone trail heads off to the left. This trail leads to Hannaford Woods Picnic Grove. It is a pleasant but short trail that you may want to explore on the way back; it is 1.3 miles round-trip. The Virgil Gilman Trail turns into the trees at 0.8 mile, not long before an obviously short 1 mile marker. Across Ke-De-Ka Road, the path enters Bliss Woods Forest Preserve. Bliss Road at 1.6 miles can be a busy crossing. Follow the crosswalk to stay on the trail, which is paved and hilly for a while. Don't be alarmed if you hear gunshots—the Aurora Sportsman's Club is located over the hill to the right. For a half mile starting at 2.4 miles, Blackberry Creek is on the right while Prestbury Golf Course is on the left. By the time you read this, the long bridge over four-lane State Highway 56 should be finished at 3.1 miles.

At 4 miles, cross busy Galena Boulevard. Be careful since this is a diagonal crossing. Continue ahead through the parking lot and onto the trail. Here is the first of the trail's stone vehicle barriers. A high, curved wall with benches sits in the middle of the trail, while a low wall blocks the left side. Another unique feature is a sundial at each barrier, but this particular one is broken. This must have seemed like an elegant solution when the trail was built, but over time these barriers became a nuisance to bicyclists because they created blind corners. Nowadays there is a paved trail to bypass every one of them. At 4.5 miles, cross the entrance to Blackberry Splash Country, a water park. Follow the curve of the main trail to the left and cross Barnes Road. Blackberry Farm's Pioneer Village is straight ahead, but the trail turns right. The sundial at the next trail barrier, dated 1967, says, "Fox River Valley Pleasure Driveway and Park District," which has since been shortened to "Fox Valley Park District." The suspension bridge over Blackberry Creek at 4.7 miles is a popular feature of the trail.

There are a number of spurs to parks and subdivisions in Aurora, but it is easy to follow the main path. As you approach Orchard Road, turn right to cross Prairie Street. While the suspension bridge over the creek is quaint, the bridge over Orchard Road is modern. At 6 miles there is a park with a playground adjoining the trail. For some reason the path is striped to go toward the next trail barrier at 6.6 miles; you should swing to the right around it instead to avoid a potential collision. After you cross Edgelawn Drive, the Aurora Country Club is on your left for half a mile. At Terry Avenue (7.4 miles), this ride turns around. If you wish to continue, follow the red arrows for a few blocks on city streets, and then onto a path that crosses the Fox River. The trail continues to Hill Avenue on the east side of Aurora.

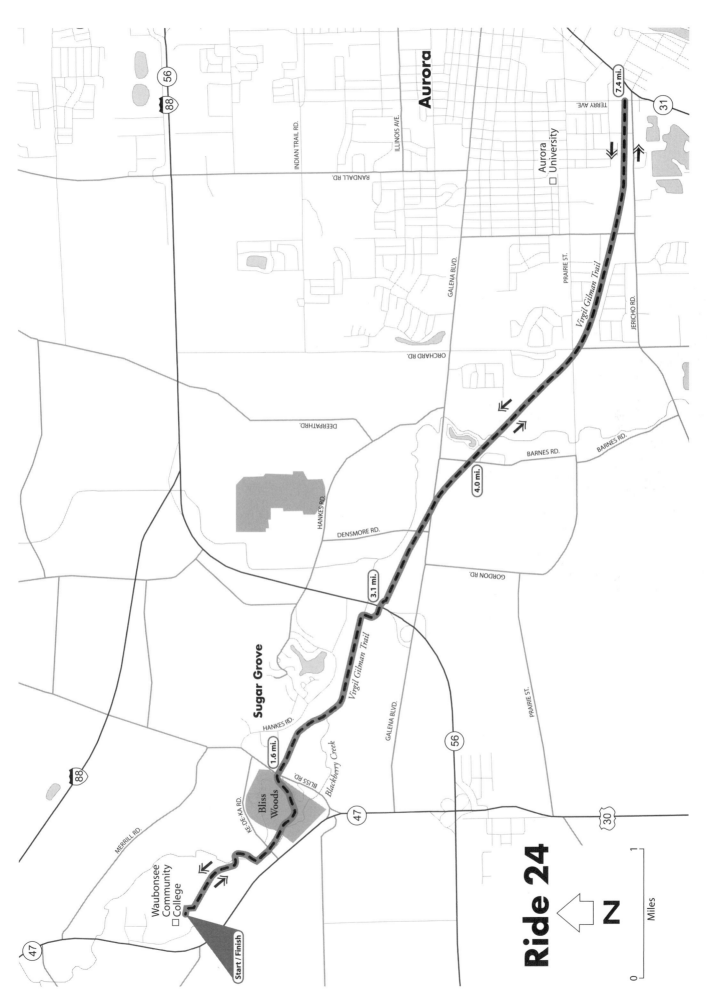

Ride 24

N

Miles
0    1

51

# RIDE 25
## Great Western Prairie Triangle

**Location:** DuPage County
**Distance:** 21 miles
**Pedaling time:** 2–2.5 hours
**Surface:** Crushed-stone trails
**Terrain:** Flat
**Sweat factor:** Low
**Trailhead:** Villa Park Historical Society Museum, Villa Avenue south of Saint Charles Road

### Kline Creek Farm

This living history farm demonstrates life in rural DuPage County in the 1890s. Besides growing crops such as corn and oats, the farm has horses, sheep, cattle, and chickens. You can take a self-guided tour, or you can plan your trip around the seasonal programs and activities held throughout the year. These include farm chores like haymaking, canning, planting, and butter making, as well as 1890s social occasions such as weddings and holidays. Call the farm office at (630) 876-5900 for more information. While the forest preserve is open daily, the farm is open Thursday through Monday 9 to 5. If you want to visit, bring a lock because bicycles are not allowed beyond the Timber Ridge Visitor Center.

The Illinois Prairie Path (IPP) is more than 60 miles long altogether. It consists of a Main Stem, two branches, and two shorter spurs. This ride follows the IPP Main Stem from Villa Park to Wheaton, then the IPP Elgin Branch to Winfield. To make a loop, the route goes north on the Timber Ridge Trail (chopping off one point of the triangle) and returns to Villa Park on the Great Western Trail.

The Villa Park Historical Society Museum is housed in a former Chicago, Aurora & Elgin train station built in 1929. There is parking on both sides of the station. Pop and water are sold here when the museum is open (Tuesday–Friday from 1 to 5, Saturday and Sunday from 10 to 4). Begin in front of the station and head west. There are frequent street crossings, but few are busy. Half a mile down the crushed-stone trail, the Villa Park Chamber of Commerce and Information Center resides in another former train station built in 1910. The trail enters Lombard after a busy street crossing at 1.3 miles. The IPP climbs to a long bridge over I-355 at 3.3 miles and then descends to a narrow, steel bridge over the East Branch of the DuPage River. West of I-355, there are fewer at-grade street crossings. The path is paved for half a mile through downtown Glen Ellyn. There is a dangerous diagonal street crossing at 6.1 miles. After crossing, follow the sidewalk to the right, then left. When the sidewalk ends, continue straight onto the crushed-stone trail. Entering Wheaton, the old DuPage County courthouse, now full of condominiums, is on the left at 7.2 miles. The trail splits briefly and comes back together; the left side is

smoother. The path is paved through Wheaton. After crossing West Street at 7.6 miles, go right on the sidewalk, then left. Less than a tenth of a mile later, veer right on the sidewalk. The Main Stem of the IPP ends just beyond the parking garage at 7.8 miles.

Turn right onto the crushed-stone trail to follow the Elgin Branch of the IPP. Immediately climb to a long steel bridge that crosses three sets of railroad tracks, narrows, and then crosses two streets. At 8.6 miles, the IPP bisects Lincoln Marsh Natural Area. You encounter a busy intersection at 10.3 miles. Use the crosswalks to go left across County Farm Road and right across Geneva Road. At the northwest corner of this intersection, turn right on the Timber Ridge Trail and cross a steel bridge with a wooden deck. At 11 miles, the trail passes Kline Creek Farm. The Timber Ridge Visitor Center has modern restrooms, drinking water, and vending machines. The Timber Ridge Trail dead-ends into the Great Western Trail at 11.4 miles. Turn right and cross County Farm Road.

The Great Western Trail (which follows the same right-of-way as Ride 23, although the two segments do not connect) is narrower than the IPP but with much less trail traffic. Watch out for metal vehicle barriers. The trail is straight except for a few detours to safer street crossings. This happens at Schmale Road and Glen Ellyn's Main Street: The trail goes south, crosses at the stoplight with Saint Charles Road, and returns north to the regular trail. Climb toward the I-355 bridge on asphalt at 17.2 miles. After the bridge, enter Lombard and return to crushed stone, and then go under State Highway 53. The trail descends to Park Avenue, then climbs to Main Street, where there is a drinking fountain on the left.

There is one tricky section of the Great Western Trail. At 18.7 miles, turn right onto the sidewalk at Grace Street. Cross Saint Charles Road, the railroad tracks, and Parkside Avenue. Then go left across Grace Street and head east on the sidewalk. Go across a park entrance, then continue straight ahead on the sidewalk. At 19.1 miles, go left across Saint Charles Road at Edgewood Avenue. After negotiating a few curves and climbing a short hill, return to the Great Western Trail right-of-way. The trail spur to the IPP goes off to the right at 20.8 miles. Start looking for this turn when you see the tall, brick smokestack of the former Ovaltine factory. After you turn, there is a Chicago Great Western Railroad Depot built in 1926 on the left, then a park with a drinking fountain. Ride across Central Boulevard and turn left at the IPP junction, finishing at the museum.

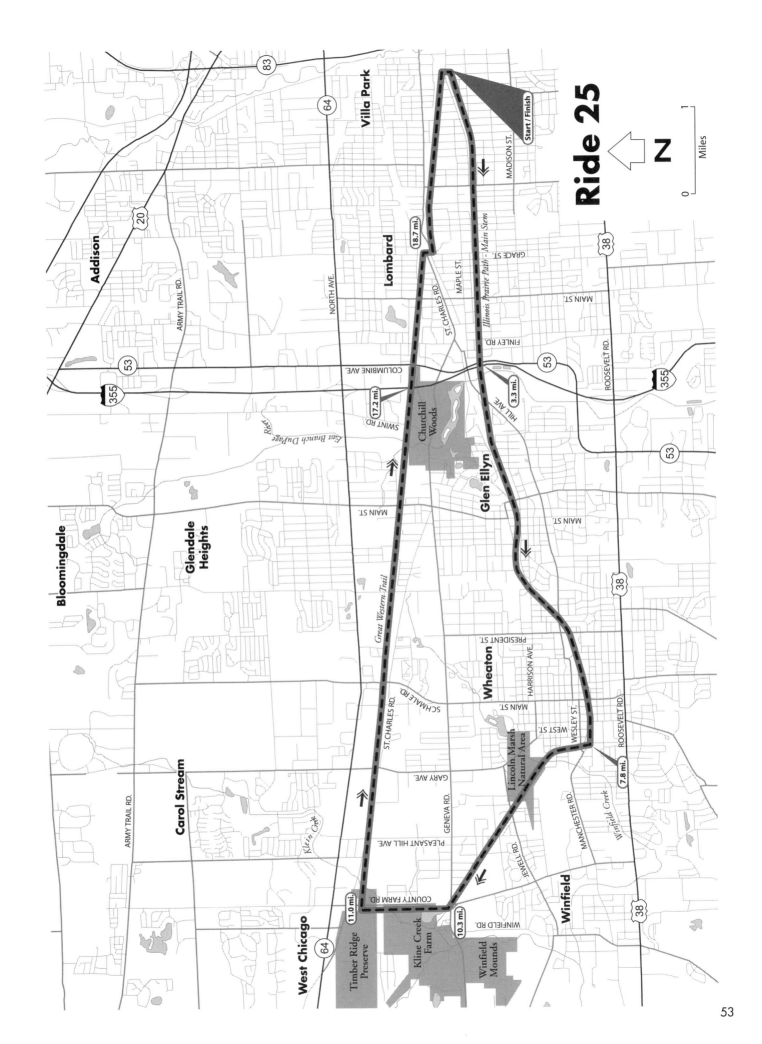

Ride 25

N

0 — Miles — 1

**Start / Finish**

Villa Park

Lombard

18.7 mi.

17.2 mi.

3.3 mi.

Churchill Woods

Glen Ellyn

Addison

Bloomingdale

Glendale Heights

Carol Stream

Wheaton

Winfield

West Chicago

Timber Ridge Preserve

Kline Creek Farm

Winfield Mounds

Lincoln Marsh Natural Area

11.0 mi.

10.3 mi.

7.8 mi.

*Illinois Prairie Path – Main Stem*

*Great Western Trail*

*East Branch DuPage River*

*Klein Creek*

*Winfield Creek*

MADISON ST.

GRACE ST.

MAIN ST.

ST. CHARLES RD.

MAPLE ST.

FINLEY RD.

COLUMBINE AVE.

SWIFT RD.

HILL AVE.

NORTH AVE.

MAIN ST.

PRESIDENT ST.

HARRISON AVE.

MAIN ST.

WESLEY ST.

WEST ST.

SCHMALE RD.

ST. CHARLES RD.

GARY AVE.

GENEVA RD.

PLEASANT HILL AVE.

COUNTY FARM RD.

WINFIELD RD.

JEWELL RD.

MANCHESTER RD.

ROOSEVELT RD.

ARMY TRAIL RD.

ARMY TRAIL RD.

83

64

20

53

355

53

53

38

355

38

# RIDE 26
## Take Me to the Zoo

**Location:** Cook County
**Distance:** 12.8 miles
**Pedaling time:** 1–1.5 hours
**Surface:** Asphalt trail
**Terrain:** Rolling hills
**Sweat factor:** Moderate.
**Trailhead:** Bemis Woods South (Groves 5–8) off
   U.S. 34 (Ogden Avenue)

### Brookfield Zoo

When Brookfield Zoo opened in 1934, it was the first North American zoo designed with "barless" enclosures that put animals in a more naturalistic habitat. Today the zoo is home to nearly 2,200 animals in 26 major exhibit areas. This includes almost 450 species. With so many animals commanding your attention, you might not realize that the zoo also grows an impressive variety of more than 500 plant species. The Forest Preserve District of Cook County owns the 216-acre zoo, but it has always been managed by the non-profit Chicago Zoological Society.

Like the Chicago Botanic Garden (Ride 20), Brookfield Zoo is a place where bicycling can save you money. To reach the zoo, ride south from the turn-around on the forest preserve road to 31st Street. This is a busy street, but the bike racks at the North Gate are less than 0.3 mile to the east. You'll save the $8 fee for car parking, but you still have to pay admission. If the weather is nice, you'll have plenty of company—about two million people visit every year. For information about the zoo, visit www.brookfieldzoo.org or call (800) 201-0784.

The Salt Creek Trail is a heavily used recreational path less than ten miles west of Chicago. It roughly parallels the serpentine course of Salt Creek as it winds its way toward the Des Plaines River. Although the path is measured from east to west, this ride starts at the west end because it is convenient to I-294 (Tri-State Tollway). The turnaround for this out-and-back ride is in Brookfield Woods, which is across the street from Brookfield Zoo. Except for the last half mile or so, most of the path is well shaded. In several places you will ride close to suburban back-yards; this trail was shoehorned into some tight spots. The surface is asphalt with a yellow centerline. It is prone to longitudinal cracks, but most of them are patched with tar. At trail junctions, follow the red arrow to stay on the path. The trail is popular with families, so watch for children. This is the same Salt Creek that flows through Busse Woods (Ride 18) about 20 miles upstream. There are long-range plans for a bike path in DuPage County running much of the way between the two trail systems.

The entrance to Bemis Woods Groves 5–8 is less than half a mile east of I-294 on the north side of U.S. Highway 34. The trail begins at the first parking area along the forest preserve road. Start at the 6.6 mile marker. The trail is actually a bit shorter than advertised, particularly between the 6.6 and 6 mile markers. The first segment of the trail is the curviest, and it is mostly downhill. At 0.4 mile the trail abruptly makes a sharp left to cross Salt Creek on the shoulder of Wolf Road and then continues across the road. After more twisty excitement, the trail joins a low-traffic road at 1.6 miles, which dead-ends into

four-lane 31st Street. The path continues across the street. The next mile is straighter than the first two, but still wooded with hills. The trail curves right at Cermak Road to cross LaGrange Road (known as Mannheim Road north of Cermak Road). Watch for turning traffic at this busy intersection. After crossing the road, go right, cross Salt Creek again, and follow a sharp left curve.

The trail enters Brezina Woods, which has a portable toilet. Cross the park road, then curve left at the trail junction. The path skirts the edge of a neighborhood

**A cyclist coasts through a tunnel as trains pass overhead.**

for a quarter mile. After 4.1 miles, the trail ducks into a tunnel under several railroad tracks, then takes a sharp left. When you cross 25th Avenue, the path continues on the right. Soon you enter 26th Street Woods and pass an-other portable toilet. At 5 miles, 17th Avenue may remind you of Wolf Road: Take a sharp left, cross the creek, then cross the road. After so much forest, the trail comes out into a meadow at 6 miles. The trail continues onto McCormick Avenue a bit later. The British Home, a retirement community founded in 1920 by the Daugh-ters of the British Empire, is on your right. Parking lots for Brookfield Zoo are behind a fence on the left. At 6.3 miles the bike path leads to the right, entering Brookfield Woods. Turn around in the park road circle just beyond mile marker 0.

What becomes of Salt Creek, your partner for the ride? About two miles from this ride's turnaround point, Salt Creek flows into the Des Plaines River, which in turn joins the Kankakee River to form the Illinois River, which eventually joins the Mississippi River north of Saint Louis. You can follow this water route via Rides 31, 46, and 47.

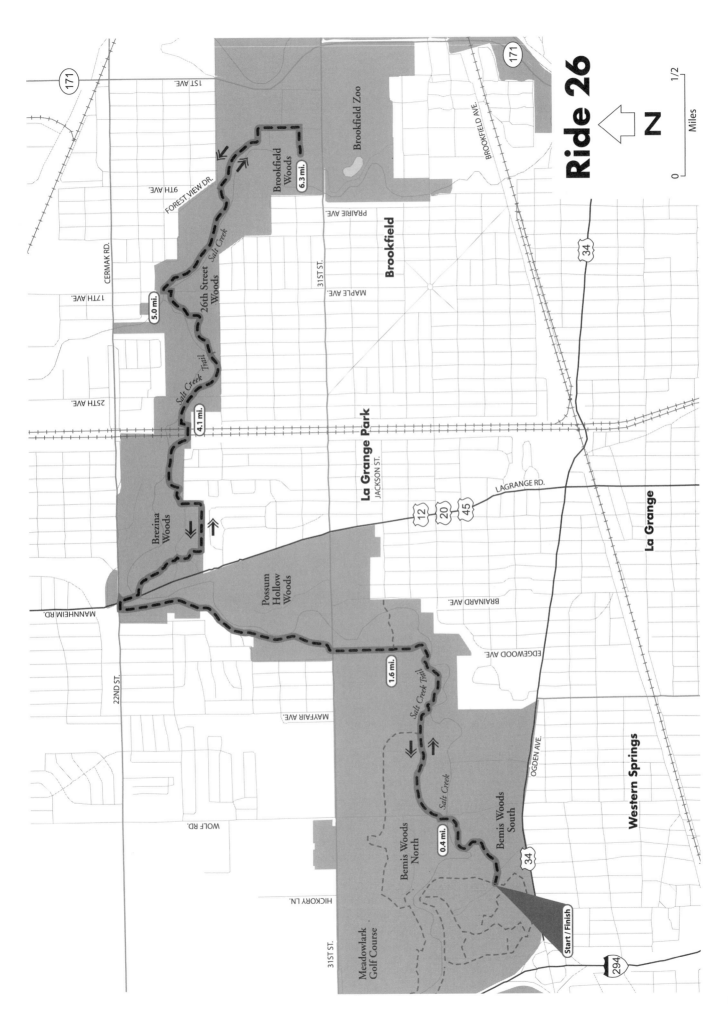

# Ride 26

**N**

0 — 1/2 Miles

171

1ST AVE.

Brookfield Zoo

BROOKFIELD AVE.

Brookfield Woods
6.3 mi.

9TH AVE.
FOREST VIEW DR.

CERMAK RD.

17TH AVE.

25TH AVE.

5.0 mi.

26th Street Woods

*Salt Creek*

*Salt Creek Trail*

4.1 mi.

PRAIRIE AVE.

31ST ST.

MAPLE AVE.

**Brookfield**

171

34

**La Grange Park**

JACKSON ST.

LAGRANGE RD.

12
20
45

BRAINARD AVE.

**La Grange**

Brezina Woods

Possum Hollow Woods

MANNHEIM RD.

22ND ST.

EDGEWOOD AVE.

1.6 mi.

*Salt Creek Trail*

MAYFAIR AVE.

WOLF RD.

31ST ST.

HICKORY LN.

Meadowlark Golf Course

Bemis Woods North

0.4 mi.

*Salt Creek*

Bemis Woods South

OGDEN AVE.

34

**Western Springs**

**Start / Finish**

294

55

# RIDE 27
## Cooler by the Lake

**Location:** Chicago along Lake Michigan
**Distance:** 13.2 miles
**Pedaling time:** 2 hours
**Surface:** Paved bike path
**Terrain:** Flat
**Sweat factor:** Low
**Trailhead:** Foster Avenue east of Lake Shore Drive

### Bike the Drive

However crowded the Lakefront Bike Path gets, it is still more appealing than the busy thoroughfare that runs beside it known as Lake Shore Drive. But for one morning a year, that changes. On Memorial Day weekend, the Chicagoland Bicycle Federation (CBF) and the City of Chicago host "Bike the Drive" (www.bikethedrive.org). This is one of the largest organized rides in America, with over 18,000 participants in 2005. Lake Shore Drive is closed to motorized traffic, and cyclists take over for several hours. The ride isn't free, but the price includes a T-shirt, rest stops, and sag support.

The CBF is a prominent bicycling advocacy group with more than 5,000 members. They have been improving cycling in the metropolitan area for nearly twenty years. If you want to explore the city or suburbs, the CBF's Chicagoland Bicycle Map shows all the best roads and trails for bikes (available at www.biketraffic.org and local bike shops).

Chicago's Lakefront Bike Path is one of the best urban paths in the world. It runs close to Lake Michigan much of the time, and the view of downtown from Lincoln Park is unforgettable. It passes near many attractions, and the people watching is fascinating. The lakefront is the city's playground, featuring museums, baseball fields, tennis courts, golf courses, marinas, beaches, a zoo, and even a Ferris wheel. If you visit without your bike, rentals are available from Bike Chicago (www.bikechicago.com).

How popular is this trail? It is so popular that the city gives the Lakefront Bike Path the right-of-way at most intersections (but be careful—drivers don't always obey their stop signs). The path is even plowed promptly after a snowfall, although many of the facilities are closed during the winter. The Chicagoland Bicycle Federation maintains a Web page to provide information about construction and special events (www.biketraffic.org/lakefront). Public restrooms, water, and concessions are too frequent to list individually.

For the cyclist, however, this path is sometimes a little too popular. Although 20 feet wide in places, it gets crowded with bikers, runners, skaters, walkers, and beachgoers, especially on summer evenings and weekends. This is not a good place to ride fast. Take your time and enjoy the sights.

Though many trails lead off into the parks along the way, you can stay on the main path easily by following the white and yellow painted lines. Use extra caution where the centerline is painted red.

The Lakefront Bike Path starts roughly 0.8 mile further north at Ardmore Avenue, but Foster Avenue is the first place with parking. Heading south from Foster, the path stays close to Lake Shore Drive most of the time. The first mile is relatively uncrowded, but trail traffic builds as you head toward downtown. South of Montrose Avenue, the wide-open park narrows as a golf course lies between the path and the lake. A tall fence protects cyclists from stray golf balls. After Irving Park Road, there are tennis courts, baseball fields, and playgrounds. Next is Belmont Harbor, one of several marinas. The trail gets crowded here. At 2.8 miles, continue straight south past a busy underpass that leads to other trails in Lincoln Park. You will be rewarded with your first glimpse of the John Hancock Center. After you cross the boat channel that leads to Diversey Harbor, the path curves left toward the lake along the concrete shoreline. Most of the lakefront is man-made, and the giant rocks, concrete, and steel pilings that you see are necessary to prevent the lake from reclaiming the space. The path turns south again, running close to the lake for a while.

You pass the brick Theatre on the Lake building just before the path curves back inland. Here at Fullerton Avenue (3.8 miles), the path can be busy. To visit the Lincoln Park Zoo (www.lpzoo.com) or the Lincoln Park Conservatory, go west on Fullerton to Cannon Drive and turn left. South of Fullerton you pass a long, sandy beach often used for volleyball. As you approach the ship-shaped North Avenue Beach House, there is a bicycle and pedestrian bridge over Lake Shore Drive. It leads to the south end of Lincoln Park, including the Chicago Historical Society (www.chicagohs.org). Just south of this bridge, the trail splits. If you need water, food, or a public restroom, go straight ahead to the North Avenue Beach House. Otherwise, turn right to bypass this crowded area.

Less than a mile after North Avenue Beach is another popular beach at Oak Street. In the summer, signs may direct you to walk your bike in this congested area. Restrooms are concealed in the tunnel that leads under Lake Shore Drive to North Michigan Avenue's Magnificent Mile shopping district (an area best explored on foot). The Lakefront Bike Path curves sharply to the left past the Drake Hotel, followed by a curve to the right. For the next half mile, the pavement is slanted down toward the lake on a fifteen-degree angle. It's like riding on the side of a hill. Sometimes you will see dedicated swimmers training in the lake here. Beyond Ohio Street Beach, head east to Navy Pier where this ride turns around at 6.6 miles.

Navy Pier (www.navypier.com) is Chicago's most popular family entertainment center. It has a carnival atmosphere with restaurants, shops, and attractions for all ages. The most prominent feature is the 150-foot-high Ferris wheel. It pays homage to the first Ferris wheel, which entertained visitors at Chicago's 1893 World's Columbian Exposition. Bicycles are allowed on Navy Pier, but there are a lot of pedestrians. Bike racks are provided at the south entrance. From here you can return west and north to Foster Avenue, or you can continue south toward Ride 28, crossing the Chicago River on the sidewalk beside the lower level of Lake Shore Drive.

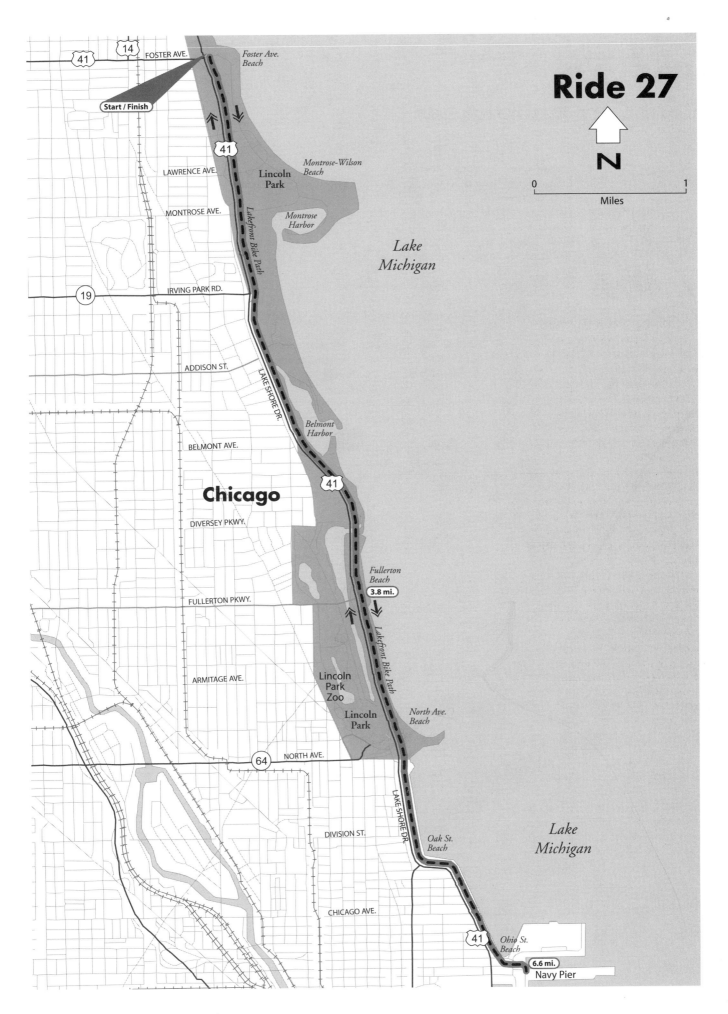

# Ride 27

N

0      1
Miles

41   14   FOSTER AVE.    *Foster Ave. Beach*

Start / Finish

41

LAWRENCE AVE.

*Lincoln Park*

*Montrose-Wilson Beach*

MONTROSE AVE.

*Lakefront Bike Path*

*Montrose Harbor*

*Lake Michigan*

19   IRVING PARK RD.

ADDISON ST.

LAKE SHORE DR.

*Belmont Harbor*

BELMONT AVE.

41

**Chicago**

DIVERSEY PKWY.

*Fullerton Beach*

FULLERTON PKWY.    3.8 mi.

*Lakefront Bike Path*

ARMITAGE AVE.

*Lincoln Park Zoo*

*North Ave. Beach*

*Lincoln Park*

64   NORTH AVE.

LAKE SHORE DR.

DIVISION ST.

*Oak St. Beach*

*Lake Michigan*

CHICAGO AVE.

41   *Ohio St. Beach*

6.6 mi.

Navy Pier

57

# RIDE 28
## Museums and Beaches

**Location:** Chicago along Lake Michigan
**Distance:** 18.2 miles
**Pedaling time:** 1.5–2 hours
**Surface:** Paved bike path
**Terrain:** Mostly flat with a few short hills
**Sweat factor:** Low
**Trailhead:** Monroe Street and Lake Shore Drive

### Chicago by Bike

In spite of its size, Chicago has achieved the distinction of being named a Bicycle Friendly Community (silver level) by the League of American Bicyclists. Longtime Mayor Richard M. Daley enjoys bicycling, and he has supported many initiatives to make getting around by bike easier in Chicago.

Bike carriers are installed on the front of every CTA bus (suburban PACE buses have racks as well). Bicycles are allowed on CTA and Metra trains except during rush hours. While the Chicagoland Bicycle Federation sells a fine regional map, the city prints its own map showing bike lanes, paths, and recommended routes within the city limits (it's free—call (312) 742-2453). More than a hundred miles of bike lanes have been painted, with many more planned. And when you're ready to park your bike somewhere, odds are good that you won't be far from one of over 10,000 bike racks in the city.

The annual Bike Chicago program is a collection of more than 125 events to promote bicycling from May through July. These include Bike the Drive (see Ride 27), the Bike to Work Rally and Commuter Challenge, and the L.A.T.E. Ride (a ride after midnight), plus parades, safety days, neighborhood rides, races, and seminars. There is even valet bike parking at the summer's biggest Grant Park festivals. The "City That Works" is becoming the "City That Bikes."

Aside from sharing Lake Michigan, the bike paths on the North Side and the South Side seem very different. The most obvious difference is the congestion—or the lack of it. While the North Side trail is packed with people sometimes, the South Side trail is much more open, particularly south of McCormick Place. The lack of crowds makes the path safer for riding, but you may want to bring a riding partner for company. As mentioned in Ride 27, the Chicagoland Bicycle Federation maintains a Web page that provides information about construction and special events along the bike path at www.biketraffic.org/lakefront.

This ride begins on the east side of Grant Park. Paid parking is available in the underground lots east of Michigan Avenue. Cross Lake Shore Drive at Monroe Street and head south on the concrete path. The first notable sight is Buckingham Fountain on the right at 0.3 mile. It was built in 1927 and restored in 1995. Although its design is based on the Bassin de Latone at Versailles, it is twice the size of the French original.

Looking south, the Field Museum of Natural History (www.fieldmuseum.org) is straight ahead. This area is known as the Museum campus. As you get closer, the path descends and curves left. Watch for pedestrians coming out of the tunnel at the bottom of the hill. The path climbs up toward the Shedd Aquarium (www.sheddaquarium.org) and curves around the left side along the lake. Continue south across Solidarity Drive, which leads east to the Adler Planetarium (www.adlerplanetarium.org). The next six miles of long, narrow green space along the lakefront is known as Burnham Park. Architect Daniel Burnham developed the visionary 1909 Plan of Chicago, which influenced transportation and recreation planning in the city for decades. As you head south, Soldier Field is on the right and Northerly Island, former home of the small airport Meigs Field, is on the left. This area hosted the 1933-34 Century of Progress Exposition, which marked the hundredth anniversary of Chicago's incorporation as a town. The massive Lakeside Center at McCormick Place lies ahead. Several other buildings of this monstrous convention facility lie on the other side of Lake Shore Drive. The path goes past a man-made waterfall on the east side of the Lakeside Center. South of here, the crowds dissipate. The path is generally set back from the lake, although it gets closer around 4.2 miles.

A popular recreational spot is Promontory Point to

**The South Shore Cultural Center used to be a country club.**

the left at 6.6 miles. Soon after, you see the Museum of Science and Industry (www.msichicago.org) straight ahead. This is the only building remaining from the 1893 World's Columbian Exposition. Other buildings in the fair stood south of the museum in Jackson Park. The path runs close to the lake approaching the broad Jackson Park Beach House, built in 1919. Curve left before the stoplight at Marquette Road at 8.1 miles. Cross La Rabida Drive at another stoplight. A golf course is separated from the trail by a fence from 8.6 miles to the South Shore Cultural Center entrance at 9.1 miles. This beautiful, Mediterranean Revival-style structure was built in 1916 for a private country club. The Chicago Park District purchased the property in 1974 with plans to tear it down, but community support led to its restoration instead. The bike path officially ends only a few hundred feet beyond the entrance, so just turn around here and ride back to Grant Park.

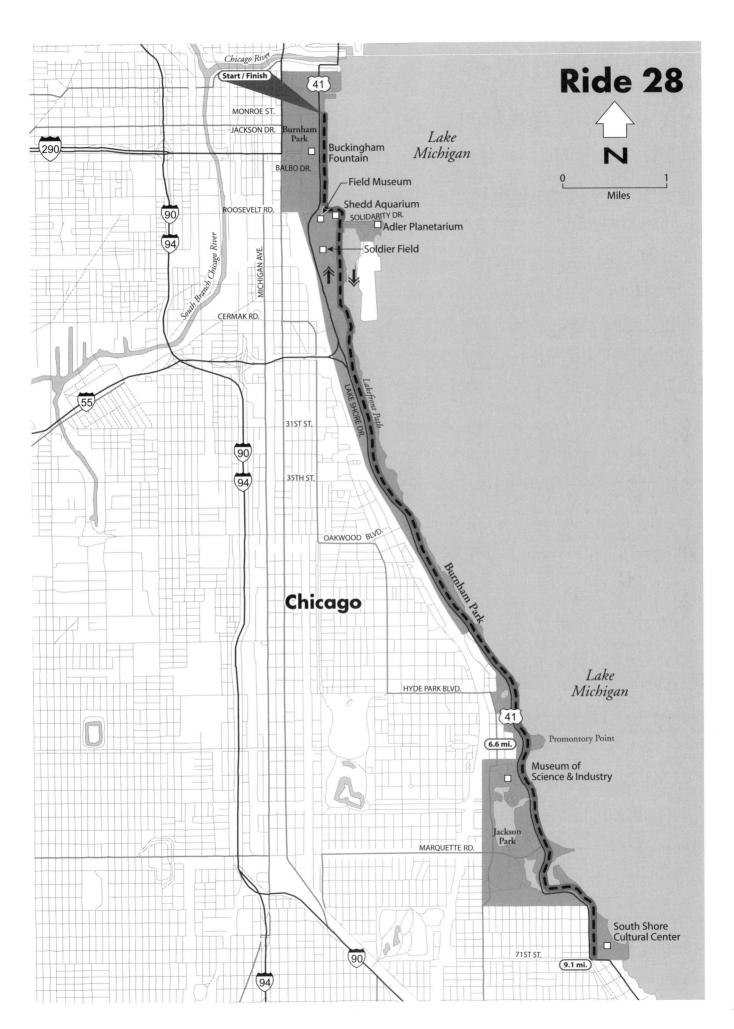

# Ride 28

**N**

Chicago River

**Start / Finish**

41

MONROE ST.

JACKSON DR.

Burnham Park

Buckingham Fountain

BALBO DR.

Field Museum

Shedd Aquarium

SOLIDARITY DR.

Adler Planetarium

Soldier Field

*Lake Michigan*

290

ROOSEVELT RD.

MICHIGAN AVE.

90

94

CERMAK RD.

South Branch Chicago River

55

*Lakefront Path*

LAKE SHORE DR.

31ST ST.

35TH ST.

90

94

OAKWOOD BLVD.

**Chicago**

*Burnham Park*

HYDE PARK BLVD.

*Lake Michigan*

41

Promontory Point

**6.6 mi.**

Museum of Science & Industry

Jackson Park

MARQUETTE RD.

90

94

71ST ST.

South Shore Cultural Center

**9.1 mi.**

# RIDE 29
## Lap Around the Lab

**Location:** Southeastern DuPage County
**Distance:** 9.6 mile
**Pedaling time:** 50–75 minutes
**Surface:** Crushed-limestone trails
**Terrain:** Rolling hills
**Sweat factor:** Moderate
**Trailhead:** Information kiosk at parking area on
Northgate Road

Waterfall Glen Forest Preserve forms a green ring around Argonne National Laboratory. It is a favorite of cyclists, runners, and even model airplane enthusiasts. Its eight-foot-wide, crushed-limestone main trail bounds over hills and sweeps through forest and prairie. There is a great diversity of plant life (600 species), and there are several man-made features to see, too. Few stands of pine trees exist in northeastern Illinois, but you will see several along the trail (they were planted by Argonne National Laboratory).

To reach the trailhead, take I-55 to Cass Avenue south. Turn right on the second street south of the interchange (Northgate Road) at the sign for Argonne. Then turn right into the "Ski-Equestrian Trail Head Area." Zero the odometer at the information kiosk near the toilets and the water pump. Follow the asphalt trail behind the kiosk and onto the crushed limestone. Keep right at the trail junction. There are a couple of steep hills in the first mile or so, but they are not long. At 2.2 miles, go around the barricade and turn right onto the shoulder of Westgate Road (unmarked). After a short distance, hook to the left across the road. Go through a hilly, forested area, and then make a sharp left at 3.2 miles to ride parallel to the railroad tracks. At 3.7 miles, turn right on the crushed-stone access road, then left onto the trail at the portable toilet. Nearby, a sign warns of low-flying model

aircraft; the model airfield is on the left. The trail continues through Poverty Prairie, which gets its name from the poverty oat grass that grows there.

At 4.2 miles, you begin a long descent into the Des Plaines River valley. Turn left at the T and continue downhill until you rejoin the railroad tracks. Naturally, a long, gradual climb begins soon after. Near 5.2 miles, you can see the stone remnants of the Old Lincoln Park Nursery. The plant nursery was small; most of the 107 acres purchased by the Lincoln Park Commission were used to gather topsoil to be trucked to Chicago's Lincoln Park (Ride 27). At 5.3 miles, go left on a crushed-stone road, then right on the trail. Keep left on the asphalt at 5.8 miles to cross the bridge over Sawmill Creek. At 6.1 miles, go left, then right on the trail. The Rocky Glen Trail intersects the main trail at 6.5 miles. This short spur goes down a steep hill to a waterfall built by the Civilian Conservation Corps in the 1930s. Incidentally, Waterfall Glen was not named for this waterfall. Seymour "Bud" Waterfall, a president of the DuPage County Forest Preserve District's Board of Commissioners, is the preserve's namesake. Take the trail either to see the waterfall or to test yourself on the challenging climb on the way back to the main trail. Round-trip will add half a mile to your ride. Otherwise, continue east on the main trail. Go up a steep hill and come to a parking area. If you don't need to use the toilets here, keep left on the trail.

At 7 miles is the somewhat busy crossing of Bluff Road (99th Street). At 8.3 miles you can see the 91st Street Marsh through the trees. Shortly after, make a sharp left at the information kiosk. At 9.3 miles, turn right onto the shoulder of Cass Avenue, go over a small bridge, then go left across the road on the crosswalk. Cross Northgate Road at 9.5 miles, then turn right on the trail spur back to the parking lot.

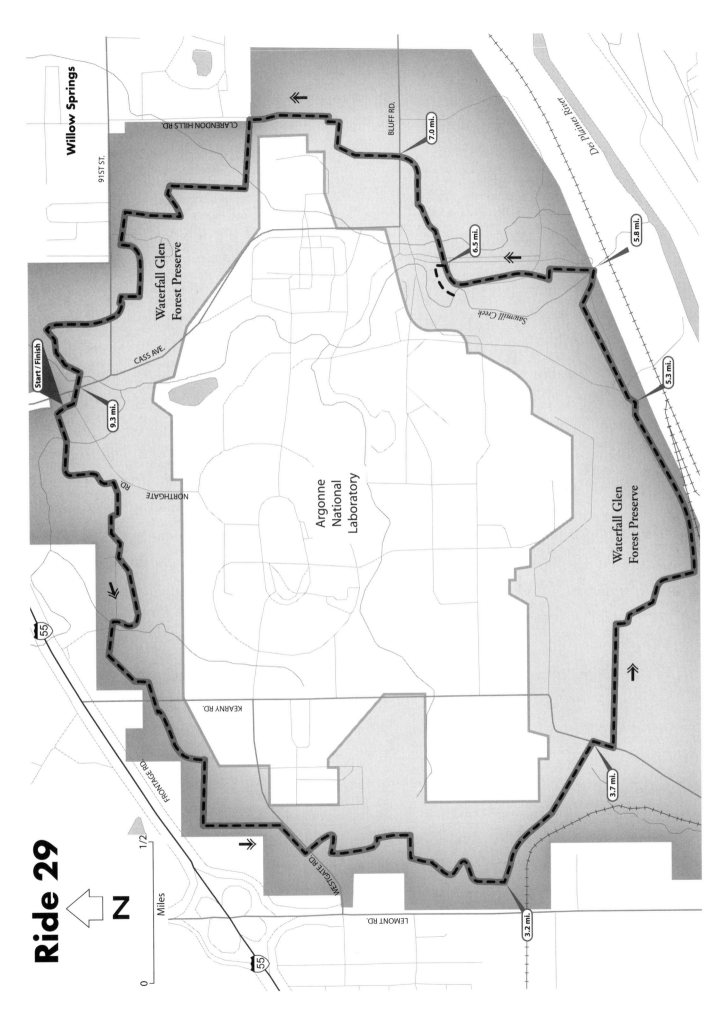

# Ride 29

N

Miles

0   1/2

**Willow Springs**

91ST ST.

CLARENDON HILLS RD.

BLUFF RD.

Waterfall Glen
Forest Preserve

CASS AVE.

Start / Finish

9.3 mi.

7.0 mi.

6.5 mi.

5.8 mi.

Sawmill Creek

Des Plaines River

5.3 mi.

NORTHGATE RD.

Argonne
National
Laboratory

Waterfall Glen
Forest Preserve

55

KEARNY RD.

FRONTAGE RD.

WESTGATE RD.

LEMONT RD.

3.7 mi.

3.2 mi.

55

# RIDE 30
## Tinley Creek Trail

**Location:** Southwestern Cook County
**Distance:** 16.3 miles
**Pedaling time:** 1.5–2.5 hours
**Surface:** Crushed-limestone trails
**Terrain:** Rolling hills
**Sweat factor:** Moderate
**Trailhead:** Yankee Woods, Tinley Park

**This ride begins in Yankee Woods.**

The Tinley Creek Trail is the name given to a system of trails in south suburban Cook County. The northernmost section is a big loop that crosses Tinley Creek twice. This is linked to a couple of smaller loops in Yankee Woods and Midlothian Meadows. There are plans to eventually connect an isolated loop several miles further south to these loops. This ride starts at Yankee Woods. It goes around two sides of the George W. Dunne National Golf Course and follows a connector trail to the big 9.4-

mile loop. Then the trail comes back south and wraps around the rest of the golf course. Trail markers are colored to correspond to trail names. The vegetation alternates between open meadows and forests, and there are lots of small hills. Although there are numerous street crossings, most coincide with traffic lights and walk signals. In general, this trail system seems to be more popular with walkers and runners than with cyclists.

To reach Yankee Woods, exit from I-57 at 167th Street, head west to Central Avenue, and turn right. Yankee Woods is the first entrance on the left. You'll cross the trail as you enter. Zero your odometer and head north on the Blue Trail Spur. Go right at the Y onto the Purple Trail Loop and up a hill, crossing the golf course entrance at 0.2 mile. Here the trail is hilly and mostly in the open. At 1.6 miles, go straight onto the Green Trail Spur where the Purple Trail Loop goes left. This connector turns right to cross 159th Street and runs north, west, and north for a total of 1.7 miles. Watch for turning traffic when you cross 151st Street. After you cross, the Green Trail Spur connects to the Red Trail Loop. Go to the right on the Red Trail Loop, heading northeast. After several street crossings, you ride into Rubio Woods. There is a trailside portable toilet at 5.7 miles. Go under buzzing power lines at 6 miles. This area is mostly open meadows. When you cross Ridgeland Avenue, there is a convenience store on the northeast corner. Be careful at 7.8 miles when you cross 135th Street; there are no traffic signals. Shortly after crossing 135th Street, you see the small Sauerbier-Burkhardt Cemetery on the left. At 8.4 miles, go straight ahead where a trail joins from the left. Arrowhead Lake, named for its shape, is on the left side of the trail just ahead.

Go left at the Y at 9.3 miles and cross a creek bridge. At 9.7 miles, cross 135th Street (unprotected by stoplights again). Soon after, the trail encounters more power lines. Turtlehead Lake appears on your left a bit further on. This lake owes its existence to the Tri-State Tollway, for which it was a borrow pit. Go straight at the trail crossing at 10.3 miles. Finally get away from the power lines at 10.9 miles for a long downhill. Go left at the T at 12.3 miles. After you cross Oak Park Avenue at 12.9 miles, go south across 151st Street to follow the Green Trail Spur again. This time turn right at 14.6 miles to follow the southern half of the Purple Trail Loop around the golf course. Around 15.7 miles, go up a steep hill, and then back down. At 16.2 miles, turn right at the Y onto the Blue Trail Spur back to the Yankee Woods parking lot.

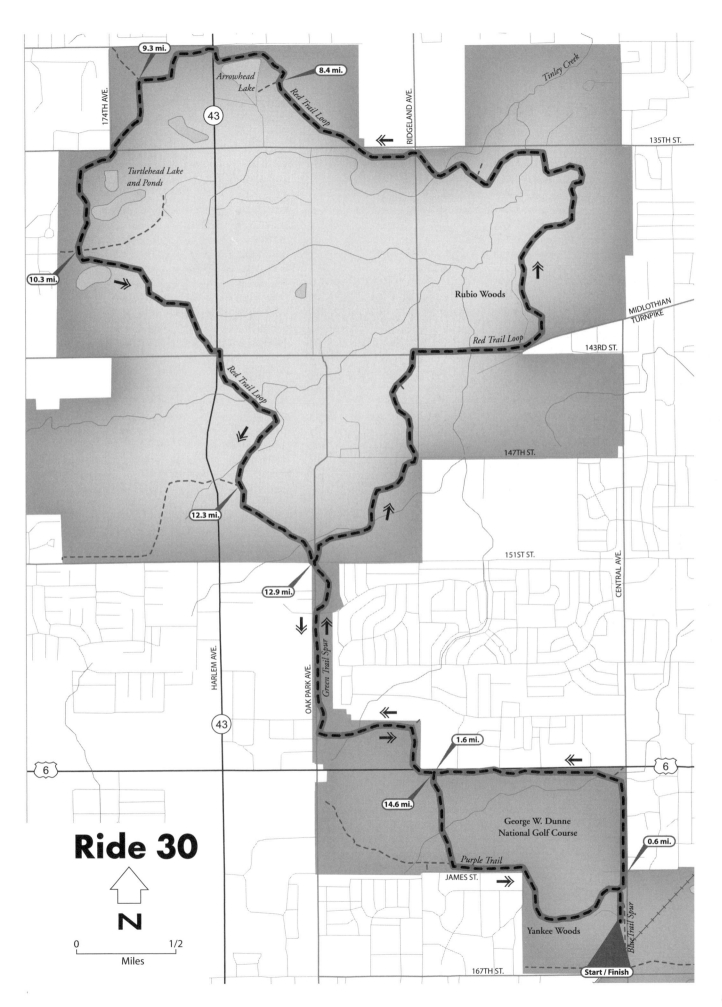

**Ride 30**

N

0 ——— 1/2
Miles

# RIDE 31
## Make Like a Mule

**Location:** Will and Grundy counties
**Distance:** 29.6 miles
**Pedaling time:** 2.5–3.5 hours
**Surface:** Mostly crushed-limestone trail, some paved trail
**Terrain:** Flat
**Sweat factor:** Low
**Trailhead:** Channahon State Park

### The Canal That Built a City

Looking at the I & M Canal today, it is hard to imagine the impact that this waterway had when it was completed more than 150 years ago. After all, it was only 60 feet wide and six feet deep. Its locks are dwarfed by those on today's Illinois River. A boat on the I & M Canal could carry a mere 150 tons; a modern river barge carries 1,500 tons, and one tugboat can push 15 barges.

Canal construction began in 1836. A nationwide financial crisis caused funding problems and stopped construction for several years, but the canal finally opened in 1848. Although railroad tracks were being laid by this time, the canal had many productive years of service. Chicago became a shipping and distribution center, it's population growing by 600 percent in the decade after the canal opened. The goods best suited for water transport then and now are bulk commodities like coal, stone, corn, and other grains. Chicago's position made it an efficient market for exchanging these products. This made the Chicago Board of Trade a leader in commodities trading. The presence of the canal got the attention of eastern railroads, and soon Chicago became a railroad hub as well.

The 1860s saw the most canal traffic, an average of 30 boats per day, but commercial traffic declined at the end of the 19th century, particularly when the Chicago Sanitary and Ship Canal opened. The I & M Canal closed in 1933.

Channahon takes its name from a Potawatomi word meaning "meeting of waters," because the DuPage and Des Plaines Rivers merge here. Bicyclists are drawn to Channahon not for this confluence, but to ride beside the legendary Illinois & Michigan Canal where mules once toiled on the towpath. To reach the trailhead, take U.S. Highway 6 through town to Canal Street south to Story Street and turn right. The trail is well developed with a solid surface, interpretive signs, and mile markers that give facts about the canal.

From the south end of the parking lot, go west up a steep hill of loose gravel—you may need to walk your bike. Lock 6 is right here, as is one of only two locktender's houses that have survived the years. This one was restored by the Civilian Conservation Corps in the 1930s. Zero your odometer and head south on the finely crushed limestone trail. A long bridge goes over a dam on the DuPage River. Lock 7 is just beyond the river. These two locks and the dam created a slack-water pool that let canal boats cross. Follow the trail to the right under a bridge. Continue into a paved parking lot, and then follow an asphalt drive for half a mile. After you return to the crushed-limestone trail, the Des Plaines River is on your left while the canal is on your right. This section of the path has ample shade in morning and evening, but not quite enough midday. At 3 miles there is a bridge across the canal to

McKinley Woods Forest Preserve. Though it is not marked on the trail, you enter Grundy County around 3.7 miles.

At 5.5 miles the path joins a paved road. The road to the left goes to Dresden Island Lock and Dam. Across the canal on the right is a red mule barn. Prior to 1871, when canal boats were pulled by mules, such barns could be found at every lock or every 10 to 15 miles. The mules were slow, but they matched the design of the canal. When steam-powered boats took over, they had to limit their speed so their wakes wouldn't damage the canal's earthen banks. West of Dresden, the trees shade the trail more completely. A half mile later the paved road ends at a parking area. Go right on the stone trail and duck under the bridge.

Approach Aux Sable at 8.2 miles. The trail crosses Aux Sable Creek on a bridge beside a canal aqueduct. The original was made of wood and stone, but this replacement aqueduct is steel. Lock 8 is here, as is another locktender's house. Aux Sable was once a village, but everyone moved away when the canal closed. At 12.6 miles the trail briefly follows a driveway after crossing a road. A mile later, William G. Stratton State Park, named for the 34th governor of Illinois, provides four boat launches and a huge parking lot beside the river on your left. Here in Morris, many homeowners have built docks in their backyards on the canal. After passing the toilets at the west end of the park, go left, downhill, under the State Highway 47 bridge, then right and back up to the trail. The trail bridge to downtown Morris at 14 miles is marked by fountains in the canal. This is a big town, so all services are available. Past the fountains, the path climbs to the right. Keep following the curve onto a steel truss railroad bridge that crosses diagonally over the canal. In Gebhard Woods State Park, there are trails on both sides of the canal. The Nettle Creek Aqueduct was another Civilian Conservation Corps restoration. The trail crosses alongside the canal. The forest downhill to the right reminds you that constructing the canal was not always about digging—sometimes the waterway had to be built up higher than its surroundings.

At 14.7 miles, a fork to the right leads downhill to toilets and water. Go straight and then cross over the bridge to the south side of the canal. As the sign says, Channahon is 14.8 miles to the left. On the return trip, be careful at the Highway 47 bridge. The descent is steep and bumpy. With all the history, one might forget what a beautiful greenway the old canal has become. On the way back, check out the reflections of the trees in the placid canal water. Look for a variety of birds, including great blue herons, on both the canal and the river.

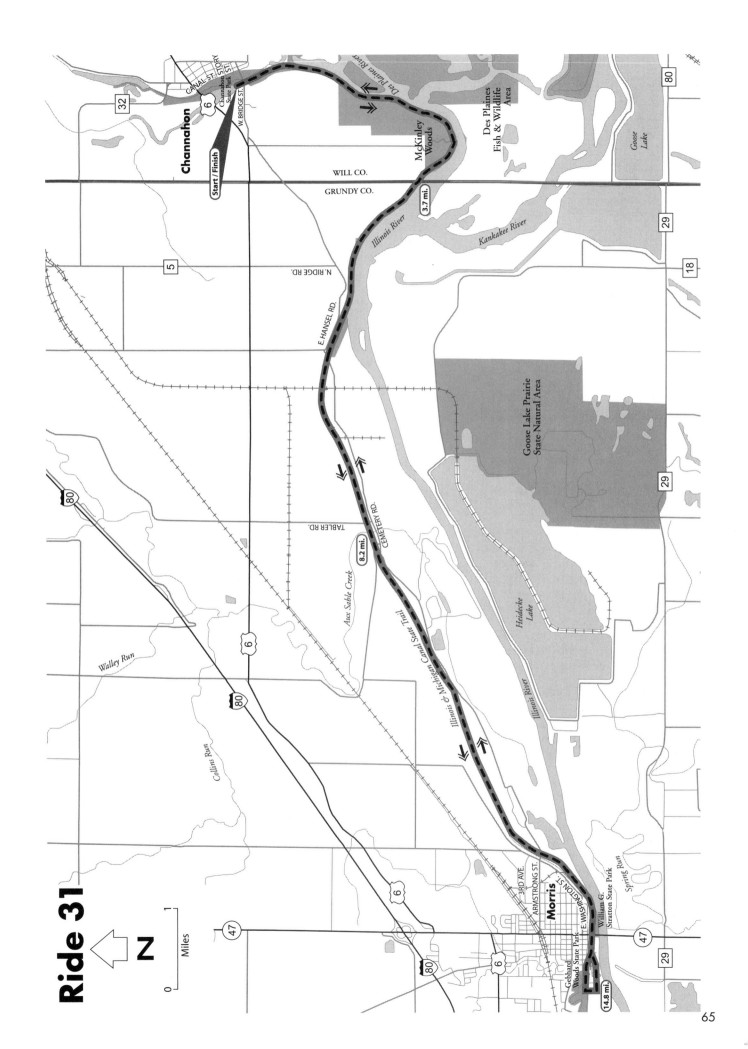

# Ride 31

**N**

Miles
0    1

**Channahon**

Start / Finish

Channahon
State Park

CANAL ST.

STORY ST.

W. BRIDGE ST.

32

6

Des Plaines River

McKinley
Woods

WILL CO.

GRUNDY CO.

3.7 mi.

Des Plaines
Fish & Wildlife
Area

Goose
Lake

80

29

18

Illinois River

Kankakee River

N. RIDGE RD.

E. HANSEL RD.

5

Goose Lake Prairie
State Natural Area

29

TABLER RD.

CEMETERY RD.

8.2 mi.

Aux Sable Creek

Illinois & Michigan Canal State Trail

Heidecke
Lake

Illinois River

Walley Run

Collins Run

80

80

6

47

6

47

29

Spring Run

**Morris**

3RD AVE.

ARMSTRONG ST.

E. WASHINGTON ST.

William G.
Stratton State Park

Gebhard
Woods State Park

14.8 mi.

80

6

# RIDE 32
## Ride the Plank

**Location:** Cook and Will counties
**Distance:** 24.6 miles
**Pedaling time:** 2–2.5 hours
**Surface:** Asphalt trails
**Terrain:** Flat with six hilly miles in the middle
**Sweat factor:** Moderate
**Trailhead:** Target parking lot on Cicero Avenue (State Highway 50) in Matteson

### Still the Prairie State?

Illinois' state nickname comes from the 22 million acres of prairie that once grew here, covering more than 60 percent of the state. That number eventually dwindled to less than 2,300 acres. In other words, for every acre remaining, nearly 10,000 have been lost, mostly to agriculture. Riding the Old Plank Road Trail gives you a chance to see an example of the concerted effort to restore the state's prairies.

Fast-moving fires from lightning strikes were commonplace in the Midwest before settlers arrived. Native Americans also set fires deliberately as a hunting and land management technique. This cycle of burning and regeneration helped to create the fertile soil where Illinois farmers grow corn and soybeans. Restoration is sometimes just a matter of setting land aside, planting native seeds, and conducting prescribed burns at regular intervals. Such burns kill off nonnative and woody species while sparing prairie plants, which have deep roots (incidentally, that feature also makes prairie grasses drought-resistant). For more information about Illinois prairies, check out Ken Robertson's Web site at www.inhs.uiuc.edu/tallgrass.

Today environmental groups and all levels of government are undertaking prairie restoration projects throughout the state. The Illinois Department of Transportation is creating prairie environments along highways. Trail builders are doing the same along recreational paths. Midewin National Tallgrass Prairie is a massive, federal prairie restoration project on the site of the former Joliet Army Ammunition Plant. While Illinois has come too far in development to ever return to the vast grasslands of the past, at least examples are being preserved and restored to show future generations why this is called the Prairie State.

The Old Plank Road Trail or OPRT (www.oprt.org) is a straight, flat rail-trail built on a former Penn Central right-of-way. The Hickory Creek Trail is a twisty and hilly path through a forest preserve. They are as different as night and day, but together they make for a great ride through the south suburbs of Chicago.

From I-57, take U.S. Highway 30 Lincoln Highway east to State Highway 50. Go south past the Target store to Gateway Drive and turn right. Park in the northeast corner of the Target parking lot. A dirt trail leads from the lot to the paved OPRT, where the ride begins. Turn left onto the trail and pass the Trail Depot gazebo. The natural area along the trail is designated as the Old Plank Road Prairie. Continuing west for a mile, enter Dewey Helmick Nature Preserve, which features a lake on the south side of the trail and cattails on the north side. Although the preserve is less than 13 acres in size,

it is home to 221 species of plants and 175 species of birds. Harlem Avenue at 3 miles is a busy crossroad that also marks the county line. Past Harlem Avenue in Will County, there are more trees to shade the trail.

The trail skirts the southern edge of Frankfort Prairie Park around 5.6 miles. Examples here show how prairie vegetation differs by soil moisture. Frankfort is a town that has really embraced the OPRT, as you might suspect while riding under the OPRT arch and onto Frankfort's Breidert Green. The strip mall beside the trail has food, drink, and a bike shop. Portable toilets are also available. The traditional downtown is located just south of the trail. On the west side of town, the OPRT climbs up to a distinctive, award-winning bridge over U.S. Highway 45. That is the path's only notable hill.

There are a number of unmarked trails connected to the OPRT, which serves as a hub for recreational paths and parks. Fortunately, the trail to Hickory Creek Forest Preserve is labeled—follow the curve to the right at 8.6 miles. Take the bridge over U.S. Highway 30 half a mile later and enjoy a long downhill into the forest preserve. As you approach a picnic area with toilets and water, turn right to follow the trail. Hickory Creek Forest Preserve alternates between prairie and woods on a hilly trail. There is a particularly long climb after crossing Hickory Creek for the second time at 11.7 miles. Shortly after the path emerges from the woods, follow the trail to the right and turn around at the parking area, which has toilets. Schmuhl School, the last one-room schoolhouse in Will County, stands to the west.

If you want to ride further, head west when you get back to the OPRT. The trail continues for at least seven miles to Joliet. Back in Matteson, you can ride more than three miles further east on the OPRT to Park Forest. Plans are underway to extend the OPRT to connect to the Wauponsee Glacial Trail in the west and the Thorn Creek Trail in the east.

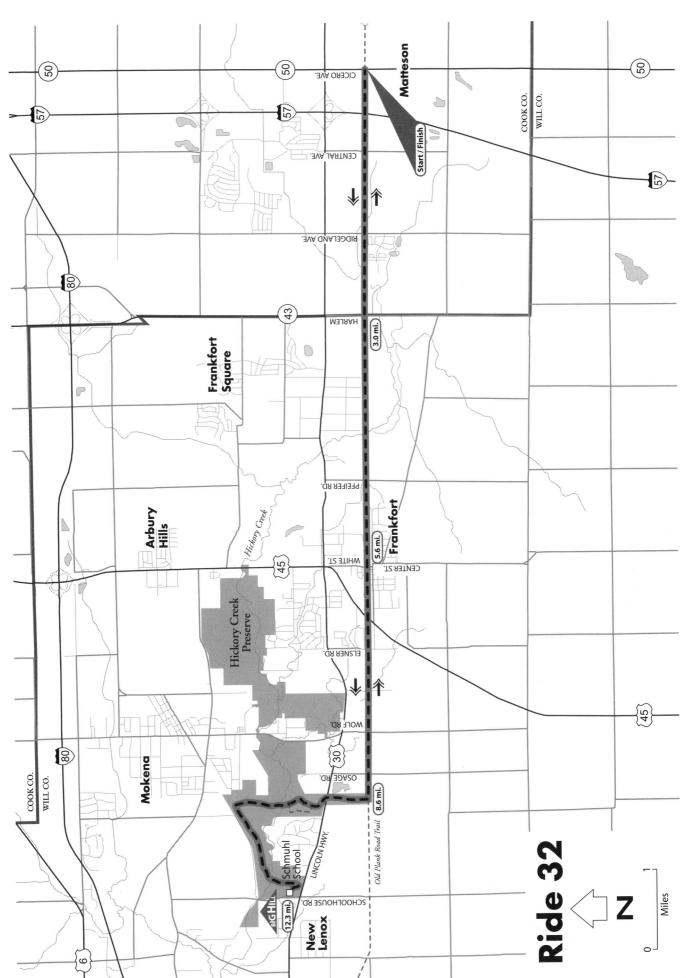

# Ride 32

N

0    1
Miles

# RIDE 33
## Bring Your Quiver to the River

**Location:** Kankakee and Will counties
**Distance:** 21 miles
**Pedaling time:** 2–2.5 hours
**Surface:** Asphalt and crushed-limestone trails
**Terrain:** Rolling hills
**Sweat factor:** Moderate
**Trailhead:** Davis Creek at east end of park

### Dairy Queen

Most people know that Ray Kroc opened his first McDonalds in Des Plaines, Illinois. Fewer know that another popular fast food chain got its start in Illinois, too. It started in Kankakee at an ice cream shop called Sherb's. That was the nickname of store owner Sherwood Dick Noble.

Noble hooked up with J. F. McCullough, who had created a semi-frozen "soft-serve" ice cream. He unveiled this new concoction on August 4, 1938, and it was an instant success. In 1940, Noble opened another store in Joliet, IL, using a name that McCullough thought of: Dairy Queen. Since then, more than 5,900 Dairy Queens have opened in nearly two dozen countries.

The restaurant chain has a special place in the hearts and bellies of many cyclists. Someone once asked Greg LeMond, America's first Tour de France winner, what he thought about during his races in Europe. He replied, "Dairy Queen. God, I dream about Dairy Queens."

And if this whets your appetite, you will be pleased to learn that there is a Dairy Queen in Bourbonnais at 121 South Main Street just five miles from this ride's trailhead.

The bicycle trail through Kankakee River State Park offers a tour of the park's north side, including some good views of the river, before turning around at the archery range. The woods and hills conspire to make this a scenic ride and a good workout. To reach the trailhead, take State Highway 102 to County Road 3000W south. After this road turns sharply left; follow the sign for Davis Creek. There are toilets at the parking area. The crushed-limestone trail at the south end of the parking lot leads west to the start of the Kankakee River Trail. The beginning of the trail is crushed limestone with occasional concrete sections in areas prone to erosion. There are mile markers every half mile, and the first mile is pleasantly downhill. The trail surface becomes asphalt from 3.5 miles on to the end. A sign across the road describes the early settlement of Altorf and the mill that operated there in the second half of the 19th century. From here on, the yellow centerline on the asphalt makes it easy to follow the main path. Signs warn of most steep hills, both up and down.

Although you get a peek a bit earlier, you don't get a good look at the Kankakee River until mile marker 4. At 4.1 miles, curve left at a trail junction. There are pop machines behind the building on the right and at 4.9 miles, where you will also find toilets. A plaque on a boulder at mile marker 5 honors C. A. Bert Stevens, the park's first superintendent. Ahead on the left, a scenic overlook offers a better view of the river. A narrow, covered bridge crosses a ditch. The Rock Creek Outpost at 5.2 miles offers food, drinks, and ice cream on summer weekends (Friday–Sunday from 11 to 5). When the concession stand is closed, you may opt for the pop machines outside. There are toilets across the parking lot. When the trail comes to a T at 5.3 miles, turn left to cross the suspension bridge over Rock Creek. One has to give the trail's designers credit for using a variety of bridges, but this one could be wider. You may not be able to enjoy the view of Rock Creek's pretty bluffs if someone else wants to get across the bridge. After the bridge, the trail goes downhill to the left and back into the woods.

One of the steeper climbs going west comes at 6.5 miles, followed by a fast descent. The trail returns to the riverside to duck under Warner Bridge Road. Just past mile marker 7, the trail crosses a park road and passes an old, limestone bridge support. This was supposed to be a railroad bridge, but it was never completed. A couple of steep climbs follow, and then you enter Chippewa Campground. A gas pipeline goes under the trail at 9.7 miles; you can see the pipes and valves on the right. The trail ends at 10.5 miles in the parking lot of the K³ River State Park Archery Facility.

On the way back around 18.3 miles, there is a descent on the crushed-limestone trail that has a loose surface near the bottom, so watch your speed. And don't forget the easy first mile you had on the way out; you have to climb it on the way back.

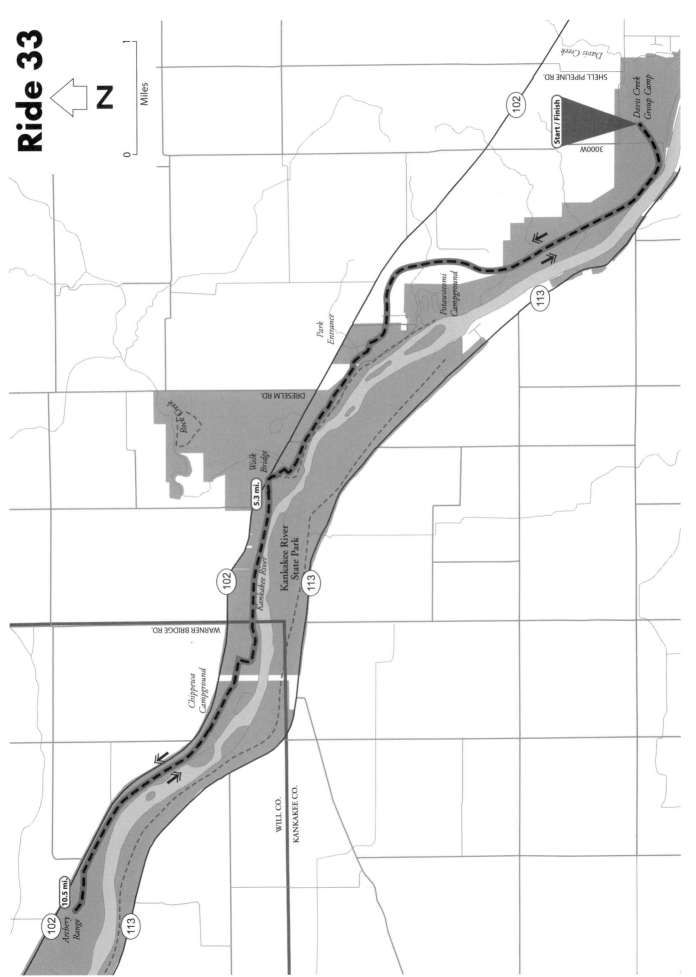

# Ride 33

N

Miles
0   1

Davis Creek

SHELL PIPELINE RD.

102

Start / Finish

3000W

Davis Creek
Group Camp

Davis Creek

102

113

Potawatomi
Campground

Park
Entrance

DRESELM RD.

Rock Creek

Walk
Bridge

5.3 mi.

Kankakee River
State Park

102

Kankakee River

113

113

WARNER BRIDGE RD.

Chippewa
Campground

WILL CO.
KANKAKEE CO.

10.5 mi.

102

Archery
Range

113

# RIDE 34
## Goodbye Norma Jean

**Location:** Henderson and Mercer counties
**Distance:** 29.7 miles
**Pedaling time:** 2.5–3 hours
**Surface:** Chip-seal roads
**Terrain:** Gently rolling hills
**Sweat factor:** Moderate
**Trailhead:** Corner of Schuyler Street and Second Street in Oquawka

This ride has nothing to do with Norma Jean Baker, better known as Marilyn Monroe. No, this ride honors a much bigger star. Norma Jean was a circus elephant who was chained to a tree in Oquawka during a thunderstorm on July 17, 1972. Lightning struck the tree and killed her instantly. Since she weighed 6,500 pounds, she had to be buried where she fell. One local man worked hard to create a decent memorial to the unfortunate pachyderm, and you'll see the fruits of his labor near the end of the ride. First, you'll see the Mississippi River, a house as old as Chicago, Big River State Forest, and the small river town of Keithsburg.

**Here lies Norma Jean.**

Most visitors will approach Oquawka from the east or south on State Highway 164. Head west from the corner where this state route turns. This is Schuyler Street, the main road through downtown. Near the Mississippi River, there is a park with a totem pole on the northeast corner of Schuyler Street and Second Street. There is plenty of on-street parking. Begin heading north on Second Street, but turn left on Warren Street at the next block to head toward Riverside Park. As you ride north through the park, the Alexis Phelps house is on the right at 0.3 mile. Phelps

was a fur trader who happened to be friends with Abraham Lincoln and Stephen Douglas. The house was built in 1833, the same year Chicago was incorporated. It can be reached from Second Street, but it is only open by appointment. When the road curves away from the river, go to Third Street, turn left, and follow it north out of Oquawka. Be careful at intersections in town because not all have traffic control signs. The road ends with a stop sign at the road to Delabar State Park. This park offers camping, boating, and picnicking along the river. Go right and pass through a grand, pine tree-lined promenade. Turn left at the T, then turn right on County Road 2300N. Turn left on County Road 1400E, which stair-steps its way into County Road 1500E. Follow this road for more than 8 miles. Big River State Forest is on the left at 6.7 miles, set apart by a firebreak. Many parts of this 2,900-acre forest have been converted from scrub hardwood to white and red pines. There are rolling hills on 1500E, especially before you cross County Road 2650N. At 9.3 miles is either a replica of a Flintstones car or the world's largest Pinewood Derby car. The forest is not one continuous tract, so it disappears for a while, and then it reappears just before you cross the Mercer County line (not signed) at the intersection with County Road 3000N.

At the stop sign for 20th Avenue, turn left to head toward Keithsburg. There are two cemeteries at the east end of town. Follow the curve of the road gently to the right onto Main Street at 15.1 miles. The Great River Road junction is at the second stop sign in town. Continue east past the only amenities on this ride: a gas station/mini-mart, a bar, a Tastee-Freez (open only in summer), and a hotel. Then go up on the levee for another look at the Mississippi. As you go north, you'll see a railroad bridge that is damaged near the east bank of the river. Just a block later, come back down from the levee. Continue east on Jackson Street to the stop sign at 10th Street. Take 10th Street south out of town. Pass Saint Mary's Catholic Church, which dates back to 1868. This road has slight curves and gentle hills with little traffic. Go through Big River State Forest again, passing campgrounds, the ranger station, a lookout tower, and a hiking trailhead.

Watch for the entrance to Delabar State Park with its rows of pines. Go past this entrance and turn right on the next street, which is unmarked. As you reach the woods and the sign for "asparagus by the pound or the ton," the road curves left to head south into Oquawka. Turn right on Henry Street, and then turn left on Fifth Street. Norma Jean's grave is located at a gravel turnout on the left side of Fifth Street at 29.1 miles. An information board tells the story of the elephant and Wade Meloan, the man who sought to honor her memory. After paying your respects to this big star, it's a short run down Fifth Street to Schuyler to get back to your starting point.

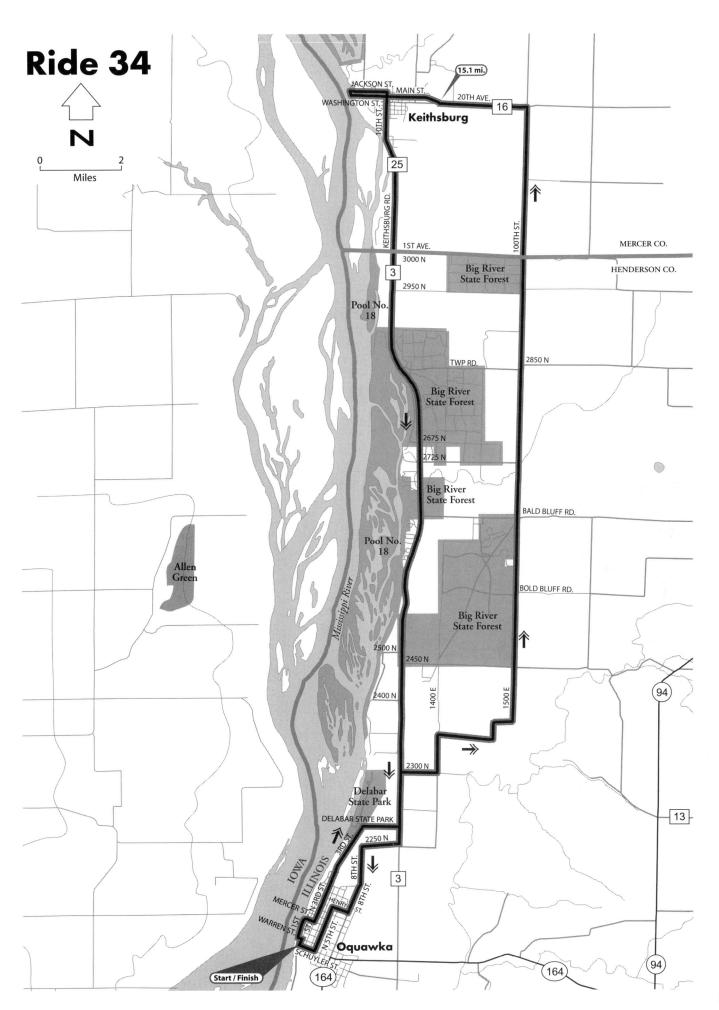

# Ride 34

N

0       2
Miles

JACKSON ST.
MAIN ST.
WASHINGTON ST.
20TH AVE.
15.1 mi.
**Keithsburg**
16
25
10TH ST.
KEITHSBURG RD.
1ST AVE.
100TH ST.
MERCER CO.
3000 N
Big River State Forest
2950 N
HENDERSON CO.
3
Pool No. 18
2850 N
TWP RD.
Big River State Forest
2675 N
2725 N
Big River State Forest
BALD BLUFF RD.
Pool No. 18
Allen Green
BOLD BLUFF RD.
Big River State Forest
Mississippi River
2500 N
2450 N
94
2400 N
1400 E
1500 E
2300 N
Delabar State Park
DELABAR STATE PARK
13
3RD ST.
2250 N
8TH ST.
3
IOWA
ILLINOIS
8TH ST.
MERCER ST.
5TH ST.
3RD ST.
HENRY ST.
WARREN ST.
1ST ST.
**Oquawka**
SCHUYLER ST.
Start / Finish
164
164
94

# RIDE 35
## Spoon Lake

**Location:** Knox County east of Galesburg
**Distance:** 30.7 miles
**Pedaling time:** 2.5–3.5 hours
**Surface:** Chip-seal roads
**Terrain:** Gently rolling hills
**Sweat factor:** Moderate +
**Trailhead:** Galesburg Visitor Center, 2163 East Main Street

Spoon Lake is a residential development ten miles east of Galesburg. Although the lake and its facilities are private, the roads are public. This ride cruises through prime Illinois farmland, goes halfway around Spoon Lake, and returns. To get to the Galesburg Visitor Center from I-74, get off at Exit 48 headed west. The Visitor Center is on the north side of the road as you enter town. The trick is that you have to turn right at the Mobil gas station sign to get there. It is okay to leave your car, but the Visitor Center staff would like to know about it.

Begin by turning left on Main Street, going under I-74. In East Galesburg, be careful going through the narrow railroad underpass at 0.7 mile. Soon after, make a sharp left turn onto Lakeview Drive. There is loose stone in the intersection. Go uphill and curve to the right, passing Saint Mary's Cemetery (1860) on the left. At 1.7 miles, bear left on Blaze Road as you cross State Street. This road has lots of rolling hills for the first three miles. After you pass Knox Station Road, however, the road is more flat except for one steep descent and climb beginning at 5.5 miles. At the end of Blaze Road, turn right on Barefoot Road. The road stair-steps through a series of left and right curves. At 7.7 miles you have to turn right to stay on Barefoot Road. Follow the paved road left at 8.9 miles. Soon after the road curves right, you begin a steep descent on rough pavement. Turn left at the bottom of the hill onto Old Wagon Road (do not cross the creek bridge). This road runs parallel to railroad tracks for half a mile. There is a sign for a railroad crossing, but you will avoid it by curving left on the paved road. A caboose sits on a hill to the left as if it had been flung from the tracks below. Keep right at the intersection with County Road 1350E, although the wider pavement curves left. The road ends at County Highway 12, which is busier. You won't be on it for long, though. Turn right and follow the curve to the left, then turn left when the road curves to the right. This road, County Road 1550N, is another stair-step road like Barefoot Road, but with some steeper hills thrown into the mix. Turn left at the stop sign onto County Road 1720E, which is County Highway 15. Go through a couple of curves, then turn left on Oak Run Drive before the next series of curves starts.

Oak Run Drive has plenty of curves of its own, plus rolling hills. After a glimpse of Spoon Lake at 16.9 miles, you get a better look as you ride across the earthen dam that makes it possible. After 19 miles of mostly chip seal, the half mile of asphalt on Oak Run Drive before the stop sign at County Road 1725N is a welcome sight. Turn left to go past a golf course, a gas station, and most important to cyclists, the Oak Run Food Mart (open daily from 7 AM to 9 or 10 PM). This is the only place for refreshments on the ride. Turn right on County Highway 12 at the T, then take the first left on County Road 1760N. Maxey Chapel is to the right at 1350E, but you want to turn left. Make the first right turn on Ward Road. There is a steep descent into a creek valley at 23 miles followed by the requisite climb, which lasts until the end of the road. Turn left on Barefoot Road, and then go right on Blaze Road. From this point on, you are retracing the beginning of the ride. You get to experience the hills on Blaze Road from the opposite direction. On Lakeview Drive, watch for those loose stones when you go downhill to Main Street at the end. Negotiate that narrow underpass again, climb a bit, and cruise back to the Galesburg Visitor Center.

**These grazing cattle show little interest in a passing cyclist.**

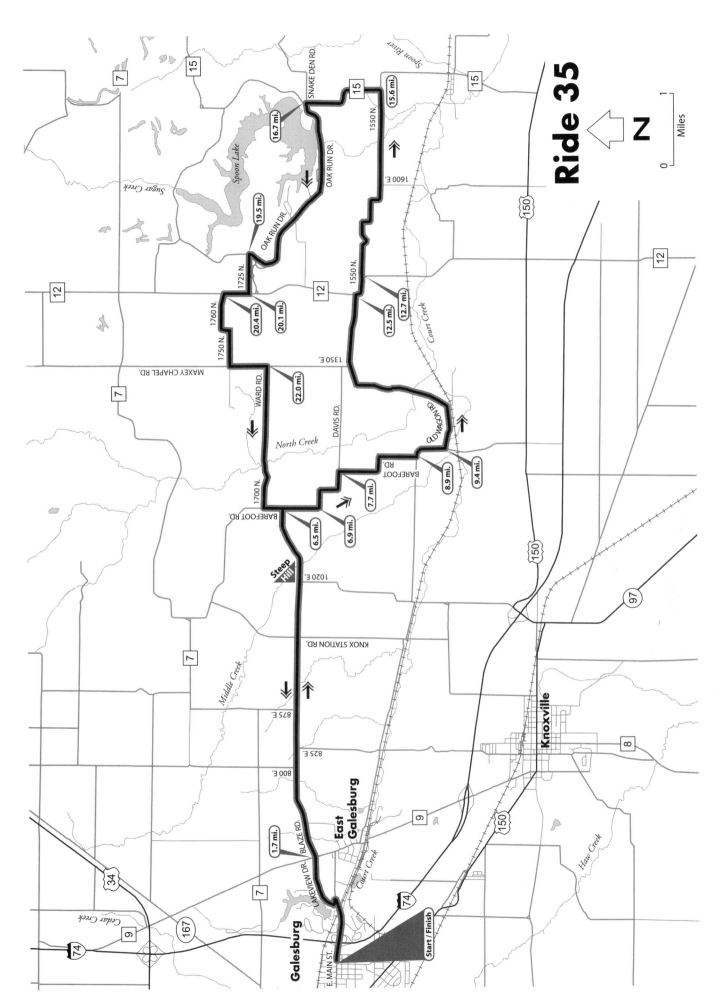

# Ride 35

N

Miles

# RIDE 36
## Historic Galesburg

**Location:** Galesburg
**Distance:** 17.7 miles
**Pedaling time:** 1.5–2 hours
**Surface:** Chip-seal roads, asphalt path
**Terrain:** Mostly flat
**Sweat factor:** Low +
**Trailhead:** Corner of Seminary Street and
Mulberry Street

Don't be surprised if you have to wait for a train or two on this ride. Galesburg is a big railroad town. In fact, Galesburg is the future home of the National Railroad Hall of Fame. Something important to cyclists is that most of the railroad crossings are diagonal, so be careful not to get a tire stuck in the tracks. There are plenty of other things besides trains to see on this ride, including Carl Sandburg's birthplace, Lake Storey Recreational Area, many old homes, several beautiful churches, a classic courthouse, and a Lincoln-Douglas debate site.

This ride begins at the south end of the Seminary Street Historic Commercial District. To get there, head south on Seminary Street from U.S. Highway 34 or Main Street (U.S. Highway 150). There are several public parking lots. Ride east on Mulberry Street toward the railroad tracks. The Galesburg Railroad Museum is on your right, and the Amtrak station is a bit further south. In the middle of the crossing, turn right on Chambers Street. Go south to Second Street and turn right. This road is brick, but only for a block. Cross Seminary Street and turn left on Kellogg Street, followed by another left on Third Street. Carl Sandburg State Historic Site is on the north side of the street. This is both the writer's birthplace and final resting spot. Prominent in Illinois literature, Sandburg is best known for his six-volume biography of Abraham Lincoln and his poems, including "Chicago," which christened the city as "Hog Butcher for the World" and "City of the Big Shoulders."

Now it's time to see some trains! Head south on Seminary Street to Davis Street. Turn right and follow the curve to the left onto Saluda Road. Heading out of town, you have railroad tracks on your right and cornfields on your left. At the four-way stop, the Burlington Northern Santa Fe Galesburg Classification Headquarters is on your right. Turn left on Old Thirlwell Road, then turn right on County Highway 10. Although this road has some traffic, there is a paved shoulder as you climb toward the overpass. The bridge is even wider, offering ample opportunity to stop and look at the trains spread out across this huge rail yard. After you come down from the bridge, turn right on Henderson Street. This is a major thoroughfare on the north side of town, but here it is a wide, two-lane road. Expect truck traffic on weekdays since this is an industrial park.

Turn right on Louisville Road before the railroad crossing at 4.6 miles. The intersection with Academy Street is tricky. You have to turn left, but cross traffic doesn't stop. Once you're on Academy Street, there is a two-way

stop before the railroad crossing. Follow the city's signed bike route north on Academy Street past Main Street and another pair of railroad tracks to North Street. The bike route goes left on North Street, right on Maple Avenue, and left on Losey Street. After crossing Henderson Street at a stoplight, leave the bike route by turning right on Hawkinson Avenue. Galesburg High School is straight ahead at Fremont Street where you turn left. Cross the bridge over U.S. Highway 34 and turn right on Log City Trail. At 9.8 miles, follow the bike route sign left on an unmarked road into Carl Sandburg College. Go left at the stop sign to loop around the campus.

This road ends at 10.6 miles at South Lake Storey Road, but a hilly, curvy, asphalt bike path continues straight north into the woods across the road. Ride carefully through the gravelly boat launch area at 10.9 miles. The path runs on a levee and crosses a spillway on a long bridge. At 12.3 miles the asphalt ends at the Lake Storey Pavilion. Follow the sidewalk between the building and the lake and continue on the asphalt path. The asphalt gives way to another sidewalk that runs right up to some restrooms. Go left on another sidewalk, then turn right at the shelter to follow the asphalt path once more. Cross busy U.S. Highway 150 at 13.2 miles and ride through the small parking area to rejoin the path. The trail narrows into single-track briefly and crosses a small, wooden bridge. Watch for gravel as you turn right on the park road. At the stop sign, turn left on Treadwell Drive. Keep right at an unmarked intersection at 13.6 miles.

Turn right on Lincoln Park Drive, which has a grassy median. Cross a bridge over U.S. Highway 34 and turn left on Carl Sandburg Drive when the road ends. Turn right on Broad Street. Past Fremont Street, you might wonder who would put a bike route on a brick street. The parallel streets are also brick, however, and as the name implies, Broad Street is wider. Besides, there are some large, beautiful homes on this street. Cross the railroad tracks again to leave this residential area. Notice the handsome National Guard Armory on the left. Traffic-wise, the hardest part of this ride comes at Public Square. Turn right, then keep left to avoid turning onto Main Street. Turn right on Broad Street at the imposing Central Congregational Church. At the end of Broad Street, you can see the Knox County Courthouse ahead to the left. To the right is Standish Park Arboretum, which you circle by turning right on Tompkins Street, left on Cedar Street, and left on South Street. The oldest part of Knox College is on the right, including Alumni Hall. Set back from the street, you can see Old Main, the building where Lincoln and Douglas debated in 1858.

To finish, turn left on Prairie Street at Corpus Christi Catholic Church, and then turn right on Simmons Street. After turning, you can look across the parking lot to the left to see the restored Orpheum Theatre on Kellogg Street. Simmons Street ends at Seminary Street where you turn right to return to the start.

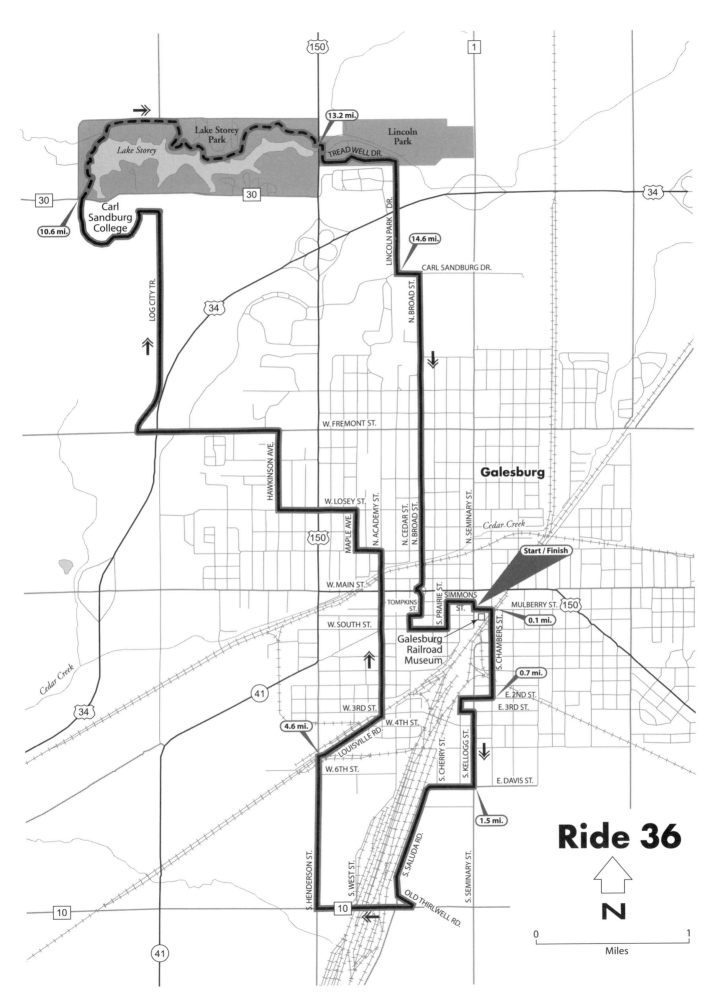

Lake Storey

Lake Storey Park

Lincoln Park

13.2 mi.

TREADWELL DR.

30

30

Carl Sandburg College

10.6 mi.

LINCOLN PARK DR.

14.6 mi.

34

CARL SANDBURG DR.

LOG CITY TR.

34

N. BROAD ST.

W. FREMONT ST.

**Galesburg**

HAWKINSON AVE.

W. LOSEY ST.

N. ACADEMY ST.

N. CEDAR ST.

N. BROAD ST.

N. SEMINARY ST.

Cedar Creek

150

MAPLE AVE.

W. MAIN ST.

Start / Finish

S. PRAIRIE ST.

SIMMONS ST.

MULBERRY ST. 150

Tompkins ST.

0.1 mi.

W. SOUTH ST.

Galesburg Railroad Museum

S. CHAMBERS ST.

0.7 mi.

Cedar Creek

41

E. 2ND ST.

E. 3RD ST.

W. 3RD ST.

34

4.6 mi.

W. 4TH ST.

LOUISVILLE RD.

S. CHERRY ST.

S. KELLOGG ST.

E. DAVIS ST.

W. 6TH ST.

1.5 mi.

**Ride 36**

S. HENDERSON ST.

S. WEST ST.

S. SALUDA RD.

S. SEMINARY ST.

10

10

OLD THIRLWELL RD.

41

N

0          1

Miles

# RIDE 37
## A Mighty Good Trail

**Location:** Northwest of Peoria
**Distance:** 40 miles
**Pedaling time:** 3.5–4.5 hours
**Surface:** Crushed-stone trail
**Terrain:** Mostly flat, a few hills
**Sweat factor:** Low
**Trailhead:** Middle of parking lot at Alta trailhead

### An Out-of-This-World Ride

Peoria's Lakeview Museum of Arts and Sciences (www.lakeview-museum.org or (309) 686-7000) features a unique attraction—the world's largest scale model of the solar system. The model's objective is to demonstrate the vastness of space. Most models of the solar system don't even attempt to show scale, and those that do either show planets to scale or their orbits to scale. Lakeview's model proportionally shows the size and distance of the planets, with west-central Illinois cornfields representing the vastness of space.

The museum's planetarium serves as the Sun with its 36-foot diameter. Nine locations throughout the region host planets sized and positioned to the scale of the Sun. In this model, Earth is only four inches in diameter, and it is located 0.75 mile from the Sun. The orbits of several planets are marked on the Rock Island Trail, but you won't see any of the actual spheres.

If you come in August for the Interplanetary Ride, you can traverse the entire solar system by bicycle, covering 17 billion miles in only two days. The Saturday ride visits the outer planets with a 14-billion-mile century ride turning around in Kewanee where Good's Furniture hosts Pluto. There are shorter options available for those who may want to linger on a certain planet. Some of the routes use roads but others use the Rock Island State Trail. This is one day when the park office/depot/museum in Wyoming is sure to be open. On Sunday morning, a shorter ride explores historic Peoria and swings through the inner solar system on a 3-billion-mile jaunt (actually 24 miles on your bike). There is a fee for the ride, but this includes museum admission, support vehicles, and plenty of food before, during, and after the ride. Visit the museum's Web site for details.

The aptly named Peoria and Rock Island Railroad built this rail line from Peoria to Rock Island after the Civil War. The railroad was in decline by the beginning of World War I, and the trains stopped running by the late 1950s. Peoria's Forest Park Foundation took control of the corridor and gave it to the state in 1969. This was a controversial project, and it took 20 years to finally open the trail.

The Rock Island State Trail begins in Alta, which is north of Peoria. There is a long parking lot off Alta Lane. If you park somewhat close to the entrance and start on the path at the middle of the lot, you will be in synch with the trail's mile markers. These markers are accurate except when a mile is passed within a town; then the marker appears north of town. After passing toilets and water on this trail spur, turn left to go north on the main trail. From Alta to Princeville the trail cuts a diagonal path. That means most street crossings are diagonal too, so be especially careful at intersections. Most of the ride to Dunlap is shaded by a canopy of trees. The corridor is narrow, and farmland is visible through the trees.

Just before mile 2, there is a sign marking the orbit of Saturn on the Lakeview Museum's scale model of the solar system (see sidebar). The highlight of this trail segment is the bridge over Kickapoo Creek at 2.6 miles. At 3.7 miles you enter Dunlap, passing the library. Follow the bike route signs through town. When you reach the T at Hickory Street, turn right, then left onto gravel, then left again onto the trail. The next street crossing, State Highway 91, is especially dangerous, so be alert.

Most of the grades are easy, but a few are steeper than you might expect on a rail-trail. Around 4.8 miles is a descent to the bridge over Harlan's Creek, followed by a street crossing and a steep climb through a trail parking lot. Shortly after mile 6, signs on the right describe farming techniques that can be observed from the trail.

At 9.8 miles, curve left to go parallel to the railroad tracks (separated from you by a fence). At the south end of Princeville, turn right on Mendenhall Road/Walnut Street. There is a rough crossing over the railroad tracks. Cutters Grove Park on the left has a public toilet building that features a Rock Island Trail mural. Walnut Street takes you past several restaurants and stores. After downtown, turn right at the first stop sign, which is North Avenue, then go left at the next stop sign onto Town Avenue. At 11.4 miles, turn left onto a one-lane road, then turn right onto the trail just before the stop sign (mile marker 11 here is obviously out of place). The trail runs along a high embankment north of Princeville, which is especially noticeable on the creek bridge. At 13.3 miles the shade disappears as the trail runs through the Rock Island Trail Prairie Nature Preserve. Cross into Stark County at 13.8 miles (no sign) and back into the shade.

At 19.8 miles is the sign for Neptune's orbit (the orbit of Uranus is somewhere between Saturn and Neptune, but the sign gets stolen often). The old Wyoming Depot at 20 miles serves as the park office and as the turnaround point for this ride. The depot, which actually served the Chicago, Burlington & Quincy rather than the Peoria and Rock Island, holds some interesting railroad memorabilia. Unfortunately, it is often closed. The maintenance building just south of the depot has drinking water and toilets. If you want to ride further, it's another six miles to the end of the line in Toulon.

On the way back, you can count down the miles. If you get tired, just start singing the "Rock Island Line" song. Its chugging beat will carry you home.

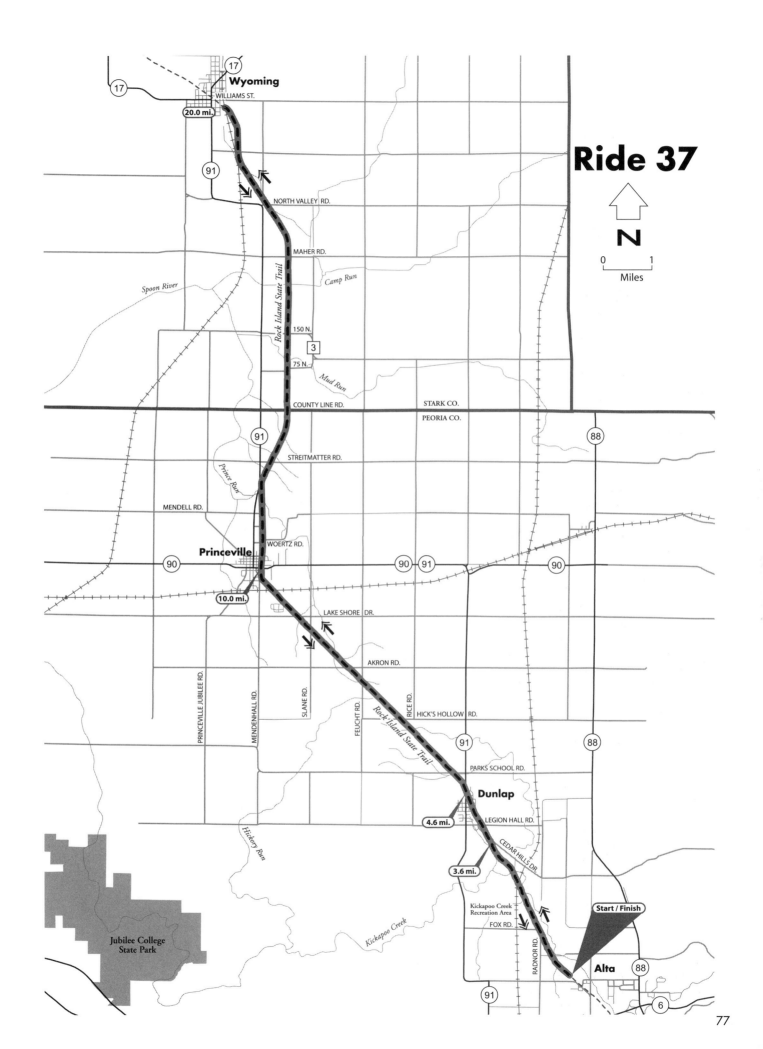

# Ride 37

N

0 — 1
Miles

# RIDE 38
## Around the Lake and Down Memory Lane

**Location:** McLean County
**Distance:** 29.4 miles
**Pedaling time:** 2.5–3 hours

**Surface:** Paved country roads, paved trail
**Terrain:** Gently rolling hills
**Sweat factor:** Moderate
**Trailhead:** Lexington City Hall, 329 West Main Street, Lexington

### Get Your Kicks on Route 66

U.S. Route 66 has always evoked a sense of adventure, whether on a family vacation or en route to a new life in California. Bobby Troup was headed for Los Angeles to pursue a songwriting career when he penned his biggest hit along the way. Released in 1946, "(Get Your Kicks On) Route 66" became one of jazz artist Nat "King" Cole's most popular numbers. It has been covered by countless other performers since. When Americans began vacationing by car in large numbers after World War II, Route 66 was a popular route to southwestern destinations ranging from the Grand Canyon to Disneyland. There was a Route 66 television series in the early sixties, too. Although little of it was actually filmed on Route 66, it cemented the road's reputation for adventure in the public mind.

The road was a victim of its own success, however, becoming choked with traffic. When the Interstate Highway System was built, Route 66 was replaced by I-55 in Illinois. The state removed its Route 66 signs in 1977, and the entire route was decommissioned in 1985. With thousands of supporters, however, the old road has refused to die. Organizations have formed in every state touched by the road to promote, celebrate, travel, and study the old highway. The Illinois Historic Route 66 Association runs a motor tour between Chicago and Saint Louis every June, one of the few times when Lexington's Memory Lane is open to cars. For more information, visit www.il66assoc.org.

This ride begins with a cruise on tree-lined country roads to Lake Bloomington. After looping around the west side of the lake, the ride returns to Lexington. Outside of town, it follows a bicycle path laid over former lanes of Historic Route 66. The grand finale is a ride into a time warp that will take you back to the glory days of old Route 66 on Memory Lane.

Ride west from the Lexington City Hall at 329 West Main Street, which is also called the Frank J. Feigl Municipal Building. There is a parking lot next door as well as on-street parking. Be careful crossing the diagonal railroad tracks. As you leave town after a four-way stop, the road curves to the right. Make the first left turn, following signs toward I-55 (you probably drove into town this way). As you cross I-55, you are on P. J. Keller Highway, a two-lane road with gentle, rolling hills. Go past Clarksville Road at 2.4 miles; you'll join it further down the road where it's paved. Turn right on County Road 2225E at 3.2 miles, then left on Clarksville Road. Clarksville is a collection of houses with no services for cyclists. After a sharp curve to the right, turn left at 4.1 miles to stay on Clarksville Road.

West of Clarksville, the road zigzags. Continue to County Road 1725E at 9.7 miles and turn left. The road curves to the left and becomes County Road 2600N. Turn right on County Road 1750E at the stop sign.

This road ends at County Highway 8. Ahead to the left, the road through North Park offers portable toilets and a view of Lake Bloomington. To continue the ride, turn right on County Highway 8 and go over a bridge. Lake Bloomington is a favorite route for local cyclists.

The only services outside of Lexington on this ride are a restaurant and a convenience store at the four-way stop sign with County Road 2500N. Continue straight ahead to the stop sign at Carver Road (2450N). Turn left and go over a bridge. At the four-way stop, continue straight ahead. Curve left at Iroquois Lane at 13.8 miles. Go through the gate to enjoy the hilly, curvy Lampe Lane Scenic Drive. The road is narrow, but the speed limit is low. This is a forested area with some picnic tables and portable toilets. Just past the end of the drive you return to a familiar four-way stop. Continue straight ahead to the T at 16.4 miles. Turn left to follow the lakeshore. At County Road 1825E, turn right to leave Lake Bloomington (if you want a longer ride, you can do a complete lap around the lake using the map). Head south on 1825E and follow the chip-seal road to the east, then to the south. At 19 miles, turn left on County Road 2200N.

Turn left on County Road 2100E, then right on Dameron Road. This low-traffic road takes you back across I-55. The stop sign ahead is Historic Route 66. Turn left onto the multiuse path just before the stop sign. You are now riding on what used to be the southbound lanes of Route 66. After most traffic moved to I-55, four lanes were no longer warranted here. In other towns the extra lanes were torn up, but in Lexington they became the Ollie and Dorothy Myers Walkway instead. Follow the path across Main Street at 27.1 miles. Don't be tempted to take a shortcut back to City Hall—you'll miss a special treat.

At 28.1 miles, the bike path ends. Go to the right across Old Route 66, watching for traffic. There is a small park here with picnic tables and dozens of bird feeders painted with Route 66 themes. The road ahead is usually gated, but cyclists and pedestrians are allowed to go through. You are about to step back in time on a ride down what they call Memory Lane. This is a section of the original 1926 Route 66 that has been closed to regular traffic for decades. Time has taken its toll on the surface, but it winds through a pleasant forest. Your nostalgic trip is made complete by old-time billboards representing local businesses.

This flashback ends too soon as the road enters Lexington. Follow it to the right, then left. At the stop sign, turn left on Main Street and ride back to City Hall.

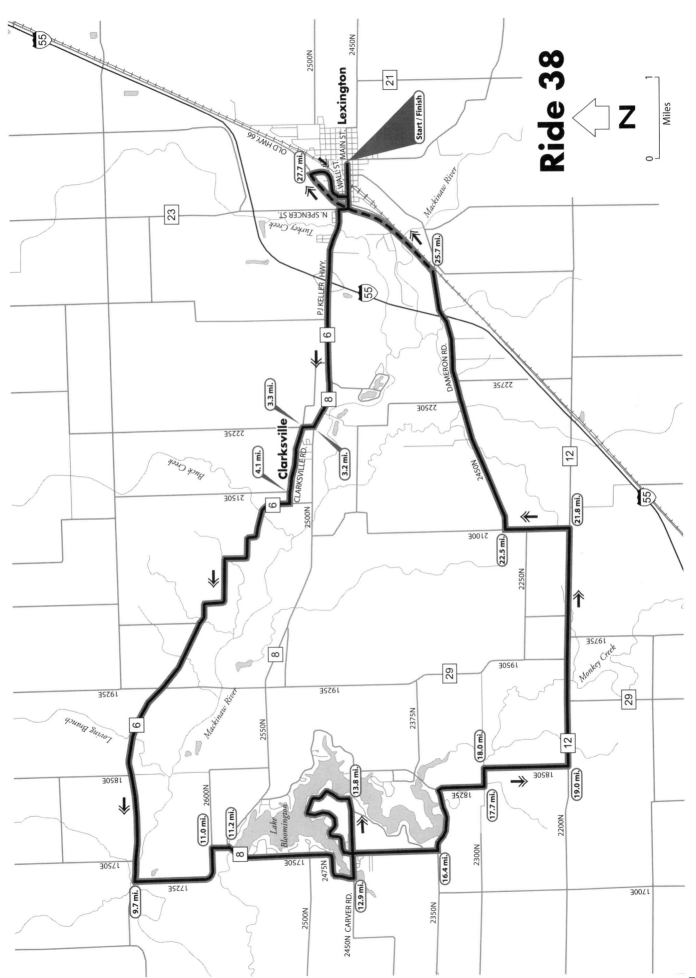

# Ride 38

N

Miles
0          1

Lexington

Start / Finish

27.7 mi.
25.7 mi.

Clarksville
3.3 mi.
4.1 mi.
3.2 mi.

9.7 mi.
11.0 mi.
11.2 mi.
12.9 mi.
13.8 mi.
16.4 mi.
17.7 mi.
18.0 mi.
19.0 mi.
21.8 mi.
22.5 mi.

WALLS ST.
N. MAIN ST.
N. SPENCER ST.
OLD HWY. 66
Turkey Creek
Mackinaw River
PJ KELLER HWY.
DAMERON RD.
CLARKSVILLE RD.
Buck Creek
Loving Branch
Mackinaw River
Lake Bloomington
CARVER RD.
Monkey Creek

55
21
23
6
8
55
6
8
6
8
29
29
12
12
55

# RIDE 39
## Havana

**Location:** Mason County
**Distance:** 37.1 miles
**Pedaling time:** 3–3.5 hours
**Surface:** Paved roads, mostly chip seal
**Terrain:** Gently rolling hills
**Sweat factor:** Moderate
**Trailhead:** Corner of Main Street and Broadway in Havana

Havana's most famous feature is its water tower. Still in use, the water tower was built in 1889 and has been named an American Water Landmark by the American Water Works Association. The area northeast of Havana includes a state forest and a national wildlife refuge. Agriculture is king in Havana. A sign on the main highway through town reports daily whether corn and soybean markets are up or down. Irrigation is used extensively in Mason County; you may need to dodge the overspray.

Main Street is brick through downtown, but this ride starts at the east end of the bricks, on the southeast corner of the Mason County Courthouse Square. Head uphill on Main Street and pass the water tower. The first stop sign is at Promenade Street. Turn left onto this well-traveled but wide street. After you pass a cemetery, turn right on Franklin Street, which becomes County Road 1700N when it leaves town. There is a park with baseball fields outside of town. Beyond, the scenery is a mix of farmland, scattered homes, and trees. Turn left on County Road 1950E at 4.1 miles, then turn right on County Road 1800N a mile later.

At 9.6 miles, a sign shows a curve to the right—instead, turn left on County Road 2400E. After curving east, this road passes Mason State Tree Nursery around 10 miles. The road stair-steps until you are on County Road 2730E. Go north over an unprotected railroad crossing at 15.6 miles, then continue across Manito Road. There is a sign announcing Forest City at 16.5 miles. This ride skirts the western edge of town. At the end of 2730E (Dierker Road), turn left on Eyman Road. After passing the first of several equestrian trail crossings, you are welcomed to Sand Ridge State Forest, which is Illinois' largest state forest at 7,200 acres. This forest mixes 3,900 acres of native oak and hickory with 2,500 acres of pine plantations dating back to the late 1930s. The rest of the space is comprised of open fields or sand prairies (also seen on Ride 6). There are hiking and equestrian trails, but bicycles must stay on roads. At 18.8 miles, there is a stop sign at Sand Ridge Road. Turn left, and then immediately turn right onto Cactus Drive (County Road 2600E). This road ends at a T. Go west and tackle some long, rolling hills for the next few miles. The Jake Wolf Memorial Fish Hatchery visitor center, which features an upper-level viewing area where you can see the different stages of fish production, is off to the right at 21.8 miles. This is the largest hatchery in Illinois. Every year it produces millions of fish in sixteen species. It is open from 8:30 AM to 3:30 PM, (309) 968-7531.

At 25.9 miles, you pass the town of Goofy Ridge. There is no sign for the village limits, but there is a sign pointing to the Goofy Ridge Café. At 26.7 miles, curve to the left, but don't turn left at the Hialeah Club. You are on North Buzzville Road. You may think you see the Illinois River through the trees, but actually it's Chautauqua Lake, which lies beside the river. Turn right at the end of this road onto County Road 2250N, which curves to the left through trees. Chautauqua National Wildlife Refuge Eagle Bluff public access area at 28.9 miles has toilets. There is a bar and grill half a mile further down the road. When this road ends at Manito Road, turn right. The road curves to the left and crosses Quiver Creek. Make the first right turn on County Road 1950N toward the river. At 33.2 miles is a sign for Forbes Biological Station—this is named for the same person as Stephen A. Forbes State Park (see Ride 50). This road curves left, becoming Quiver Beach Road and passing a tavern called the Squirrel Pit. At 35.4 miles you return to Manito Road and turn right. Go over a rail yard on a bridge with paved shoulders. A lot of the railcars are filled with coal. Manito Road turns into Promenade Street in town. The first stop sign at 36.9 miles is Main Street. Turn right, go past the water tower again, and go downhill to the start.

The Havana water tower has been in use since 1889.

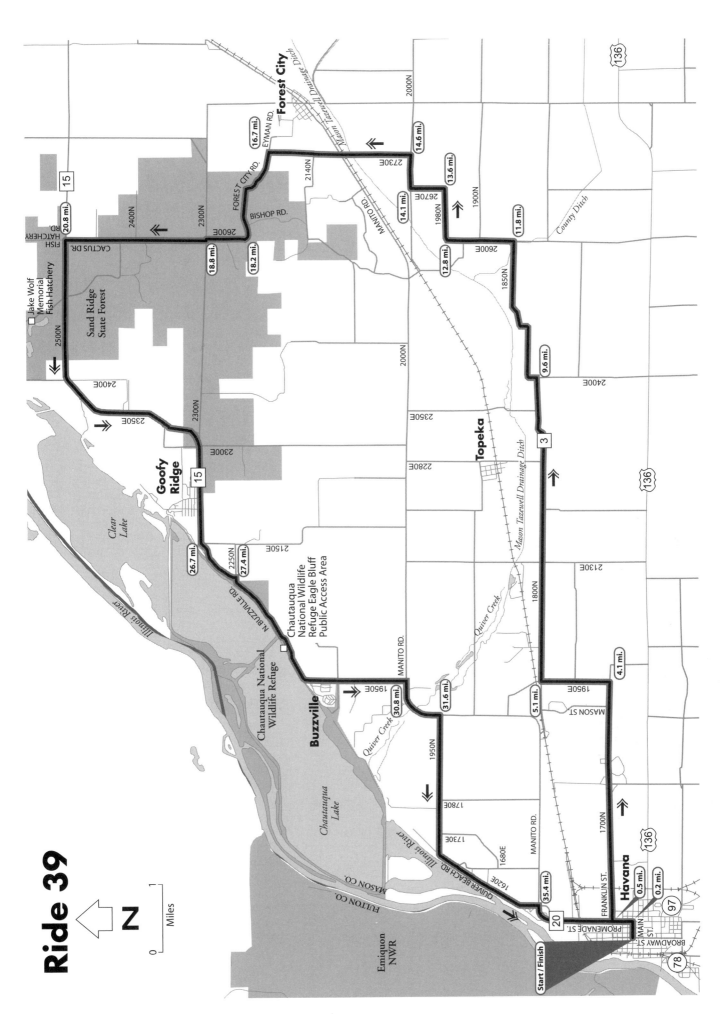

# Ride 39

N

Miles
0    1

Forest City

Goofy Ridge

Buzzville

Topeka

Havana

Start / Finish

Jake Wolf Memorial Fish Hatchery

Sand Ridge State Forest

Chautauqua National Wildlife Refuge

Chautauqua National Wildlife Refuge Eagle Bluff Public Access Area

Emiquon NWR

Chautauqua Lake

Clear Lake

Illinois River

Mason Tazewell Drainage Ditch

Quiver Creek

County Ditch

20.8 mi.
18.8 mi.
18.2 mi.
16.7 mi.
14.6 mi.
13.6 mi.
14.1 mi.
11.8 mi.
12.8 mi.
9.6 mi.
26.7 mi.
27.4 mi.
30.8 mi.
31.6 mi.
5.1 mi.
4.1 mi.
35.4 mi.
0.5 mi.
0.2 mi.

FISH HATCHERY RD.
CACTUS DR.
FOREST CITY RD.
EYMAN RD.
BISHOP RD.
MANITO RD.
N BUZZVILLE RD.
QUIVER BEACH RD.
MASON ST.
FRANKLIN ST.
PROMENADE ST.
MAIN
1ST
BROADWAY ST.

2400N
2300N
2600E
2140N
2730E
2670E
1980N
1900N
2600E
1850N
2000N
1800N
1950N
1700N

2500E
2400E
2350E
2300E
2150E
1950E
2350E
2280E
2130E
1950E
1780E
1730E
1680E
1620E

15
15
136
136
3
20
97
78

Fulton Co.
Mason Co.

81

# RIDE 40
## Short But Sweet

**Location:** Lake of the Woods Forest Preserve, Mahomet
**Distance:** 6.6 miles
**Pedaling time:** 40–50 minutes
**Surface:** Asphalt trail
**Terrain:** Gently hilly
**Sweat factor:** Low +
**Trailhead:** Crowley Road parking lot, Mahomet

The bike path through Lake of the Woods Forest Preserve is only 3.3 miles long, but it packs a lot into those miles. You'll see prairie and forest with botanical gardens in between. The trail flows over rolling hills, but none of them are difficult. This is a nice ride to go slow. There are lots of walkers and runners on the trail, and the scenery is worth savoring.

**Bicycles cross outside the walls of this covered bridge.**

The hardest part of this ride is finding the start of the trail. Go south on State Highway 47 from I-74 to the stoplight at Franklin Street and turn right. Keep right at the stop sign, and then turn left on State Street. At the three-way stop, turn right on Crowley Road. Go north over I-74 and watch for the entrance on the right. This parking lot only holds about a dozen cars, but the lot at the east end of the trail is even smaller. Signs warn against parking on Crowley Road, so if the lot is full your best bet is to use the museum entrance on Highway 47 and join

the trail in the middle.

This bike path is very well marked with yellow dots on the pavement every tenth of a mile. Begin with a long descent. The vegetation between Crowley Road and Highway 47 is mostly restored prairie. In spring and summer, you can see a variety of wildflowers in bloom. The maintenance crew has wisely mowed a wide path near the tighter curves in order to maximize visibility. There are many mowed grass trails in this section of the park, but they are intended for foot traffic. Just before Highway 47 there are toilets on the right. Be careful crossing the busy highway, then head south parallel to the road before turning left through a gap in the fence at 1.3 miles. The Mabery Gelvin Botanical Gardens are on the left. An award-winning feature is the Miriam H. Davies Enabling Garden, dedicated in 2001. By using raised beds, the garden is not just accessible for disabled visitors—it is designed so people with limited mobility can actually work in the garden. If you wish to wander through the gardens, walk or lock up your bike.

Most of the trail east of Highway 47 is forested. At 1.7 miles the path joins a park road to cross the Sangamon River. The Lake of the Woods Covered Bridge only dates back to 1965, but it adds a rustic touch to the scene. Cross the bridge on the outside (cars drive through the middle) and yield to pedestrians.

As you approach Hartwell C. Howard Golf Course on the park road, turn left onto the trail at 2 miles. There aren't any killer hills on the trail, but the hardest climbing is probably near the end in each direction. Cross a road at 3.1 miles and enter a section of the park known as Stidham Woods. The trail ends at 3.3 miles. On the way back, you get to ride mostly downhill for the first half mile, but you'll have to make up for it at the end. If you want to ride further, you can explore the park roads.

Most towns would be happy just to have a forest preserve with a pleasant trail like this, but the citizens of Mahomet are really spoiled. You've already seen the gardens and the golf course, but there is even more. The Early American Museum (www.earlyamericanmuseum.org or (217) 586-2512) has two floors of exhibits that interpret local pioneer living, including a hands-on room for kids. The HI-Tower, named for Forest Preserve District founder H. I. Gelvin, has an observation deck six stories up as well as a bell carillon that plays throughout the day. There are numerous picnic areas, shelters, and pavilions. And of course, the Lake of the Woods itself has fishing and boating.

The Champaign County Forest Preserve District has more information about Lake of the Woods at www.ccfpd.org. For a map of greenways and trails throughout Champaign County, call (217) 328-3313 or visit www.ccrpc.org.

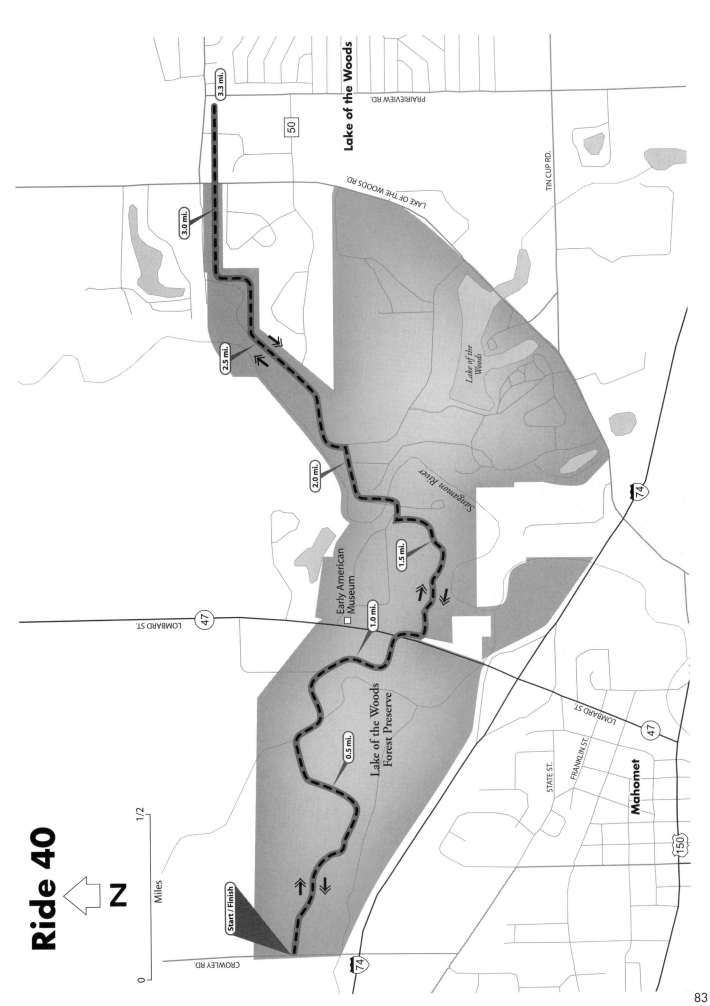

# Ride 40

N

Miles
0    1/2

Start / Finish

CROWLEY RD.

Lake of the Woods Forest Preserve

0.5 mi.

1.0 mi.

Early American Museum

LOMBARD ST.

47

1.5 mi.

2.0 mi.

2.5 mi.

3.0 mi.

3.3 mi.

50

Sangamon River

Lake of the Woods

Lake of the Woods

LAKE OF THE WOODS RD.

PRAIRIEVIEW RD.

TIN CUP RD.

74

STATE ST.

FRANKLIN ST.

LOMBARD ST.

47

Mahomet

150

74

# RIDE 41
## The Palace and the Hall of Fame

**Location:** Brown County
**Distance:** 21.2 miles
**Pedaling time:** 2–2.5 hours
**Surface:** Chip-seal roads
**Terrain:** Rolling hills
**Sweat factor:** Moderate
**Trailhead:** Corner of Second Street and Main Street (State Highway 99) in Versailles

The climb up from the Illinois River is one of the biggest hills on this ride.

The first thing you need to know is that in the Illinois vernacular, the name of the town where this ride begins is pronounced "ver-SALES." While you won't find the tourist attractions of the more famous Versailles and Cooperstown, this ride is still worth seeking out. Traffic is light and the roads are hilly enough to keep things interesting without exhausting you. It is also easy to follow—there are essentially just two turns. En route, you will see a wetland area, a brief view of the Illinois River, and lots of farmland (this is central Illinois, after all).

Start at the corner of Main Street (State Highway 99) and Second Street in downtown Versailles. For food and drink, there is a small grocery a few doors down. You will pass a mini-mart at the north end of town when you return to Versailles. Head east on Second Street out of town. The road climbs most of the way to 2.3 miles, and then plunges down into the Illinois River bottomland. There is a scenic overlook on the right at 4.1 miles provided by The Nature Conservancy. This 2,026-acre area is known as the Merwin Preserve at Spunky Bottoms (Spunky Ridge is on the north side of the road). The wetlands below were drained for farming, but the Conservancy has allowed more water to remain, providing a habitat for ducks, geese, songbirds, grassland birds, wading birds, hawks, and bald eagles. If you enjoy bird-watching, bring your binoculars. Access is restricted, but you can contact the Conservancy's Lewistown office at (309) 547-2730 for more information. There is also a portable toilet here.

The first town outside of Versailles is La Grange, not to be confused with the much larger suburb of Chicago with the same name. There are no services in La Grange, just a small cluster of homes along the road near the La Grange Dam and Lock. Notice the size of the lock posted on the sign—600 feet by 110 feet—and compare this to an Illinois & Michigan Canal lock as in Rides 12 and 31. A modern Illinois Waterway lock is nearly six times the size of an I & M Canal lock. The U.S. Army Corps of Engineers runs this facility, and visitors are not welcome. A posted sign warns the curious not to take pictures, write notes, or make sketches. Look down the gravel road just to glimpse the Illinois River, and then move on.

Leaving La Grange, the road curves to the left and climbs a steep hill up from the river bottoms for half a mile. More hills follow. Approaching Cooperstown, the town cemetery is on the right. Enter Cooperstown at 13.5 miles. Though the village is small in population, it stretches for half a mile along the road. The Crooked Creek White-tails Lodge is a Quonset hut with pop machines in front. Outside of town, the road curves sharply to the left, then right. At 15.5 miles, turn left at the stop sign to head south toward Versailles. There is another cemetery at 17.8 miles. The bridge over Camp Creek at 19.3 miles is followed by a half-mile climb. At the intersection with Highway 99, the mini-mart/gas station is on the right. Continue across the highway onto Chestnut Street. Pass the library and turn left at the first stop sign, Second Street, to return to Main Street.

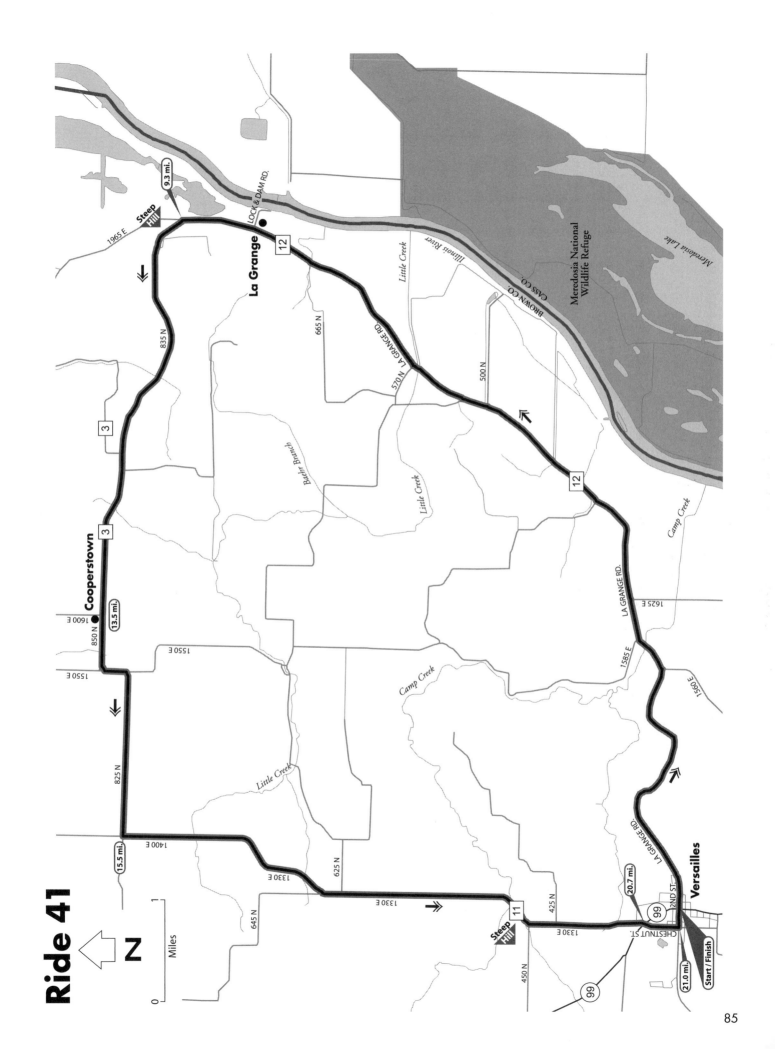

# Ride 41

# RIDE 42
## Follow in Young Abe's Footsteps

**Location:** Menard County
**Distance:** 17.5 miles
**Pedaling time:** 1.5–2.5 hours
**Surface:** Chip-seal roads
**Terrain:** Rolling hills
**Sweat factor:** Moderate +
**Trailhead:** Southeast corner of parking lot, Lincoln's
    New Salem State Historic Site

Bicycles weren't around in Abraham Lincoln's day, but if he had pedaled one while living in New Salem, he would have had mighty strong legs. This ride starts at Lincoln's New Salem and follows part of the Lincoln Trail toward Springfield. Then it completes the loop by following country roads to the unmarked rear entrance of the park. This ride is both scenic and physically demanding. Unfortunately, street signs are in short supply around here. With so many unmarked intersections, you'll have to keep an eye on the odometer so you don't miss a turn.

Abraham Lincoln came to the pioneer town of New Salem in 1831 when he was 22 years old. Like many young adults, he was trying to find his place in life. During his six years here, he was a laborer, shopkeeper, postmaster, soldier, surveyor, legislator, and lawyer. New Salem faded away shortly after he left, and it would have been forgotten completely if not for its famous former resident. The abandoned town site was rebuilt as a living history village in the 1930s, a century after its demise. Two dozen buildings have been reproduced and furnished in 1830s style. People in period dress demonstrate the chores and lifestyle of the time. Depending on your perspective, this is a great place to spend the afternoon or a good way to keep your family occupied while you enjoy a bike ride. For hours and other information, call (217) 632-4000 or visit www.lincolnsnewsalem.com.

The easiest part of this ride is the beginning. From the visitor center parking lot, swoop down a curvy, wooded descent. Alas, there is a stop sign at the bottom for busy State Highway 97. That's a shame because you could use the momentum for what comes next. Go across the highway and climb a tough hill. When you reach the top, curve to the right toward Sangamon Picnic Area. Then turn right on the first of many unmarked roads at 0.8 mile. Turn left at the end of this road, then keep right when the road splits at a cluster of homes. Plunge down a steep, shaded hill, then curve left onto Boy Scout Trail at the bottom. A wooden post by the side of the road marks the Lincoln Trail with Abe's silhouette. This part of the ride offers the most shade, but you have to work hard for the reward.

A mild climb at 2.8 miles gets steeper in the trees, followed by a series of easier rollers. At 4.4 miles, turn left at the intersection marked Big Dog Trail (you're still on Boy Scout Trail). There is another steep, forested climb at 5.2 miles. Turn right at 5.9 miles onto unmarked Knoles Road, and then turn right on another unmarked road a mile later after a sharp left curve. There is an auto repair shop at 7.1 miles, which proves that a business doesn't always need a high-traffic location. If the shop is open, the pop machine inside is your only chance to get refreshments along the route. A steep descent at 7.5 miles is followed by a sharp left curve. At 8.8 miles, turn left on State Highway 97. Just a quarter of a mile later, make the first right on Rock Creek Road. There is a steep climb at around 10 miles. Rock Creek Presbyterian Church is on the left at 10.4 miles. The road turns sharply to the right at 11.3 miles. After the tortuous roads you've been on, this one is surprisingly straight. The ride north is broken up only by a stop sign at State Highway 123 and a gentle S-curve a mile later. At 14.9 miles, turn right at an unmarked crossroad, Reimer Road. Curve sharply to the left at 16.5 miles, pass some new homes, then go right at 17 miles. The first road heading south, County Road 790E, is the rear entrance into Lincoln's New Salem. Turn right, go through the wooden gates, and ride past the campground. You reach the parking lot at 17.5 miles.

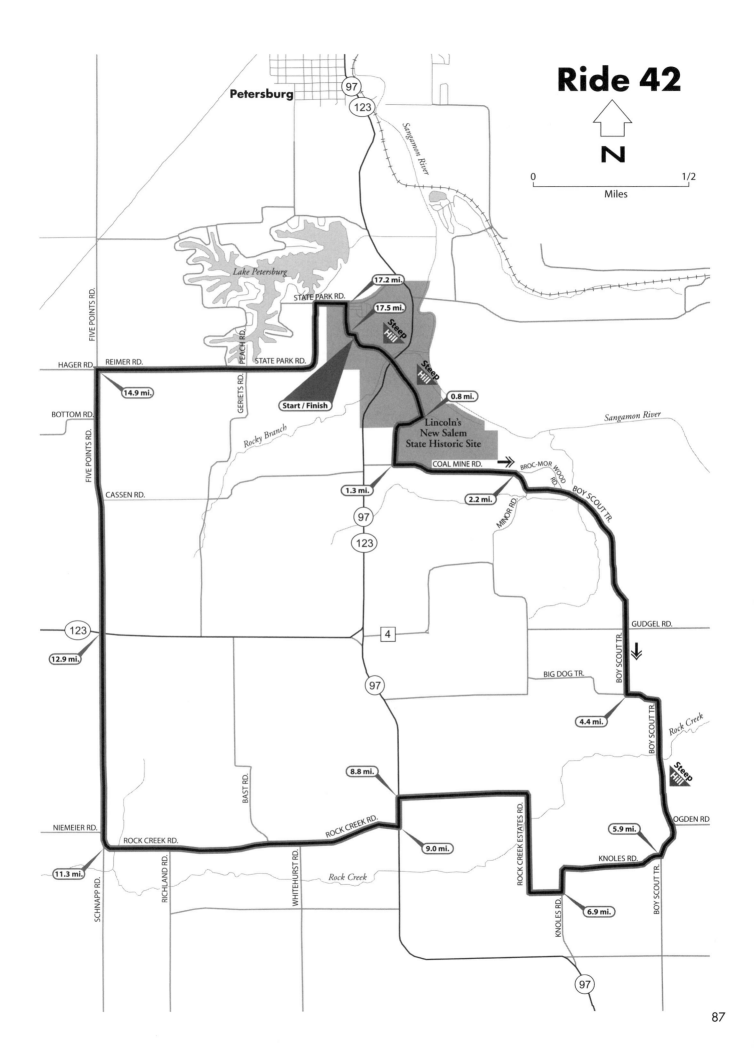

# Ride 42

**N**

0        1/2

Miles

**Petersburg**

97
123

*Sangamon River*

*Lake Petersburg*

STATE PARK RD.

17.2 mi.

17.5 mi.

**Steep Hill**

**Steep Hill**

0.8 mi.

HAGER RD.  REIMER RD.

14.9 mi.

FIVE POINTS RD.

GERIETS RD.

PEACH RD.

STATE PARK RD.

**Start / Finish**

*Sangamon River*

BOTTOM RD.

FIVE POINTS RD.

*Rocky Branch*

**Lincoln's New Salem State Historic Site**

COAL MINE RD.

BROC-MOR WOOD RD.

BOY SCOUT TR.

CASSEN RD.

1.3 mi.

2.2 mi.

MINOR RD.

97
123

123

12.9 mi.

4

GUDGEL RD.

BOY SCOUT TR.

BIG DOG TR.

97

4.4 mi.

BOY SCOUT TR.

*Rock Creek*

**Steep Hill**

BAST RD.

8.8 mi.

5.9 mi.

OGDEN RD

NIEMEIER RD.

ROCK CREEK RD.

ROCK CREEK RD.

ROCK CREEK ESTATES RD.

9.0 mi.

11.3 mi.

SCHNAPP RD.

RICHLAND RD.

WHITEHURST RD.

*Rock Creek*

KNOLES RD.

KNOLES RD.

6.9 mi.

BOY SCOUT TR.

97

# RIDE 43
## Where's the Bridge?

**Location:** Springfield
**Distance:** 9.8 miles
**Pedaling time:** 50–60 minutes
**Surface:** Paved bike path, one mile on street
**Terrain:** Flat
**Sweat factor:** Low
**Trailhead:** IDOT Headquarters, 2300 South Dirksen Parkway, Springfield

**South Fork Bridge is a highlight of the Lost Bridge Trail.**

The Illinois Department of Transportation's main headquarters is one of the most attractive buildings visible from I-55/72 in the state capital. From the interstate, one can also see an asphalt path sweeping between the building and a lake. This could be mistaken for a mere office park walking path, but in fact it is the beginning of the Lost Bridge Trail. This trail is built on the old bed of the Baltimore and Ohio Railroad from Springfield to Rochester. This is the same right-of-way that is used by the Lincoln Heritage Trail from Taylorville to Pana, and someday the trails may be connected.

To reach the trailhead, exit I-55/72 at State Highway 29 north, and then turn left on Dirksen Parkway. A brown sign for the trail points the way into the IDOT parking lot. Go all the way to the south end of the lot,

turn left, and then keep right to get to the trail parking area. There is a drinking fountain just north of the trailhead, along with a telephone and some picnic tables. The Lost Bridge Trail begins with its only hill of note, a short descent toward the lake and to the left. There is a bike rack down by the lakeshore near several picnic tables. The path curves around the north side of the lake. At 0.6 miles, it heads straight southeast on the old railroad right-of-way and goes under I-55/72. The Lost Bridge Trail is lined with trees that provide a shady canopy and muffle the road noise from nearby four-lane Highway 29. It is a popular walking trail, too. There are markers every half mile, and several small trailside signs describe the vegetation along the way, but you might miss them at cycling speed.

The name of the trail is intriguing. Apparently the Baltimore and Ohio Railroad secretly removed the bridge over Sugar Creek before it sold the rail line to the Illinois Department of Natural Resources. Luckily for you, a replacement was installed so you won't have to ford the creek. Cross Sugar Creek Bridge at 1.2 miles. There are farm fields on the right much of the way between Springfield and Rochester. Go through a short tunnel under Hill Top Road at 2 miles.

The architectural highlight is South Fork Bridge, the one the railroad didn't remove. This steel truss bridge over the South Fork of the Sangamon River at 3.1 miles has a wooden deck and railings. As you near Rochester, you can see a park on the right. Go past the access trail at 3.9 miles; you will come back on that trail. According to the signs on Highway 29, you enter Rochester at 4.1 miles. Although the trail extends a bit further into town, make a tight right turn at the first stoplight onto West Main Street (4.6 miles). This wide, flat street is easy riding. When the street narrows, move onto a parallel bike trail on the right. This path goes past two schools and a cemetery, and then it heads downhill into Rochester Community Park. Keep to the right when the trail splits around 5.4 miles, passing J. Marshall Bell Field. Ride past toilets, drinking water, and a small lake. After this pleasant jaunt through the park, curve right and go uphill at 5.8 miles to the railroad grade of the Lost Bridge Trail. Make a sharp left turn to head back toward Springfield on the trail. It's a flat, easy cruise home except for that little hill up to the parking lot. The picnic tables beside the lake near the trailhead are an ideal place to relax after the ride.

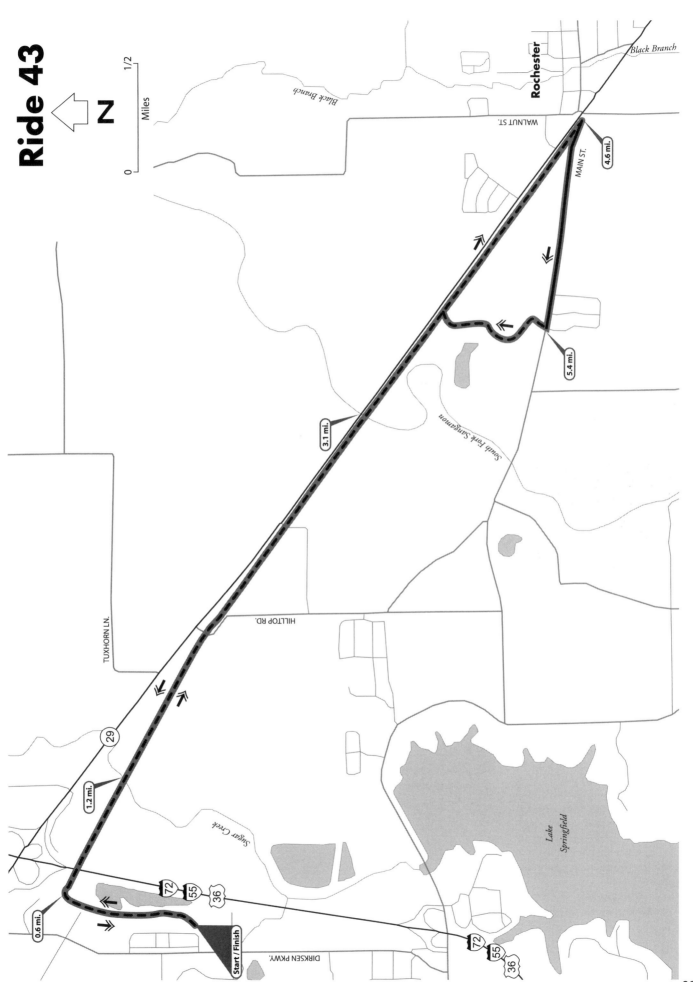

# Ride 43

N

0   1/2
Miles

*Black Branch*

*Black Branch*

**Rochester**

WALNUT ST.

MAIN ST.

4.6 mi.

5.4 mi.

3.1 mi.

*South Fork Sangamon*

TUXHORN LN.

HILLTOP RD.

29

1.2 mi.

*Sugar Creek*

*Lake Springfield*

72
55
36

0.6 mi.

**Start / Finish**

DIRKSEN PKWY.

72
55
36

# RIDE 44
## Ambling Among the Amish

### Amazing Arcola

If you want to learn more about the Amish, the Illinois Amish Interpretive Center on Locust Street is one place to start. They have a museum and they also arrange tours of Amish homes and businesses, including meals (www.amish center.com). The Amish settlement in western Douglas County is not the only reason to visit Arcola, however.

The area's most popular attraction is Rockome Gardens. Besides the rock and floral gardens that give it its name, they have specialty shops, entertainment, buggy rides, a train, a petting zoo, an antique museum, a restaurant, and more (www.rockome.com or (217) 268-4106).

Johnny Gruelle was born here in 1880. His family moved to Indianapolis when he was only two years old, but Arcola still claims him with pride. Arcola's Raggedy Ann & Andy Festival is held annually the weekend before Memorial Day weekend, and the Johnny Gruelle Raggedy Ann & Andy Museum on Main Street is open most of the year (www.raggedyann-museum.org or (217) 268-4908).

Arcola is also the official "Broom Corn Capital of the World." Broom corn is actually a long-tasseled variety of sorghum. The story goes that a Massachusetts farmer made the first broom of broom corn in 1797 (an alternate story claims that Benjamin Franklin brought it here from Europe). As the country expanded westward, settlers discovered that broom corn grew particularly well in the Midwest. Broom corn has been grown in the Arcola area since at least 1859. The town celebrates a Broom Corn Festival in September, and the Depot displays a large collection of antique brooms and brushes.

For more information about these and more, go inside the Depot Welcome Center, call (800) 336-5456, or visit www.arcola-il.org.

**Location:** Douglas County
**Distance:** 25.3 miles
**Pedaling time:** 2–2.5 hours

**Surface:** Paved roads, mostly chip seal
**Terrain:** Mostly flat with a few hills
**Sweat factor:** Low +
**Trailhead:** Arcola Depot/Tourist Information Center, 135 North Oak Street

Although one usually associates the Amish with horses and buggies, they also use bicycles to get around. In fact, the "employee parking lot" of a large woodworking shop near Arthur consists of several dozen bikes side by side. This makes Illinois' Amish Country a natural place to visit for a bike ride. Most of the rural roads are paved, and the locals are accustomed to sharing the road with cyclists. There are few hills, and none are steep. The wind blowing across the open fields is more of a challenge than the terrain. Be attentive at rural intersections, as many do not have stop signs in any direction. You will see a number of Amish homes and businesses along the way, as well as a few bikes and buggies.

Take I-57 to State Highway 133 and drive west into Arcola. Just before the railroad tracks, turn right on Oak Street. Start in front of Arcola's tourist information center, a former railroad depot. The helpful staff there can tell you about road construction in the area and where the bike shops are. They can also give you a free map of Amish business locations; this ride passes at least two dozen. A small monument south of the depot remembers Raggedy Ann and Andy creator Johnny Gruelle. Riding north, "America's One and Only Hippie Memorial"

stands on the left. This abstract art by Bob Moomaw is explained on a sign bearing his wife's dedication speech from June 29, 1999. Turn left on Jefferson Street. As you approach the railroad tracks, watch for railcars being shuffled around—they don't actuate the signals as far in advance as fast trains do. At the edge of town, turn right on Highway 133, a busy road with wide, paved shoulders known locally as buggy lanes. Leave this road midway through the first curve, turning right on County Road 250N. This, like most roads in the area, has a chip-seal surface. At 1.3 miles, continue north through a zigzag at County Road 300N. At 2.4 miles, turn left on County Road 400N, which curves to the left at 5.8 miles.

As you reach Chesterville, cross the Kaskaskia River on a steel truss bridge with a rough, wooden deck. The longest river within Illinois' borders, the Kaskaskia begins about 30 miles north of here and meanders 280 miles southwest to the Mississippi. Along the way, it feeds water into Lake Shelbyville and Carlyle Lake, the largest man-made lake in the state. After the bridge, go straight at the stop sign and follow a couple of curves to the right until you are heading north on County Road 400E. At 8 miles, the pavement narrows considerably. Traffic is light, but if you see a car it would be a good idea to pull over to the side. At the end of this road, turn left on County Road 600N. At 9.4 miles there is a diagonal railroad crossing. When this road ends, turn left, cross a small bridge, and keep left at the Y. Turn right on County Road 500N at the T. Pass a bike shop at 12.8 miles, then cross over the railroad tracks again.

At 14.1 miles, turn left on busy but wide County Road 000E, which marks the border shared with Moultrie County. This road leads into the heart of Arthur. Cross the railroad tracks once more and ride into downtown. The Arthur Visitor Center is on the left. A misleading sign says that bicycles are not allowed, but it refers only to the sidewalk, not the street. The next few blocks are rather congested. Be especially wary of cross traffic. At the south end of Arthur is a stop sign at Highway 133. This is only a two-way stop, so proceed across with caution. One mile later, turn left on County Road 300N. This is a quiet road where you are more likely to encounter a buggy than a car. Turn left on County Road 425E at the end of 300N and revisit Chesterville. Turn right at the stop sign on Highway 133, which again has buggy lanes. Highway 133 cuts a straight course back to Arcola. After the road curves to the right at 24.8 miles, turn left on Jefferson Street and ride back to Oak Street.

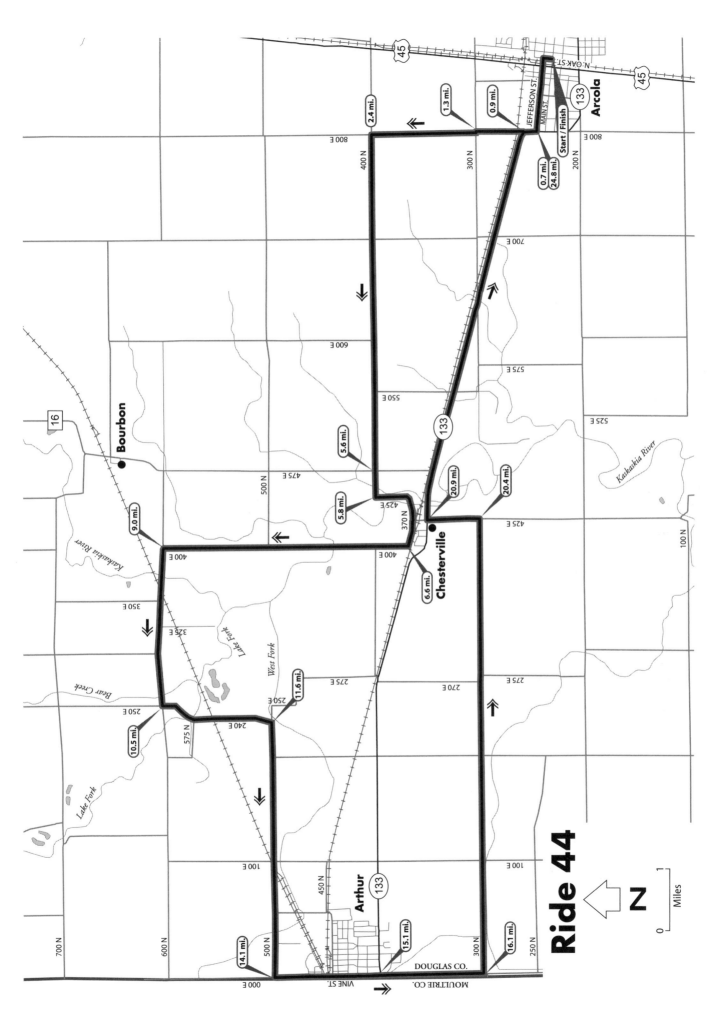

# Ride 44

N

0 —— 1
Miles

# RIDE 45
## Moonshine Run

**Location:** Clark County
**Distance:** 23.8 miles
**Pedaling time:** 2–2.5 hours
**Surface:** Chip-seal roads
**Terrain:** Mostly flat with some hills
**Sweat factor:** Low +
**Trailhead:** Fairview Park in Casey

### George Rogers Clark

This ride takes place in Clark County, which is named for Revolutionary War hero George Rogers Clark. Clark was the most important American leader in the Northwest Territory, which included Illinois. His exploits within Illinois were actually some of his easiest conquests. When he marched on Kaskaskia in the summer of 1778, he took the town without firing a shot. Although ostensibly under British rule, most of the settlers were French and had no allegiance to the British. Clark and his men similarly took Cahokia and Vincennes, Indiana. The British, under Henry Hamilton, took back Vincennes in December. Then, as was customary in those times, Hamilton let many of his soldiers return home for the winter. He planned to take back Kaskaskia and Cahokia in the spring.

A trader named Francis Vigo (note that Vigo County is across the Indiana border from Clark County) learned of Hamilton's intentions and reported them to Clark. Clark decided to attack Vincennes in February 1779. His men marched 240 miles in 17 miserable days through cold floodwaters from Kaskaskia to Vincennes. There, they surprised the British, who surrendered two days later. The British never recaptured Vincennes, Kaskaskia, or Cahokia, and Clark's victories gave the United States a claim to the Northwest Territory, which was formalized in the Treaty of Paris in 1783. Without Clark's leadership, Illinois could have been part of Canada.

Contrary to the title of this ride, you won't be engaging in illegal activities. You won't need a whiskey still, and the revenuer won't be on your tail. All you need is an appetite, especially for a good burger. The famous Moonshine Store has been featured on national television, and people have visited from around the world. Just don't get a late start; the place is open Monday–Saturday from 6 AM to 1 PM (same menu all day), and the grill closes at 12:30 sharp.

The Moonshine Run starts at Fairview Park in Casey. To get there from I-70, exit at State Highway 49 and go south past downtown to Van Buren Avenue and turn left. This street runs right into Fairview Park. A fine city park that once hosted horse racing events, Fairview has ball fields, a swimming pool, picnic shelters, and camping. The annual Casey Bluegrass Festival is held here in June. There is ample parking scattered throughout the park. Ride to the southeast corner of the park at Eighth Street and Tyler Avenue and reset your odometer. Head south on Eighth Street, which turns into 150 Street outside of town. Go east on 800 Road, then south on 250 Street.

This route has many turns, but once you get on 250 Street, most of them are simply a matter of staying on the paved road. Most roads are narrow, but traffic is light. Pavement is all chip seal. A cluster of homes and a church make up the town of Moriah at 7.1 miles. When 350 Street ends at 8.5 miles, turn left onto 400 Road, which seems very wide compared to the other roads on this ride. The bridge at 9.2 miles crosses the North Fork of the Embarras River. To avoid embarrassment in front of the locals, be aware that the

name is pronounced "Ambraw." There is only one steep hill on this ride, at 9.8 miles. Since you'll be going slowly at the top, look left to see one of the oil pump-and-tank combinations common in parts of southern Illinois. Though it is no match for Texas or Alaska, Illinois ranks 14th among oil-producing states.

Turn left onto 300 Road at 10.2 miles. The vacant, yellow-tile building on the corner used to be the Hogue Town store. As you approach the stop sign at 11.9 miles, you'll see the Moonshine Store, (618) 569-9200, on the left. The store was built in 1912, and the front was remodeled in 1990. Nowadays it is more of a sandwich shop/snack bar than a general store. In addition to their legendary Moonburgers, the owners prepare several other hot and cold sandwiches. They also sell snacks, including Moon Pies, and soft drinks. If you arrive after hours, there is a pop machine outside. You can enjoy your meal on a bench inside (no tables), or you can sit at a picnic table outside. Pay for your sandwich after you finish. If you need to use the restroom, there is an outhouse labeled "Sitty Hall" across the street.

**Reward yourself with a Moonburger from the Moonshine Store.**

So, is the Moonshine Store named for an illicit past of making hooch? Maybe, but another story says that the name comes from a nearby church that was built by farmers after their workday was done, literally "by moonshine." Even the proprietors are not certain of the origin.

After your visit, the best way to return to Casey is the way you came since there are a lot of gravel and dead-end roads in the area.

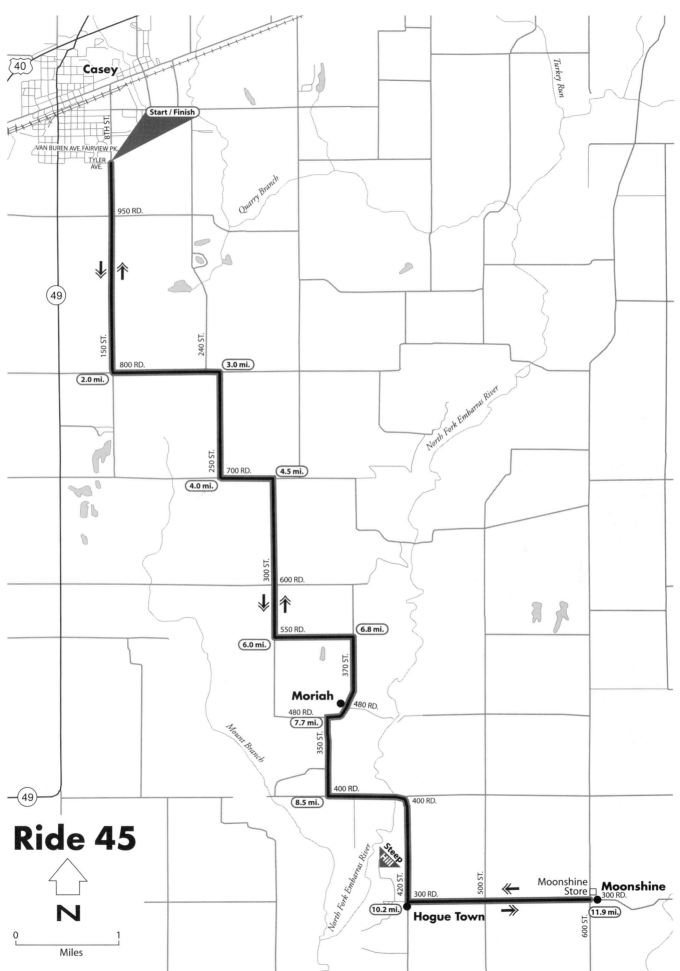

# Ride 45

N

0          1

Miles

# RIDE 46
## Bluffing on the Mississippi

**Location:** North of Saint Louis
**Distance:** 41.6 miles
**Pedaling time:** 3.5–4.5 hours
**Surface:** Paved trails
**Terrain:** Mostly flat with four hilly miles
**Sweat factor:** Low +
**Trailhead:** Piasa Park, State Highway 100 west of Alton

The Illinois Department of Transportation built the first section of the Vadalabene River Road Bikeway from Alton to Grafton as a demonstration project in 1976. More than a quarter century after our nation's bicentennial, it remains one of the most scenic bike paths in Illinois. The path is named for Sam Vadalabene, an Illinois state senator who supported bike trails. It runs beside the Meeting of the Great Rivers National Scenic Byway along the Mississippi River from Alton to Pere Marquette State Park. The picturesque bluffs between Alton and Grafton make this one of the prettiest areas along the entire Mississippi River. This is a great place for a weekend getaway, and there are many bed and breakfasts in towns along the trail. If you are willing to brave the winter chill, you can see the hundreds of American bald eagles that live here from December to February. The path is well signed throughout, so you shouldn't get lost.

An ideal starting point is Piasa Park on State Highway 100 just west of Alton. It has about 40 parking spaces plus restrooms. Before you begin, take a look at the "Piasa Bird," a cliff painting of a river monster recalling a similar Indian painting that Pere Marquette and Louis Joliet saw in this area in 1673. The asphalt trail begins at the west end of the parking lot, separated from Highway 100 by a guardrail. The path is located on the former right-of-way of the Bluff Line Railroad from Alton to Grafton.

At 3.6 miles is Clifton Terrace Park, an alternate starting point if Piasa Park is full. Vintner Louis Stiritz built the stone terraces in the 1850s; a steel-barred door in one terrace reveals a wine cellar. Watch for turning traffic as you cross Clifton Terrace Drive at the stoplight. For the next mile the path is higher than Highway 100 so you can see the river. Enter Jersey County at 4.8 miles.

At 5.6 miles, the path merges onto the outer part of the shoulder of Highway 100. Cyclists ride with traffic, so stay on the north side of Highway 100 to head west. This is the fastest section of the trail, but it has the pitfalls of riding on any highway shoulder: stones, garbage from motorists, and traffic noise. Highway 100 is popular with motorcyclists on weekends. You can cross the highway anywhere there is an opening in the median, to visit attractions like the Piasa Harbor gas station, convenience store, and restaurant. At 10.2 miles, the Village of Elsah offers a restaurant, a park, and restrooms in town. In 1974, Elsah was the first village placed in its entirety on the National Register of Historic Places.

On a hot day, Raging Rivers WaterPark may tempt you at 13 miles. The Grafton Visitor Center at 13.6 miles is a great place to stop for information, water, and indoor restrooms (open 10 to 4, closed Mondays).

Bicyclists are not allowed to ride on Highway 100 through Grafton. At 14 miles, turn left toward the river, then right on East Water to follow the trail. The path passes south of the town's tourist district, but several bike racks are provided if you want to stop. One notable Grafton restaurant is the Fin Inn, which features 8,000 gallons of aquariums. Ahead to the left is the Grafton Ferry, which can take you to Missouri. Call (636) 250-3103 or visit www.graftonferry.com for rates and times. At 14.8 miles, watch for gravel and dirt for about 1500 feet. Ahead, enjoy the only place where the trail follows the contours of the Mississippi River bank.

West of Grafton, cross carefully over Highway 100 and ride west past the Illinois Youth Center Department of Corrections. A memorial cross at 16.3 miles marks the point where in August 1673 the party of Marquette and Joliet first entered what became Illinois. You can't see it through the trees, but the Illinois and Mississippi Rivers merge here.

The terrain of this ride changes at 17.2 miles with a steep climb. The next two miles are hilly and curvy. Watch for leaves, branches, sand, rocks, and oncoming cyclists rounding blind curves. At 17.9 miles, you can see the free Brussels Ferry across the Illinois River through the trees. Continue past the Pere Marquette Riding Stables. At 19.2 miles, the trail is flatter and closer to Highway 100. Although there are toilets in the camping and picnicking area at 20.2 miles, you should hold out for the indoor facilities ahead. The main entrance to Pere Marquette State Park at 20.8 miles is the turnaround point for the ride, but the park is worth exploring. The visitor center lies straight ahead, while the lodge and restaurant are a short distance to the right. Both offer drinking water and indoor restrooms. The lodge was built by the Civilian Conservation Corps during the 1930s. Bicyclists may ride on any of the park's paved roads, but not on its challenging hiking trails.

The return trip is easy to follow. The only difference is that you ride on the south shoulder of Highway 100. Don't cross Highway 100 east of Grafton—turn right to follow the path onto the shoulder. The ride east has great views of the bluffs across Highway 100, as well as waterfowl along the river's edge. At 36.1 miles, cross over to the path on the north side of the road and continue east to Piasa Park.

There is plenty to see and do in Alton after your ride. The National Great Rivers Museum features interactive exhibits and guided tours of the Melvin Price Locks and Dam 26. Alton's history is represented by a number of monuments and memorials, and there are many antique stores downtown. Phone (800) ALTON-IL or see www.visitalton.com for more information.

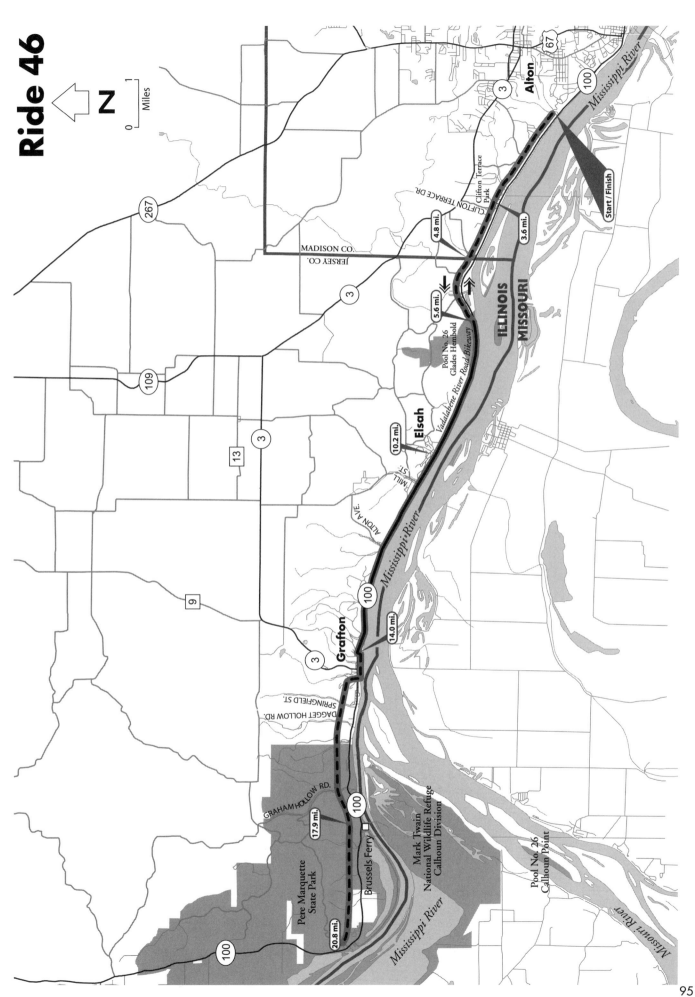

# Ride 46

N

0 — 1
Miles

Mississippi River

67

100 Alton

3

Clifton Terrace Park

CLIFTON TERRACE DR.

4.8 mi.

3.6 mi.

Start / Finish

MADISON CO.

JERSEY CO.

267

3

5.6 mi.

ILLINOIS

MISSOURI

Pool No. 26
Glades Hembold

Vadalabene River Road Bikeway

109

13

3

Elsah

10.2 mi.

MILL ST.

ALTON AVE.

Mississippi River

9

Grafton

3

100

14.0 mi.

SPRINGFIELD ST.

DAGGET HOLLOW RD.

GRAHAM HOLLOW RD.

100

17.9 mi.

Brussels Ferry

Pere Marquette
State Park

Mark Twain
National Wildlife Refuge
Calhoun Division

Pool No. 26
Calhoun Point

Mississippi River

100

20.8 mi.

Missouri River

# RIDE 47
## Lewis and Clark

**Location:** North of Saint Louis
**Distance:** 14 miles
**Pedaling time:** 75 minutes–1.5 hours
**Surface:** Paved, chip-seal, and gravel trails and roads
**Terrain:** Mostly flat with one hill
**Sweat factor:** Low
**Trailhead:** Lewis & Clark State Historic Site

### A Bridge with a History

The Chain of Rocks Bridge opened in 1929. To facilitate safe passage for shipping, the bridge had to be "bent" in the middle (it was built before the Chain of Rocks Canal, which now handles river traffic). Beginning in 1936, it carried the legendary U.S. Route 66 across the Mississippi. As auto traffic increased and trucks grew in size, the bridge was no longer adequate. Route 66 was rerouted, and the bridge was closed to motor vehicles in 1968. The bridge stood dormant for decades. It was almost torn down for scrap in the mid-1970s, but instead it became a movie star. Scenes from Escape From New York (released in 1981) were filmed on the structure, which was dubbed the 69th Street Bridge in the movie.

Aside from that moment in the spotlight, the bridge was largely forgotten except by Route 66 aficionados and people who used the site's isolation for drinking parties and worse. After one unfortunate incident, fences were erected to keep everyone off the bridge. The structure was too narrow for modern traffic, but tearing it down was too expensive. In 1989, Trailnet (www.trailnet.org), a Saint Louis-area organization, saw the potential for the Chain of Rocks Bridge as an ideal crossing point for bicyclists and pedestrians in a region where bicycle-friendly bridges were scarce. Seven years later, Trailnet agreed to a 20-year lease with the City of Madison, owner of the bridge. The surface wasn't in bad condition considering the years, but many safety features were added to prepare the bridge for riders and walkers. The bridge reopened in 1999. The gates are open every day from one-half hour before sunrise to one-half hour after sunset.

At the dawn of the 1800s, Illinois was on the western edge of the United States. In 1803, the Louisiana Purchase nearly doubled the size of the young nation. President Thomas Jefferson sent Meriwether Lewis and William Clark on their famous expedition to explore this new acquisition. The explorers traveled down the Ohio River and up the Mississippi River to the mouth of the Missouri River. They made camp on the Illinois side to wait for spring and make final preparations. Their winter home was named Camp River DuBois. On May 14, 1804, the expedition left the camp and set out on their epic adventure. Today Lewis & Clark State Historic Site has 14,000 square feet of exhibits plus a full-scale replica of the camp.

The Confluence Trail passes through this park on its way from Granite City to Alton. This ride follows that trail south to Chain of Rocks Road, which leads to one of the world's longest bridges for non-motorized traffic, the Chain of Rocks Bridge across the Mississippi River. Although the ride is relatively short, be advised that there are no services along the way, and there is little shade to provide comfort from summer heat.

The historic site is located on State Highway 3 north of I-270 and south of Wood River. The building is only open Wednesday–Sunday from 9 to 5, but the parking lot is always open. Begin at the bike parking area east of the building. Ride across the park entrance, watching for turning traffic. This trail spur meets the Confluence Greenway at 0.2 mile. Lewis and Clark Confluence Tower, which offers a view of

the mouth of the Missouri River from 150 feet up, is straight ahead (it's set to open in September 2006). Turn left on the path and cross the park road (do not go over the bridge). The asphalt trail runs along the inside base of the levee for a while, and then it climbs very gradually onto the levee road. At 1.5 miles the levee road becomes gravel, alternating between chip seal and gravel a few times over the next two miles. The waterway to your right is the Chain of Rocks Canal. This was opened in 1953 to bypass a section of the Mississippi River that was difficult to navigate. Just beyond the MCT Trails sign, turn left off the levee at 3.5 miles. Ride under I-270 but turn left before the next bridge, following the bike route sign.

At the stop sign at 4 miles, turn right, making a U-turn onto the road. The low-traffic road climbs to the canal bridge. Be extremely careful approaching the steel grid in the middle of the bridge. The joint has wide gaps that could grab a bike tire. Of course, steel grids always make for tricky riding as well. Use the same caution 0.1

**This 22-degree bend once caused fits for truck drivers negotiating the narrow Chain of Rocks Bridge.**

mile later as you ride across another joint back onto pavement. This is Chouteau Island. There is a landfill on the left at 5.4 miles. Go straight ahead toward the Chain of Rocks Bridge, entering a parking lot at 6 miles. There are several portable toilets on and around the bridge. Enjoy the great views of the river and the mile-long ride to the Missouri side. The unusual bend in the bridge may surprise you. The bridge ends at 7 miles. There used to be toll booths on this side of the river. If you are feeling ambitious, you can ride the Riverfront Trail about 10.5 miles to downtown Saint Louis. The path weaves through industrial areas and flood walls, so it isn't particularly scenic. Be sure you have plenty of water because you won't see concessions or trail amenities until you get downtown. From the end of the trail it is less than a mile to the Jefferson National Expansion Memorial, better known as the Gateway Arch.

# Ride 47

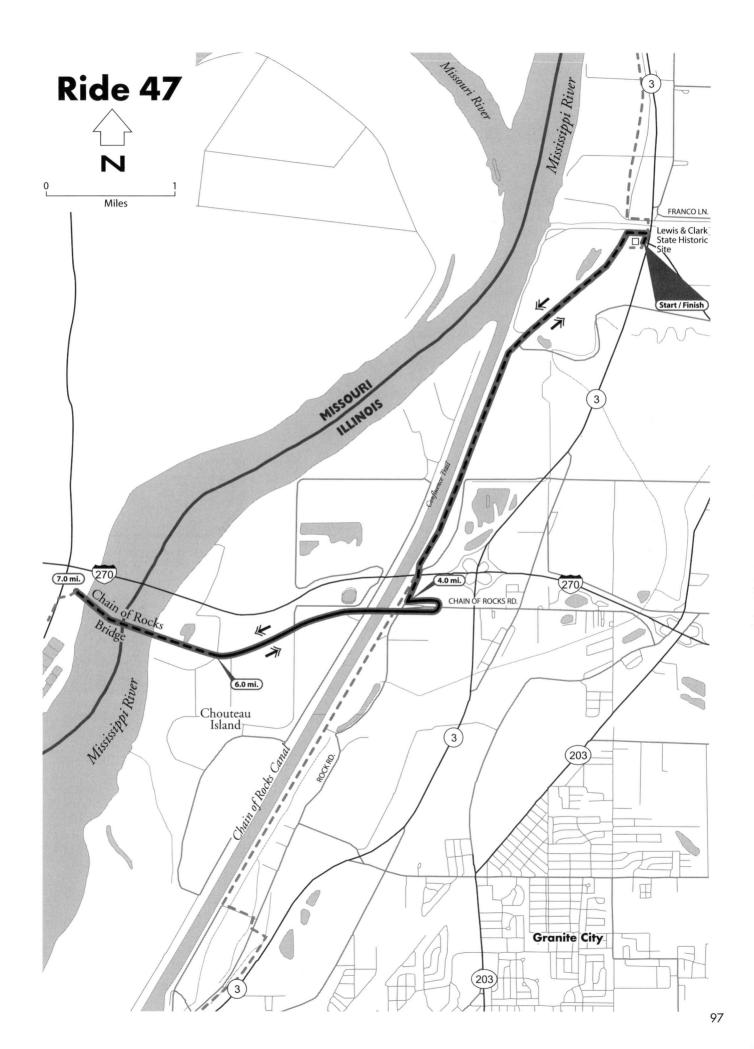

N

0       1
Miles

Missouri River

Mississippi River

3

FRANCO LN.

Lewis & Clark
State Historic
Site

Start / Finish

3

MISSOURI

ILLINOIS

Confluence Trail

7.0 mi.

270

Chain of Rocks
Bridge

4.0 mi.

270

CHAIN OF ROCKS RD.

6.0 mi.

Chouteau
Island

Mississippi River

Chain of Rocks Canal

ROCK RD.

3

203

Granite City

203

3

97

# RIDE 48
## Hillsboro-Roubaix

**Location:** Montgomery County
**Distance:** 22.4 miles
**Pedaling time:** 2–2.5 hours

**Surface:** Paved country roads, a few bricks
**Terrain:** Rolling hills, a few steep hills
**Sweat factor:** Moderate +
**Trailhead:** Main Street and Fairground Street, Hillsboro

### Paris-Roubaix

**Although many Americans think the Tour de France is the only professional race that matters, avid cycling fans know that the one-day "classics" of northern Europe are among the greatest tests of a rider's skill. Paris-Roubaix is among the toughest, the sort of race that only a fine rider can win. The race begins on the outskirts of Paris and ends with a lap of the velodrome (a banked, oval bicycle race track) in Roubaix. Along the way, riders are challenged by more than 20 sections of cobblestones known as pavé (pronounced PAHV-ay). These bumpy, cobbled sections are inevitably the decisive points of the race. In good weather they are dusty; in poor weather they are a slick, mucky mess that coats racers and their bikes with a crust of mud. In any weather they can cause a flat tire or an accident. The brick roads in Hillsboro are cleaner and more forgiving, but they might rattle you around a bit. Stand up to take the pressure off your seat as you ride over especially rough sections.**

**The wind on the wide-open plains of northern France is another challenge for the pro racers, one that you may experience on this ride as well. To spice things up, Hillsboro-Roubaix adds some short, steep hills into the mix. It's too bad that Hillsboro lacks a velodrome for the finale; the only one in Illinois is the Northbrook Velodrome near Chicago (www.northbrookveldrome.com).**

Hillsboro-Roubaix is one of the toughest bicycle races in Illinois. The course is named for and inspired by Paris-Roubaix, a legendary French race held the same weekend in April. The race starts and finishes in town, but most of the course meanders about the quiet country roads to the west. This course is challenging for racers, who often average 23 mph, but it is much easier at a leisurely touring pace.

Start out heading west from the trailhead on the bricks of Fairground Avenue. Turn left onto Seymour Avenue at the stop sign. Turn right at the four-way stop onto Kinkead to head west out of town, where the road becomes Walshville Trail. The road goes down a hill, over a creek, and back up again. At 2.7 miles, turn right onto Miller Trail, which is paved with chip seal. Be careful at 3.5 miles; there is a gravelly creek crossing at the bottom of the hill. Half a mile after Miller zigzags, turn left at the stop sign onto Interurban Circle. From 1905 to 1939, the Illinois Traction Company operated an interurban railway between Hillsboro, Litchfield, and Staunton. At 5.6 miles there is a sharp right curve in a hilly, wooded area, the first of several sharp turns. A hill near 6 miles gets steep at the end, but you'll find some extra motivation if the dogs are loose at the top. Turn left on

Chitaqua Trail, which has another gravelly creek bridge at 6.8 miles. Make another left to head south on Washboard Trail, which is much smoother than its name would lead you to believe. Be alert around 8.6 miles. You'll go down a hill, make a sharp left, and immediately start climbing a steep hill, followed by a sharp right and a creek bridge. After navigating that tricky section, turn right onto Old Litchfield Trail at the stop sign.

Only 0.4 mile later, turn left on East Sixth Road. The first mile is fairly flat and straight, but the next four miles are full of hills, curves, and turns. These roads are narrow but traffic is very light. Most of the time you can only turn one way, and as long as you stay on the paved road you'll get through just fine. After several turns, you will be heading west on Hickory Grove Avenue. Turn left on East Fifth Road at 12.7 miles, then left again on Akeman Trail half a mile later, heading east. This turns into Durbin Road at a sharp right turn. At 14.1 miles, turn left on Beckhams Trail (the sign here says "Beck Ham's"). Negotiate a couple of tight curves and a bit of gravel. After several miles of narrow roads, you'll feel like you've emerged from the wilderness when you reach the stop sign at Walshville Trail. Turn left to head northeast on this hilly, curvy road toward Hillsboro. The hill at 15.2 miles is particularly steep although the wide road makes it look milder. At 17.1 miles turn right and head east on Farm Trail, a narrow, chip-seal road with a couple of sharp curves in the middle. Turn left on East Eighth Road at 18.3 miles, then turn right onto Walshville Trail. There are several hills along the way. At 21.4 miles, you return to the four-way stop sign with Seymour Avenue on the edge of Hillsboro. The toughest hill lies directly ahead of you. Its name is Major Hill, and it is indeed a major hill. Fight the temptation to turn left to avoid it; go straight on Kinkead. When you reach the top of Major Hill at 21.8 miles, you can see all of Hillsboro spread out around you. Pay attention, though, or you'll miss the left turn onto Main Street. Main goes down a bit, then up, then down a long hill. Be forewarned that at the bottom of the hill (22.2 miles), the street gets narrower and turns to bumpy brick for the final 0.2 mile to Fairground.

When you finish, congratulate yourself for conquering this tough ride. Do you want to try the race next year? For more information about the Hillsboro-Roubaix race, visit www.stlbiking.com.

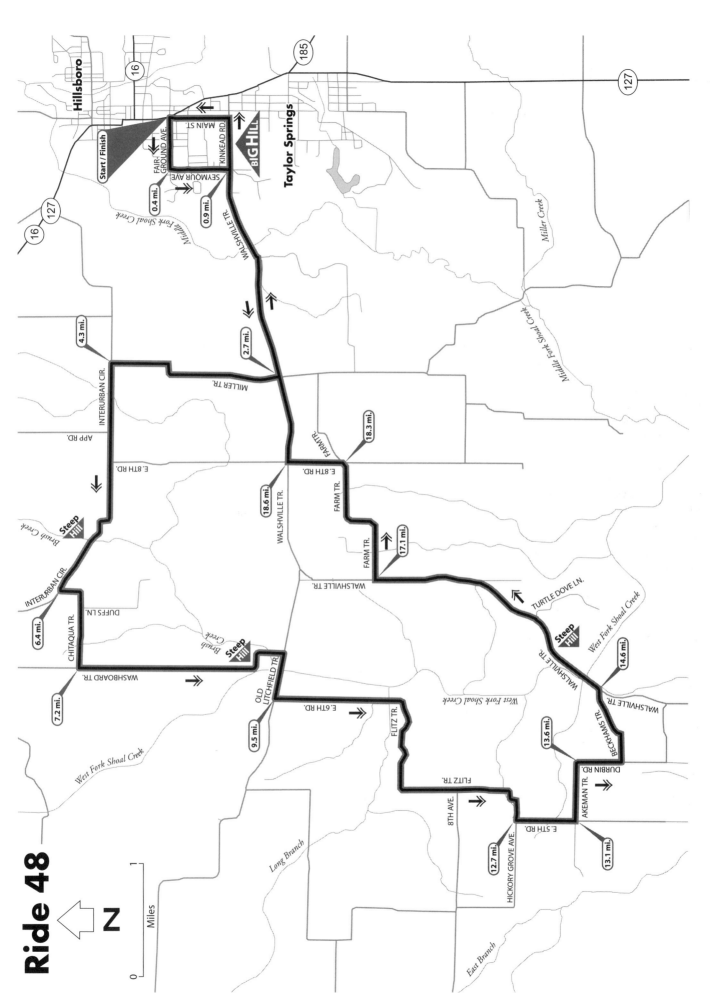

# Ride 48

N

Miles
0   1

**Hillsboro**

16
16
127
185
127

Start / Finish

FAIR-
GROUND AVE.

0.4 mi.

SEYMOUR AVE.

0.9 mi.

MAIN ST.

KINKEAD RD.

**BIG HILL**

**Taylor Springs**

*Middle Fork Shoal Creek*

WALSHVILLE TR.

2.7 mi.

MILLER TR.

4.3 mi.

INTERURBAN CIR.

APP RD.

E. 8TH RD.

*Brush Creek*

**Steep Hill**

WALSHVILLE TR.

18.6 mi.

18.3 mi.

FARM TR.

E. 8TH RD.

FARM TR.

FARM TR.

17.1 mi.

WALSHVILLE TR.

TURTLE DOVE LN.

*West Fork Shoal Creek*

**Steep Hill**

14.6 mi.

INTERURBAN CIR.

6.4 mi.

DUFFS LN.

CHITAQUA TR.

7.2 mi.

WASHBOARD TR.

*Brush Creek*

**Steep Hill**

OLD LITCHFIELD TR.

9.5 mi.

E. 6TH RD.

*West Fork Shoal Creek*

WALSHVILLE TR.

BECKHAMS TR.

13.6 mi.

DURBIN RD.

AKEMAN TR.

13.1 mi.

E. 5TH RD.

FLITZ TR.

FLITZ TR.

8TH AVE.

12.7 mi.

HICKORY GROVE AVE.

*Long Branch*

*East Branch*

*Miller Creek*

*Middle Fork Shoal Creek*

# RIDE 49
## Greenville

**Location:** Bond County
**Distance:** 27.4 miles
**Pedaling time:** 2–3 hours
**Surface:** Chip-seal and asphalt roads
**Terrain:** Some rolling hills
**Sweat factor:** Moderate
**Trailhead:** Corner of Fourth Street and Main Street, Greenville

### The National Road

The National Road was the nation's first interstate highway. It carried settlers west over the Appalachians and into what is now the Midwest. Then it provided a trade route for those settlers to send their goods back east. The road began in Maryland and eventually carried pioneers all the way to Illinois.

President Thomas Jefferson signed legislation for the National Road in 1806, but progress was relatively slow. Construction in Illinois did not begin until 1830. Although a route was surveyed all the way to Jefferson City, Missouri, the federal government only constructed the National Road to Vandalia, which was the state capital from 1820 to 1839. At that point railroads were beginning to make the National Road obsolete. Signs now mark the historic National Road all the way across Illinois. The road west of Vandalia, including the road through Greenville, follows the surveyed route and has been known throughout history as the National Road. In 1926, U.S. Highway 40 was chartered to follow the National Road corridor and beyond.

For more information, contact the National Road Association of Illinois at www.nationalroad.org or (217) 849-3188.

This is a scenic ride through farmland and forest surrounding Greenville. The trailhead is at the Greenville Public Library. More than a hundred years ago, Andrew Carnegie offered money to build libraries in towns around the world. The Ladies Library Association formed in Greenville in 1855, and in 1902 they contacted Carnegie and received a $10,000 donation. The library was dedicated in 1905. It is one of 106 Illinois libraries that Carnegie funded (other towns in this book that have Carnegie libraries include Arcola, Havana, and Vienna).

There is public parking on the northwest corner of the intersection, and a bed and breakfast is located on the southeast corner. Head south on Fourth Street to the stop sign and turn right. This is Franklin Avenue, but leaving town it becomes Old National Road. The next turn is a little tricky; you won't see it until you are almost on top of it. At mile 1.9, turn right on Rocky Mountain Avenue. This is a beautiful ride through the woods, but you'll sweat a bit on the rolling, sometimes steep hills. Turn right at the

end of the road and keep going north at the stop sign. The next stop sign is State Highway 140. This road can be busy, but you'll only be on it for 0.2 mile before you turn left on Mount Gilead Road. Mount Gilead Cumberland Presbyterian Church was organized in 1823, and this building was erected in 1867. Past the church and cemetery, the road dives downhill toward a creek bridge. Watch your speed because there is a sharp left curve at the bottom of the hill. Turn right at 8.2 miles on Plant School Avenue, another great road that winds through the woods. Go left on Schlemer Road and right on Coyote Avenue.

At 11.8 miles, stop at State Highway 127 and turn left. This road has paved shoulders, and you'll only follow it for half a mile before making almost a U-turn on Hazel Dell Road. Then take the first left, which is Ayers Road. On this road, you pass the John and Martha Ayers Science Field Station of Greenville College. You will see the school itself when you return to town. At 15.6 miles, keep left at Union Grove Avenue. The road narrows and makes a sharp left. Turn right onto Ayers Road and cross the railroad tracks at an unprotected crossing.

At Sorento Avenue, turn right. This road has some more rolling hills. Turn right on Red Ball Trail to head back toward Greenville. This is a wide road that gently curves over the hills. Watch for the narrow, rough, wooden bridge at 22.8 miles. The road skirts the west end of Governor Bond Lake, but the only evidence you'll see is a sign for a marina. Both the lake and the county are named for Shadrach Bond, Illinois' first governor (the county was actually formed in 1817 when Bond was territorial governor). After you cross a creek at 25.1 miles, there is a half-mile long, occasionally steep climb out of the valley. At the stop sign (State Highway 140), cross and veer to the right on Beaumont Avenue. Greenville College is on the left at 27.1 miles. This school was founded in 1855 as Almira College for women, but men were attending classes by the 1890s when it became Greenville College. The road splits in a Y shortly after. Keep to the right on Oak Street, then turn left on Fourth Street. The two-way stop sign, College Avenue, is busy State Highway 127. Return to the library at 27.4 miles.

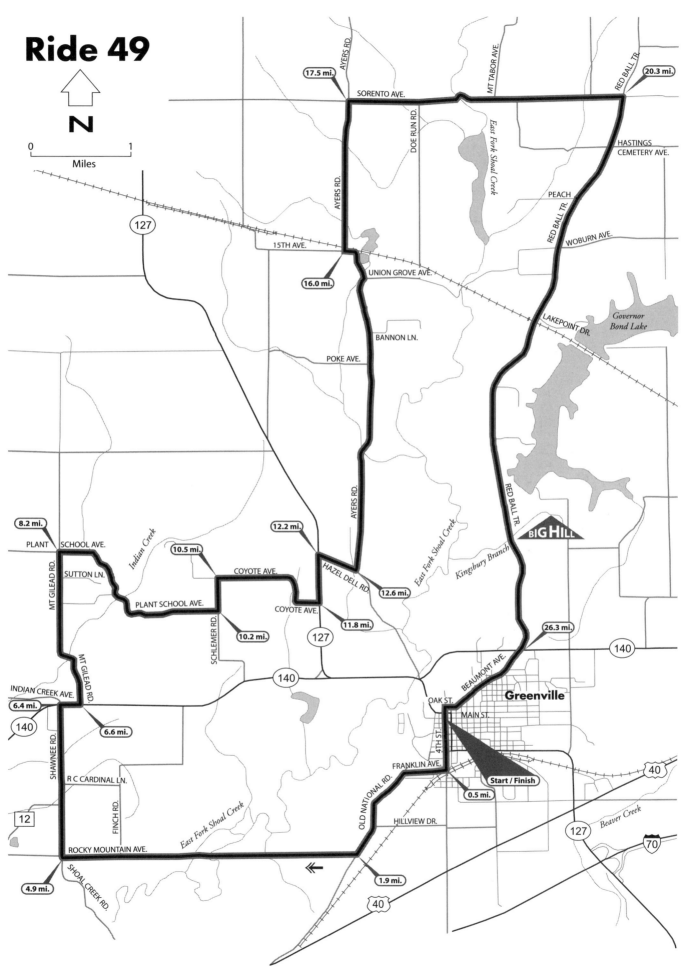

# Ride 49

N

0      1
Miles

127

17.5 mi.

AYERS RD.

SORENTO AVE.

MT TABOR AVE.

RED BALL TR.

20.3 mi.

East Fork Shoal Creek

DOE RUN RD.

HASTINGS CEMETERY AVE.

PEACH

RED BALL TR.

WOBURN AVE.

15TH AVE.

AYERS RD.

UNION GROVE AVE.

16.0 mi.

LAKEPOINT DR.

Governor Bond Lake

BANNON LN.

POKE AVE.

AYERS RD.

8.2 mi.

PLANT SCHOOL AVE.

Indian Creek

10.5 mi.

MT GILEAD RD.

SUTTON LN.

COYOTE AVE.

PLANT SCHOOL AVE.

12.2 mi.

HAZEL DELL RD.

East Fork Shoal Creek

Kingsbury Branch

BIG HILL

SCHLEMER RD.

COYOTE AVE.

12.6 mi.

10.2 mi.

11.8 mi.

127

26.3 mi.

140

140

BEAUMONT AVE.

Greenville

MT GILEAD RD.

INDIAN CREEK AVE.

6.4 mi.

140

6.6 mi.

OAK ST.

MAIN ST.

SHAWNEE RD.

R C CARDINAL LN.

4TH ST.

FRANKLIN AVE.

Start / Finish

12

FINCH RD.

0.5 mi.

ROCKY MOUNTAIN AVE.

East Fork Shoal Creek

OLD NATIONAL RD.

HILLVIEW DR.

127

Beaver Creek

70

4.9 mi.

SHOAL CREEK RD.

1.9 mi.

40

40

101

# RIDE 50
## Watch for Wild Turkeys

**Location:** Marion County
**Distance:** 17.3 miles
**Pedaling time:** 1.5–2 hours
**Surface:** Paved and chip-seal country roads
**Terrain:** Some rolling hills
**Sweat factor:** Moderate
**Trailhead:** Main (west) entrance to Stephen A. Forbes State Park

### Stephen A. Forbes

**Stephen A. Forbes (1844-1930) would probably be pleased with the biodiversity in his state park. When it came to nature, Forbes was truly a jack of all trades. A prolific researcher and writer, he studied insects, birds, fish, and other animals, publishing hundreds of papers. One paper, "The Lake as a Microcosm," was a seminal work in the field of ecology. He was the Illinois state entomologist for 35 years, and a University of Illinois professor even longer. He served as president of the Illinois Academy of Science, the Ecological Society of America, the National Society of Horticultural Inspectors, and the American Association of Economic Entomologists. Forbes would really like the Sam A. Parr Fisheries Research Laboratory used by the Illinois Natural History Survey. After all, he was once in charge of that group, too.**

Stephen A. Forbes State Park covers 3,100 acres, including a 585-acre lake. While most activities seem to focus on the lake, there is some good cycling on roads in and around the park. Wildlife abounds, especially birds of all sizes. Be prepared to yield to wild turkeys crossing the road, and keep an eye out for hawks.

Park in front of the visitor center, or at Boston Pond if that lot is full. The visitor center has bathrooms and water. Zero the odometer at the main entrance to the park and head south on Omega Road. This concrete road may have RV or boat trailer traffic since it is a main route to the park. There is a stop sign at 1.5 miles. The Omega General Store is on the southwest corner (open 7 AM-7 PM daily). This is the only place to get food and drink outside of the park. They claim to

have the best pizza in town, although there isn't much competition in tiny, unincorporated Omega.

Once you turn left on Penrod Road at 2.8 miles, you'll be on chip seal for the remainder of the ride. Follow the curves onto Landmark Road and then Allen Road. The ride thus far has been fairly flat with only slight hills. The terrain soon changes to rolling hills. After you follow another zigzag onto Ludwig Road, you'll start a steep climb through a wooded area, then a long, gradual climb through open fields until you reach Beard Road. This is the border between Marion and Clay counties, so you'll be in Clay County as you head north. This road makes a sharp left at 10.9 miles. As the road curves north again onto Lane Road, veer left on Wilcoxen Road. The rolling hills are back, including two short, steep climbs around 11.6 miles. Be careful on the following descent because there is a small, wooden plank bridge at the bottom of the hill.

As you head north on Meacham Road, you'll see the Sam A. Parr Fisheries Research Laboratory on the left. Turn left into the park at 14.1 miles, then left again at the yield sign. Ride through a large parking lot for boaters. There are toilets on the right. Like most big lakes in Illinois, this one is man-made. Ride over the dam at 14.5 miles, then head into the woods. The remainder of this ride is filled with hills and curves on the park road. The turn-off for the marina and restaurant comes at 17 miles; keep to the left. Be forewarned that if you choose to visit the marina, you'll have to climb a steep hill to get back. This ride ends at the stop sign at 17.3 miles. From here you can go left or straight depending on where you parked.

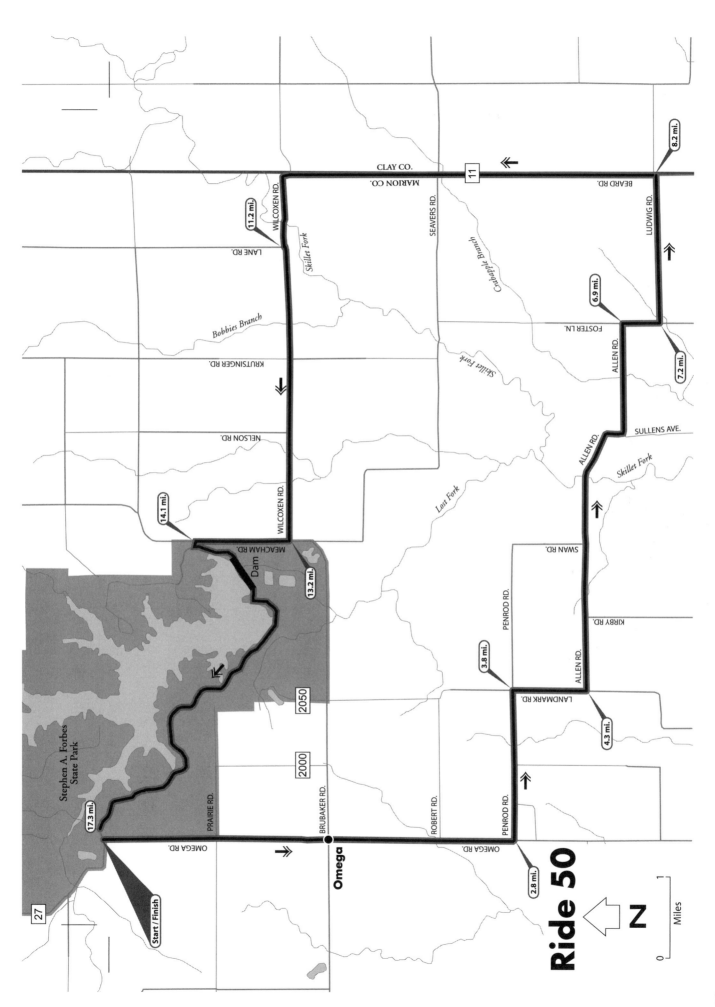

# Ride 50

Stephen A. Forbes State Park

**Start / Finish**

Omega

**N**

Miles
0 — 1

103

# RIDE 51
## Merry Miles to Maeystown

**Location:** Monroe County, south of Saint Louis
**Distance:** 32.5 miles
**Pedaling time:** 3–4 hours
**Surface:** Paved and chip-seal roads
**Terrain:** Hilly
**Sweat factor:** High
**Trailhead:** Corner of Main Street and Mill Street in Waterloo

### Waterloo's Legendary Beginning

Waterloo was the site of the first permanent American settlement in the old Northwest Territory in 1782. Five Virginia soldiers from the Revolutionary War took their pay in the form of Illinois land. They formed a town named Bellefontaine, and the restored Bellefontaine House at 709 South Church Street, (618) 939-5230, stands today as a reminder of Waterloo's roots.

Emery Peters Rogers moved into the area in 1816 and opened a store, mill, and quarry. The cluster of houses near the store became known as Peterstown. Though built years later in 1830, Peterstown House at 275 North Main Street, (618) 939-4222, represents the old village on the north side of town. This building was once a stagecoach stop on the Kaskaskia-Cahokia Trail.

A creek ran between Peterstown and Bellefontaine, and there was said to be a strong rivalry between the two settlements. According to legend, an Irishman named Charles Carroll arrived in 1818 and built his home on one side of the creek, his barn on the other. Carroll reputedly said, "It won't be Bellefontaine, and it won't be Peterstown, but begorra, I'll give ye's both your Waterloo."

The cheeky Irishman must have been successful because in 1825 Waterloo became the seat of Monroe County. The town experienced a growth spurt in the 1840s and 1850s when many Germans moved in (as in Maeystown at that time). In a nod to its heritage, Waterloo has become a sister city with Porta Westfalica, Germany, a connection celebrated in a June festival.

Maeystown was founded by Jacob Maeys in 1852 and settled by German immigrants. Many of them were Forty-Eighters, people who left Germany after the Revolutions of 1848. Drawing inspiration from the Bavarian stone buildings back home, they built sturdy limestone structures that earned the town a place on the National Register of Historic Places in 1978. Thus far Maeystown has resisted the growth that towns further north in Monroe County have experienced. It is a popular tourist destination on weekends, especially during special events, but otherwise it is pretty quiet. Maeystown, Waterloo, and Columbia are three Monroe County towns with a strong German-American heritage, but Maeystown has best retained that character.

Start in Waterloo at the northwest corner of the Monroe County Courthouse Square at Main Street and Mill Street. Head west on Mill Street to Moore Street and turn right. Go over State Highway 3 at 1.2 miles (cross traffic does not stop), then immediately turn right to stay on Moore Street. Turn left on HH Road at the four-way stop. At 4 miles, follow the curve right, and then turn left to stay on HH Road. Though most of these roads are chip seal, this road has asphalt for 1.5 miles as it passes a housing development. Then the road descends to cross a creek at 6.1 miles. Turn left on Deer Hill Road and climb a steep hill. There is a yield sign at Trout Camp Road at 9.2 miles. Turn right,

then keep left 0.6 mile later when Trout Camp Road continues west. At State Highway 156, turn left then quickly right at the Gateway Farms pig sign. This is still Deer Hill Road. At the intersection with C Road, follow the curve left. At 14.4 miles, follow the curve right onto Ahne Road. Turn right at the T onto KK Road, which leads into Madonnaville. The Immaculate Conception Catholic Church on the right is a preview of the limestone buildings you'll see in Maeystown.

The road is mostly downhill from Madonnaville to Monroe City. Turn left on Baum Road at the east edge of this tiny town. There is a long climb on this road after you cross the creek. At 17.1 miles, keep right at the Y to stay on Baum Road. You know you're approaching Maeystown when you see the Maeystown Sportsmen's Club (members only) around 18.2 miles. Turn right at Maeystown Road and descend all the way to the stop sign, where the road is also labeled Maeystown Road. Turn left into Maeystown where the road becomes Mill Street.

Most places are closed during the week, but Eschy's Bar & Restaurant at the four-way stop is open every day except Monday. In addition to the limestone buildings, another feature reminiscent of the Bavarian towns that the early settlers of Maeystown left behind are the flagstone gutters on the hilly streets. A trip to this town wouldn't be complete without a look at its famous one-lane stone bridge, which is past Franklin Street and around the bend. Like the stone buildings in town, the bridge is well over a century old. Ride to the bridge at 19.7 miles. Double back to Franklin Street and turn left up a steep hill. Saint John's Church stands at the top, but turn left on Hanover Street before you get there. The road keeps going up, passing the Josiah Ryan House (circa 1780, moved from another location) on the left and becoming Bushy Prairie Road outside of town. A mile later, the road levels somewhat into rolling hills. Curve left at Altes Road (21.9 miles). Turn right on KK Road where Bushy Prairie Road ends, but be careful because there are no stop signs at this three-way intersection.

Enter Burksville and turn left at a broad intersection onto Kaskaskia Road. This asphalt road has a little more traffic than the roads around Maeystown. Turn right on busy State Highway 3 at the T, then take the first left onto Old Red Bud Road. At 28.7 miles, turn left again to follow Old Red Bud Road north to Waterloo where it becomes Legion Drive. Turn left on Hartman Street. At the two-way stop at Market Street, veer right to continue on Hartman Street. This becomes Leo Street after a right curve. Turn left on Front Street at the T, and then turn right on Main Street back to the courthouse square.

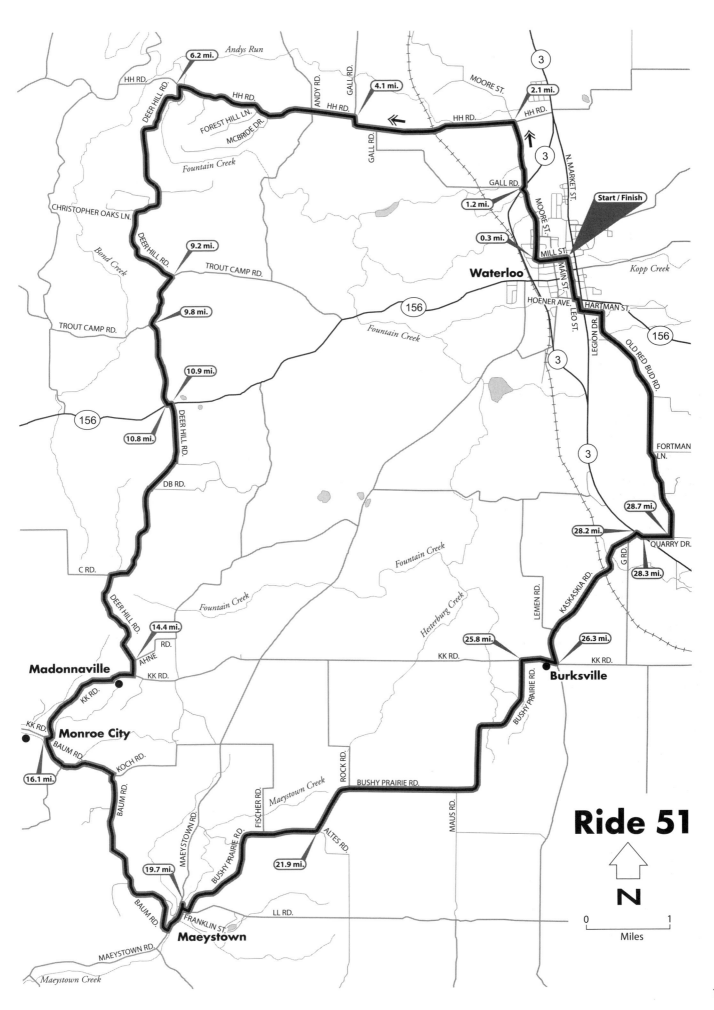

## Ride 51

# RIDE 52
## Ava Loop

**Location:** Jackson County
**Distance:** 25.2 miles
**Pedaling time:** 2–3 hours
**Surface:** Paved and chip-seal roads
**Terrain:** Hilly
**Sweat factor:** High
**Trailhead:** Corner of Main Street and Miller Street in Ava

### Adventure Cycling

The TransAmerica Bicycle Trail is a bicycle touring route dating back to America's bicentennial. In fact, the Adventure Cycling Association (ACA) was originally named Bikecentennial. The idea was to celebrate our country's 200th anniversary by experiencing its beauty and history at a slower pace. Bikecentennial produced maps and led trips for 4,100 cyclists in the summer of 1976. Nearly half of those participants rode the entire TransAmerica Bicycle Trail.

Now the ACA offers a network of routes including three east-west cross-country routes, east and west coast routes, a Great Divide mountain bike route, a Lewis and Clark route, and several other routes and connectors totaling more than 33,000 miles. With over 42,000 members, the ACA is America's largest organization dedicated to bicycle touring. In addition to producing detailed maps, the ACA publishes *Adventure Cyclist* magazine and leads a variety of tours. For more information about this organization, visit www.adventure cycling.org or call (800) 755-2453.

Winding through the northwest corner of the Shawnee National Forest, this route has too many hills to mention, but not as many trees as you might expect. It stands in stark contrast to pancake-flat Ride 53, which starts only a dozen miles to the south on the Mississippi River floodplain. Stock up on water and food in town because there are no services on the route.

Elizabeth A. Smysor Park stands where the railroad once ran through the middle of town. It features a gazebo. Park your car here along Main Street and start riding west from the intersection with Miller Street. At the stop sign, turn left on Keller Street. This is State Highway 151, the Kent Keller Highway, which was named for the congressman who was instrumental in getting it built. This road isn't as busy as many other state highways, and it has a paved shoulder. Turn right on Little Kinkaid Road at 0.7 mile. Strangely, the advance warning sign for the intersection is labeled "650 feet" instead of "Little Kinkaid Road." This road has lots of rolling hills, including a long, hard climb after crossing Little Kinkaid Creek at 3.2 miles. At Flat Rock Lane (4.1 miles), the road turns sharply to the right. Turn left on Rock Crusher Road at 5.8 miles. This road carries trucks bound for the Kinkaid Stone Company, but they turn left 0.3 mile later while you continue straight. Then traffic is light and there are gently rolling hills. At 8.2 miles, curve left past the road to Piney Creek Ravine Nature Preserve. Curve right on Hog Hill Road at 9.2 miles, and follow it to the left at 9.4 miles.

The ride enters Shawnee National Forest unannounced just before you turn left on narrow and hilly Koehn Road at 10 miles. At 11.5 miles the road dips to Kinkaid Creek, which spills over the pavement. If there is water, walk your bike because the road is likely to be slick. At the end of Koehn Road, turn right on Kinkaid Stone Road. There are more rolling hills with a few steep ones. Follow the pavement to the right at Suchman Road, then curve left onto Dry Hill Road just before the radio tower. There is a long descent at 17.2 miles, but be prepared to stop just past the bottom. Turn left on State Highway 151 and go up and down some more steep hills. Johnson Creek Recreation Area is on the right at 19.6 miles. Then you cross Kinkaid Lake on a steel bridge. Like most recreational lakes in southern Illinois, Kinkaid Lake is man-made.

Leaving the lake behind, climb a steep hill at 20.6

**This ride crosses the north end of Kinkaid Lake.**

miles. After a sign for a school bus entrance, turn right on hilly Sharp Rock Road. Start heading uphill and curve right at McBride Road. At the end of Sharp Rock Road, turn left on Ava Road. This is part of the Adventure Cycling Association's TransAmerica Bicycle Trail. Follow this road back into Ava, riding past Henry "Buck" Bower Park. Turn left on Main Street at 25 miles.

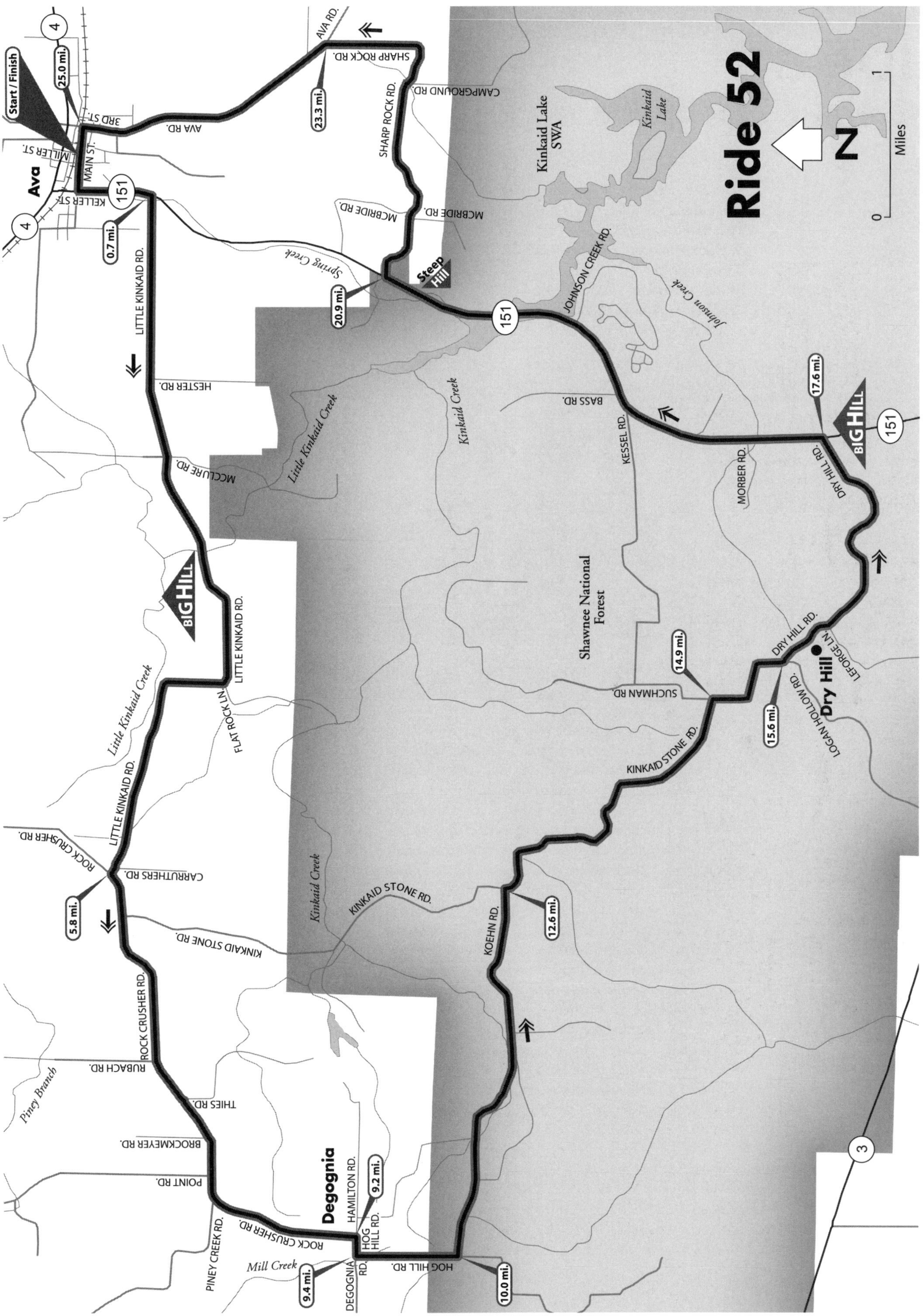

Ride 52

N

Miles 0 1

Start / Finish
25.0 mi.

4

Ava

4

151

AVA RD.
MILLER ST.
MAIN ST.
3RD ST.
KELLER ST.

SHARP ROCK RD.
AVA RD.
23.3 mi.
SHARP ROCK RD.
CAMPGROUND RD.

Kinkaid Lake SWA

Kinkaid Lake

MCBRIDE RD.
MCBRIDE RD.

0.7 mi.
LITTLE KINKAID RD.

Spring Creek

Steep Hill

20.9 mi.

151

HESTER RD.

JOHNSON CREEK RD.

Johnson Creek

MCCLURE RD.

Little Kinkaid Creek

BASS RD.

17.6 mi.

Kinkaid Creek

KESSEL RD.

BIG Hill

151

BIG Hill

MORBER RD.

DRY HILL RD.

LITTLE KINKAID RD.

FLAT ROCK LN.

Little Kinkaid Creek

Shawnee National Forest

14.9 mi.

SUCHMAN RD.

DRY HILL RD.

15.6 mi.

LOGAN HOLLOW RD.

LEFORGE LN.

Dry Hill

ROCK CRUSHER RD.

CARUTHERS RD.

KINKAID STONE RD.

5.8 mi.

Kinkaid Creek

KINKAID STONE RD.

KOEHN RD.

12.6 mi.

ROCK CRUSHER RD.

RUBACH RD.

THIES RD.

Piney Branch

BROCKMEYER RD.

POINT RD.

PINEY CREEK RD.

ROCK CRUSHER RD.

Degognia

HAMILTON RD.

HOG HILL RD.
9.2 mi.

DEGOGNIA RD.

Mill Creek

9.4 mi.

HOG HILL RD.

10.0 mi.

3

107

# RIDE 53
## Gorham Floodplain

**Location:** Near Mississippi River west of Carbondale
**Distance:** 29.6 miles
**Pedaling time:** 2.5–3 hours
**Surface:** Paved and chip-seal roads
**Terrain:** Flat
**Sweat factor:** Low
**Trailhead:** Corner of Main Street and Lake Street in Gorham

As in many small Illinois towns, the grain elevator dominates Jacob.

With all the bumpy terrain in Southern Illinois, the Mississippi River floodplain east of Gorham really stands out. It's a great place to ride without climbing, and most of the roads have very little traffic. There are a few minor warnings, though. First, because it is a floodplain with some of the roads lying at field level, it may not be passable during high water. Second, there are few trees, leaving riders exposed to wind and sun. Finally, get water and food before you reach Gorham because services are limited to a couple of taverns.

Follow the signs from State Highway 3 to Gorham. This is easily the biggest town on the ride with a population around 250. At the west end of town, there is plenty of parking either on Main Street or next to the railroad tracks. Most of the town lies on the other side of the

tracks, but Gorham is a quiet place. The only active enterprise downtown is the post office.

Start the ride at the corner of Main Street and Lake Street, the road that crosses the tracks. Head west on Main Street, which turns into Neunert Road. This road is asphalt, but the rest are chip seal. To the left is Fountain Bluff. A gravel road loops past the rock face of the bluff, which makes an interesting side trip by mountain bike or car. There are several petroglyphs (ancient drawings) on the cliff walls. If you visit them, be more thoughtful than some previous visitors who have vandalized the area. You can also drive to the top of Fountain Bluff from State Highway 3 on Happy Hollow Road. The Bottoms Up Bar and Grill is on the right as you enter Neunert. Christ Lutheran Church, built in 1906, is up the road, but this ride turns left instead (you can continue north to shorten the ride to 9.3 miles). You are still on Neunert Road, but now it is chip seal. Around 5.7 miles this road approaches the levee, but then it turns north. Go left on Indian Ridge Road at 6.9 miles (to shorten the ride to 14.3 miles, turn right here).

The only notable hills are the climbs up to the levee, which are short but steep. When you reach the top the first time at 9.5 miles, take a moment to look to your left. This is Missouri, a rare spot where the Show Me State lies east of the Mississippi River. Of course, it wasn't always that way; the river changed course after the boundary was set. Drop down to Little Levee Road at 11.5 miles because Levee Road turns to gravel. Climb up to Levee Road again at 13.7 miles, and this time you can finally see the river. Turn right off the levee at the first opportunity onto Smokey Road (no street sign). To the north you can see the wooded hills traversed by Ride 52. Turn south on Jones Ridge Road in the town of Jones Ridge, which is little more than a cluster of homes.

Return to Levee Road and Indian Ridge Road, but continue straight this time on the latter when it meets Neunert Road at 22.2 miles. At West Jacob Road, you can see Neunert to the right. Turn left on West Jacob Road instead. In the town of Jacob, turn right on East Jacob Road before the railroad tracks. This is Jacob's main street. The Old Tin Barn and Grill is on the right. At 27.7 miles, follow the curve left onto Gorham Road. Be careful at the railroad crossing (28.3 miles), which has a stop sign instead of a gate. This is an active, twin-track railroad. As you come into Gorham, curve to the right onto Lake Street, which takes you back over the tracks to the start.

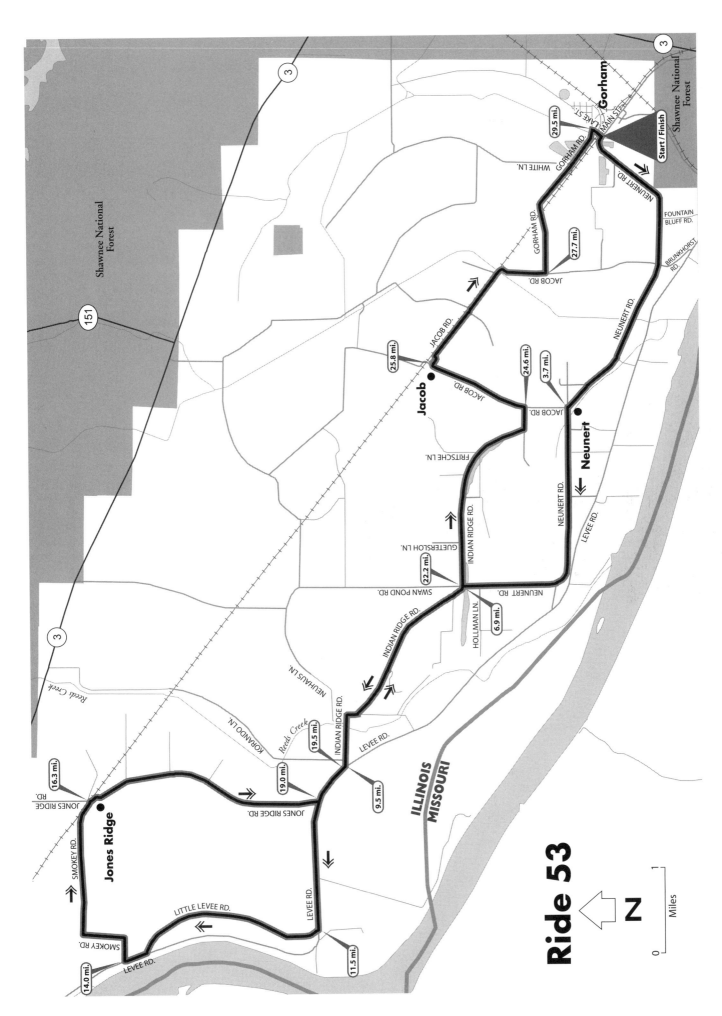

# Ride 53

N

Miles
0    1

# RIDE 54
## Giant City

**Location:** Jackson and Union counties
**Distance:** 14.1 miles
**Pedaling time:** 75–100 minutes
**Surface:** Chip-seal roads
**Terrain:** Hilly
**Sweat factor:** High
**Trailhead:** Shelter 1 parking lot, north end of Giant City State Park

### Giant City Lodge

The Civilian Conservation Corps (CCC) was a program begun by President Franklin D. Roosevelt to put people in a nation ravaged by depression and drought back to work. CCC workers were instrumental in planting and protecting forests, including Illinois' then-new Shawnee National Forest. The workers also carried out projects to build dams, prevent erosion, create campgrounds, renovate historic buildings, and develop parks. Many of Illinois' state parks benefited from the CCC. Lodges and cabins were constructed at Giant City, White Pines, Pere Marquette (see Ride 46), and Starved Rock State Parks.

Giant City Lodge is a handsome structure originally built of multihued sandstone and white-oak timber. It has been expanded and remodeled over the years, but many original features have been preserved. Although the lodge serves breakfast, lunch, and dinner, it is best known for fried chicken served family-style. There are three types of cabins for rent here, too. Twelve one-room cabins were built by the CCC, and 22 larger cabins have been added since. With an outdoor pool to complement the park's many treasures, the Lodge is a great place for a weekend getaway. Call (618) 457-4921 for reservations.

Befitting of its name, Giant City State Park is one of Illinois' largest parks, covering 4,000 acres in the middle of Shawnee National Forest. The natural feature that gives the park its name is a formation of Makanda stone that has been cut by water over the centuries to create narrow "streets" between stone "buildings" evoking the image of a city populated by giants. A hike through this area on the Giant City Nature Trail is an ideal post-ride activity. This ride begins with a big loop through forests and orchards to the south, followed by a spin around the park roads. Please note that bicycles are not permitted off-road in the park.

Park at Shelter 1 on the north side of Giant City State Park. Use the northernmost entrance or risk "spoiling" the last few miles. Ride west back to the park entrance and turn left at the stop sign to go through Makanda. This road probably has more traffic than any other on this ride, but it's still pretty light. Aside from the state park, the town's main attraction is the Makanda Boardwalk, a restored block of 1890s shops populated by artists and artisans that you pass at 0.8 mile. Vultures have been living in this area since the last ice age. During the summer they nest in the bluffs at the state park and raise their young, but the rest of the year, they are a common sight in Makanda. Every fall, the town celebrates Vulture Fest. Just past the Boardwalk, veer left on Old Lower Cobden Road before the railroad crossing—don't curve right across the railroad tracks and don't take the sharp left up the big hill. This shaded road has low traffic. It starts out easy, but the hills get bigger later. Ride past Giant City Park Road at 2.5 miles; you'll pick up this road on the way back. Go over a creek and begin a half-mile-long climb that ends with a sharp right turn in a clearing.

Somewhere along the way, Old Lower Cobden Road becomes Shiloh Road. At 4 miles, begin a descent that gets steep approaching a wooden plank bridge (some modern bridges have been constructed recently on this road, so it may be gone by the time you ride). Marvin's Garden at 4.9 miles sells fresh vegetables. There is another plank bridge at 5.5 miles followed by a stop sign at Water Valley Road. Make a hard left turn onto the eastbound road. It starts downhill, but most of the next 0.8 mile goes up. Don't go too fast on the following downhill because you have to turn left on Giant City Park Road at 6.4 miles. This road has challenging, rolling hills past orchards and forest. At 8 miles begin a long descent; you barely have to pedal for the better part of two miles. Be alert at the bridle crossing at 9.2 miles—you don't want to collide with a horse at 30 mph!

Turn right on Albert Lane at 9.7 miles and start climbing. There is another bridle crossing, but you won't be going as fast this time. Turn right at the stop sign at 10.1 miles. This road loops through the park, passing several picnic areas and hiking trailheads. The last big hill begins around 10.4 miles and keeps climbing until you reach Giant City Lodge, the highest point in the park, at 11.2 miles. The hardest part of your ride is finished, so you may wish to take advantage of the bike rack in front to stop in for a meal. At the other end of the parking lot from the Lodge, the water tower features a spiral staircase climbing 50 feet to an observation platform. From the tower you can see Bald Knob Cross (Ride 55), among other things. Half a mile later, go straight past the road leading to the visitor center. Curve right at the yield sign at 12.2 miles and go under Church Road. The rest of the ride is mostly downhill from here, but watch for moss on the road that could make it slick. There is one last bridle crossing at 12.8 miles.

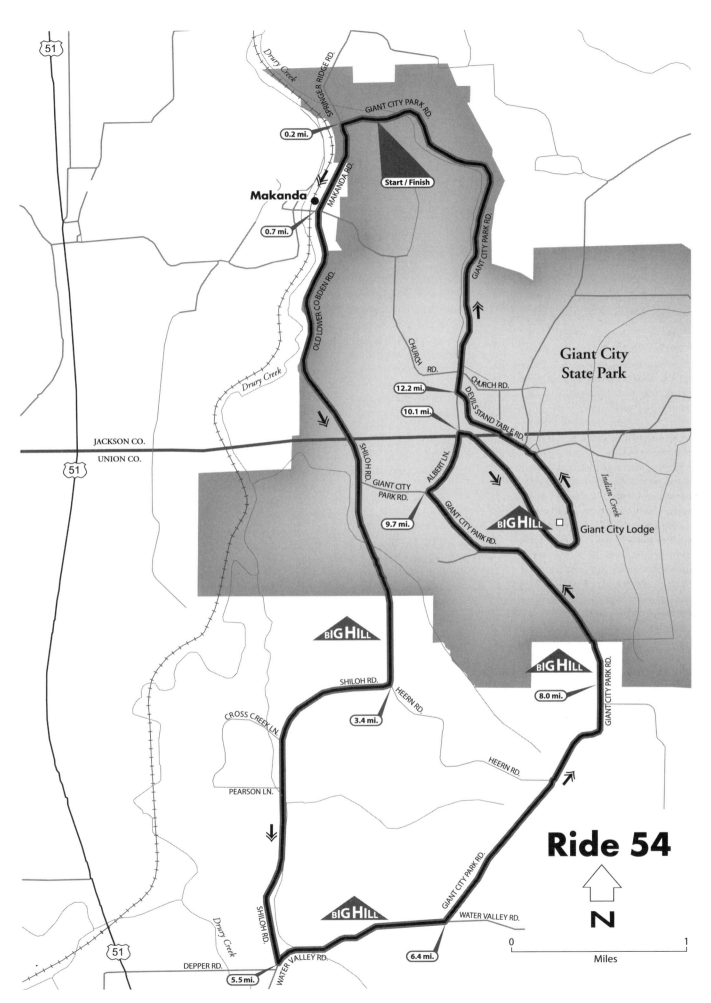

51

Drury Creek

SPRINGER RIDGE RD.

GIANT CITY PARK RD.

0.2 mi.

MAKANDA RD.

**Makanda**

0.7 mi.

OLD LOWER COBDEN RD.

GIANT CITY PARK RD.

CHURCH RD.

CHURCH RD.

12.2 mi.

**Giant City State Park**

DEVILS STAND TABLE RD.

10.1 mi.

Start / Finish

Drury Creek

JACKSON CO.

UNION CO.

51

SHILOH RD.

GIANT CITY PARK RD.

ALBERT LN.

GIANT CITY PARK RD.

9.7 mi.

**BiG HiLL**

Giant City Lodge

Indian Creek

**BiG HiLL**

**BiG HiLL**

8.0 mi.

GIANT CITY PARK RD.

SHILOH RD.

HEERN RD.

3.4 mi.

CROSS CREEK LN.

PEARSON LN.

HEERN RD.

**Ride 54**

N

Drury Creek

SHILOH RD.

WATER VALLEY RD.

**BiG HiLL**

WATER VALLEY RD.

6.4 mi.

GIANT CITY PARK RD.

51

DEPPER RD.

5.5 mi.

WATER VALLEY RD.

0    1

Miles

# RIDE 55
## Climb to the Cross

**Location:** Union County
**Distance:** 9.5 miles
**Pedaling time:** 50–70 minutes
**Surface:** Chip-seal roads
**Terrain:** Hilly
**Sweat factor:** High
**Trailhead:** Corner of Main Street and Chestnut Street in Alto Pass

### Wine in Illinois?

While it lacks the cachet of California's Wine Country, the Illinois wine industry is growing rapidly. And judging from the hundreds of awards earned by Illinois vintages, they aren't too bad. There are more than 50 wineries in the state. Illinois' climate limits the varieties of grapes that can be grown, but many winemakers say that the process is more important than the grapes. Wines are also made from berries, plums, peaches, or honey.

The Shawnee Hills are especially attractive to vintners. Alto Vineyards sold its first wine in 1987, and half a dozen winemakers have opened nearby since. The Shawnee Wine Trail is an auto route that links these wineries into one big tourist attraction. Casual drinkers can visit one or two, or avid wine drinkers can sample them all in a weekend. Just remember that if you are dehydrated from bicycling, a little wine can pack a big punch. For more information about wineries in southern Illinois, visit www.shawnee winetrail.com.

Don't be fooled by the short distance—this is a tough ride. Virtually none of it is flat, and since it is out-and-back, you'll climb every inch of it one way or the other. Your reward is a great view from Bald Knob (elevation 1,030 feet), which towers some 700 feet over the surrounding Shawnee National Forest. Bald Knob is the second-highest point in southern Illinois. It's also home of the 111-foot-high Bald Knob Cross of Peace, which is visible for miles around day and night.

In Alto Pass, you will find a restaurant on Main Street, a market on Elm Street, and parking along both. Starting from Main Street, head southwest on Chestnut Street. You face a hill immediately, but it's one of the easier ones on this ride. Follow Chestnut Street out of town, crossing a bridge over State Highway 127. Beyond the crest of another hill, Hedman Orchard & Vineyards is on the right. This farm has been growing fruit since it was established in 1880, but now it also features a winery, a Swedish café, and a bed and breakfast. Peaches are their specialty, with six varieties available from July to September (www.peach-barn.com or (618) 893-4923.) Unless you are planning a picnic on Bald Knob, you might want to wait for the return trip to take on extra weight. The only turn to make comes at a fork just before 1 mile: Veer left on the road into the woods, following the sign for Bald Knob Cross.

You might expect that since the cross is located at such a high point, the road leading to it would be one big climb. Alas, it is not that easy. In fact, the first mile of this road is mostly downhill. After that pleasant descent, it's time to get that height back; the next mile is mostly up-hill. Approaching 3 miles, you'll see a peach orchard on the right. As the road goes back into the woods, there is a trailhead on the right for a Shawnee National Forest hiking and equestrian trail. When you finally reach the top of that hill, you'll go down again for 0.3 mile, then up again. At 3.7 miles you'll pass between some communications towers—watch for loose gravel on the curve. After a bit more of this up-and-down give-and-take, you finally hit the last climb at 4.4 miles. You can see the cross on the left as you climb the big hill and round a curve to the welcome center ((618) 893-2344). The center is generally open 9 to 5 on Saturday and Sunday. Volunteers sell snacks and souvenirs, and there are restrooms inside. Continue between the brick columns to the small parking area at the foot of the cross. The cross, erected in 1963, was built to last. It is supported by 730 tons of reinforced concrete that extend 20 feet underground to bedrock, and it was engineered to withstand 150-mph winds. The cross is made of white porcelain steel panels with a base of Illinois marble, and it weighs 200 tons. The first Easter Sunrise Service was held on Bald Knob in 1937, a tradition that continues into the new century. The idea for a permanent cross on the site was born then, but it took decades to raise the funds for such a huge landmark. There is a plaque on Bald Knob honoring Wayman Presley, the prime mover in getting the cross built. An unusual fundraiser was the "Pig Program:" a woman gave her baby pigs to local farmers who raised them and donated some of the profits.

You'll have a hard time staying below the speed limit of 25 mph on the trip back to Alto Pass. A couple of steep climbs will keep you honest, especially at 7.4 and 8.1 miles. And don't forget about the easy mile you coasted down on the way to the cross—it isn't so easy on the way back. At the stop sign, look over your shoulder for fast-moving traffic, then proceed straight ahead. If you'd like to make your ride an even ten miles, turn right on Main Street (which becomes Skyline Drive) and climb to the second scenic overlook entrance and back. From the overlook, you can see Bald Knob Cross and lots of trees.

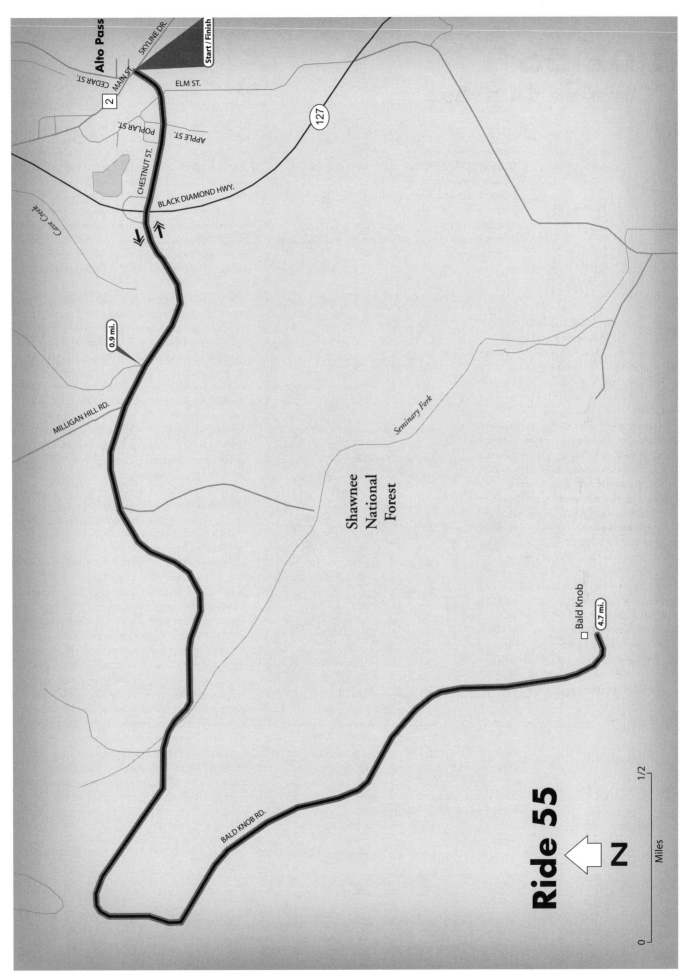

Ride 55

N

Miles

0    1/2

# RIDE 56
## Dongola Churches

**Location:** Union County
**Distance:** 20.6 miles
**Pedaling time:** 1.5–2.5 hours
**Surface:** Paved and chip-seal roads
**Terrain:** Hilly
**Sweat factor:** High
**Trailhead:** Corner of East Front Street and Cross Street in Dongola

St. John's is the oldest Lutheran congregation in Illinois.

See how many churches you can spot on this ride. Two of the main roads are named for churches that you'll ride past. Two churches are visible from the starting point, and you'll see two more on the way back into town. Whatever your religious persuasion, you'll be praying for mercy on some of these hills. It's a beautiful ride through the country on low-traffic roads, but it's not easy.

Dongola is easy to find, however. Take I-57 to the Dongola Road exit and head west into town. Drive straight ahead at the stop sign onto East Front Street, which used to be U.S. Highway 51. There is plenty of parking downtown by the railroad tracks. The ride starts at the corner of East Front Street and Cross Street. As you head north on Cross Street over the railroad tracks, the first big hill looms ahead. There are no services until you get back to Dongola, so you may want to stop by the grocery on the left for provisions. When you tackle that first hill, you will find that it continues as you go around a couple of curves. Outside of town, this turns into Saint Johns Road. This road has lots of hills, including a long climb at 2.3 miles and a descent at 3.5 miles so steep that you can coast up the next hill.

A mile later there is another steep descent toward Saint John's Cemetery. Watch your speed because there is a tight S-curve at the bottom. Saint John's Lutheran Church is at 5 miles. If the cemetery looks bigger than most country cemeteries, that is because Saint John's is older than most country churches. It was the first Lutheran congregation in Illinois Territory in 1816, predating statehood by two years. The current church building was formally dedicated in 1856, but it was extensively remodeled in the 1880s.

Continuing west on Saint Johns Road, take the first right on Boyd Road (the street sign may be facing the wrong way). This road starts with a half-mile climb followed by rolling hills. You won't see Ebenezer Church on this ride, but you pass the road bearing its name at 7.1 miles. At 8.9 miles, go downhill toward a T. Turn right on Sadler Road (the road to the left leads to the town of Anna). After passing an apple orchard, ride over some railroad tracks and a wooden plank bridge over Little Creek. After the stop sign at U.S. Highway 51, the road's name changes to Friendship School Road. At 10.4 miles, go to the right at the stop sign for Tollgate Road. A series of brutal, steep hills follows a mile later. These hills continue until you cross the bridge over I-57.

Turn right on Christian Chapel Road at 13.7 miles. There are still plenty of hills, but they are not as steep. Pass the Christian Chapel, built in 1905, and the cemetery beside it at 17.1 miles. At the end of this road, turn right on Cypress Road. After one last big climb, the road is mostly flat or downhill back to Dongola. Be alert at the interchange with I-57 at 19.7 miles (this is most likely the way you got to the start of the ride). As you ride through town, you'll see Dennis Swink Park on the left and a couple more churches on the right. At 20.4 miles, go straight at the stop sign and climb a little hill to the finish at Cross Street.

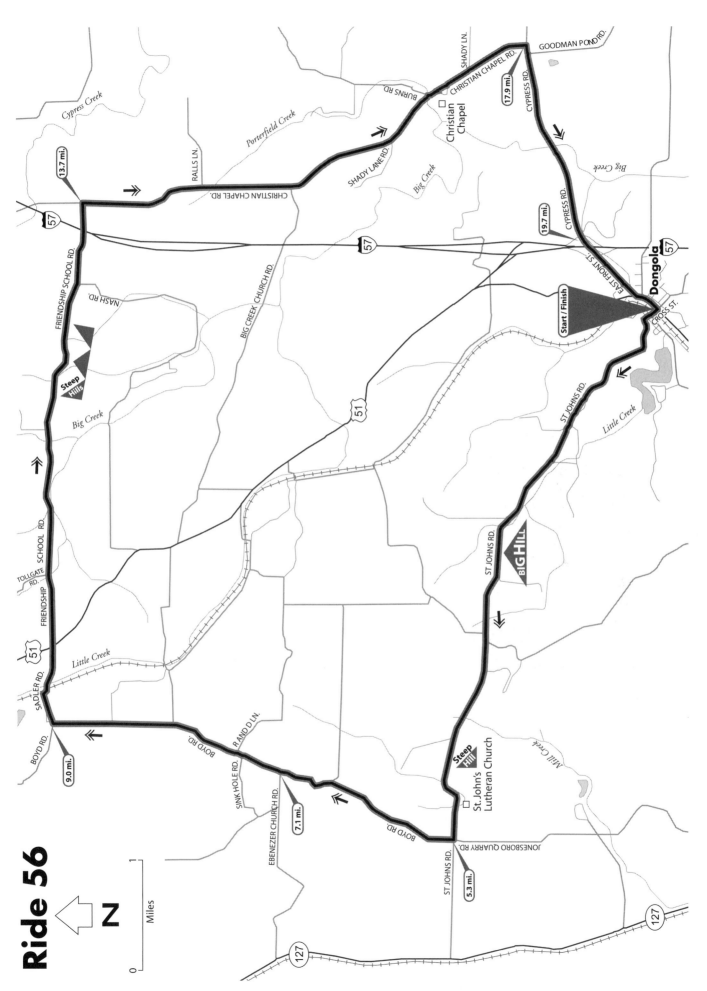

# Ride 56

N

Miles
0   1

# RIDE 57
## Tunnel Vision

**Location:** Johnson County
**Distance:** 31 miles
**Pedaling time:** 2.5–3.5 hours
**Surface:** Crushed-limestone trail
**Terrain:** Flat
**Sweat factor:** Low +
**Trailhead:** Vienna Depot, Vienna City Park in Vienna

As you might expect, the tunnel is the highlight of the Tunnel Hill State Trail.

Tunnels of any kind are uncommon in Illinois, but even rarer is a tunnel you can ride your bike through. When the Norfolk Southern Railroad ended service on the old Vincennes and Cairo Railroad and gave the right-of-way to the State of Illinois in 1991, it presented a golden opportunity for a unique rails-to-trails conversion. The Department of Natural Resources upgraded the surface to crushed limestone and created a few parking areas with water and toilets. Where freight trains once rumbled through the tunnel, now bicyclists can pedal. The Tunnel Hill State Trail runs 45 miles from Harrisburg southwest to Karnak. This ride takes in a few of the highlights, particularly the tunnel and the longest, highest trestle. Johnson County has been named the Bicycling Capital of Illinois by the state legislature, in no small part because of this popular trail.

The town of Vienna (pronounced VIE-anna) has stores, restaurants, and lodging. You should stock up before you leave town because aside from water at access areas, services are scarce. The steepest grade on the trail is only 2%, but the climbs are long. The mostly shaded trail is easy to follow. There are few street crossings and the surface is generally well maintained, though leaves and branches may clutter the trail in fall or after a storm. Watch for walkers and runners within the first few miles outside Vienna.

The trail office, which looks like a railroad depot, adjoins Vienna Community Park on State Highway 146 just a mile west of I-24. It has indoor restrooms as well as displays about the railroad. Hours are 8 to 4, but the building is locked when workers are out on the trail. There are toilets at the west side of the park, as well as at the Johnson County Chamber of Commerce Welcome Center. The Chamber resides in a red depot moved from Forman, a nearly abandoned town about five miles south along the trail.

The park also features a memorial to the Trail of Tears. In 1838 the federal government forced 15,000 Cherokee Indians to walk from the southeastern U.S. to Oklahoma. Some four thousand died in Illinois during the harsh winter. The seven faces carved on the totem pole at the center of the memorial represent the seven clans of the Cherokee Nation.

Head north from the white depot. I-24 passes overhead at 1 mile. Shelby Road at 2.9 miles marks the town of Bloomfield, which has no services. The old railroad trestles have been converted for trail use with side rails and wooden decks. The longest and highest is Breeden Trestle at 6.8 miles.

You finally approach the tunnel around 9 miles. When the railroad was built, the tunnel was more than 800 feet long. Part of the tunnel collapsed in 1929, so now it is only 543 feet long. The trail staff has done a good job of making sure the surface inside the tunnel is smooth, so you shouldn't encounter any surprises in the dark. On a hot day, you'll appreciate the coolness in the tunnel, but it can be a strange experience. An interesting phenomenon reported by trail users is that once you get into the dark, you tend to veer toward the walls instead of riding straight. A road carrying the TransAmerica Bicycle Trail (see Ride 52 sidebar) passes over the trail above the tunnel. The town of Tunnel Hill, established in 1870 when the railroad began construction, is a short distance north of the tunnel at 9.3 miles. The trail access area has toilets and water.

This ride turns around at the New Burnside access area at 15.5 miles, which also has water and toilets. The town was named for Civil War General Ambrose Burnside, one of the men who started the Vincennes and Cairo Railroad that is now the trail. Burnside is better known for his facial hair—the word sideburns was created by transposing the syllables of his name.

If you want to ride further, Harrisburg is 18.6 miles from here. Alternatively, you can continue south when you get back to Vienna. The trail extends for 10.8 miles down to Karnak, plus there is a 2.5-mile spur into the cypress and tupelo swamp of the Cache River State Natural Area.

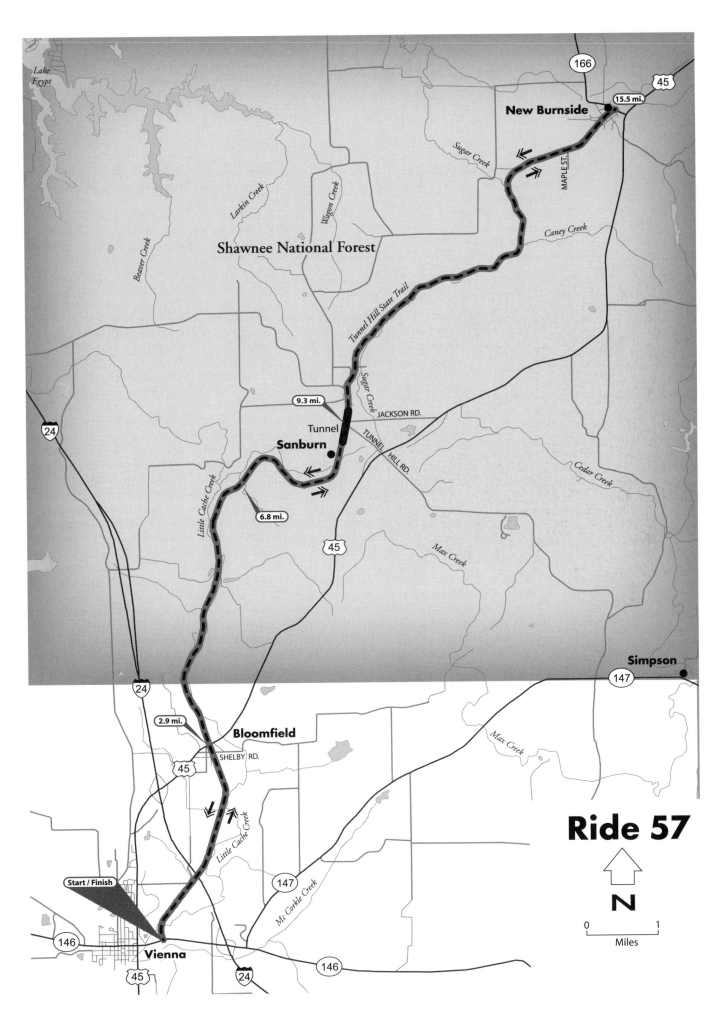

**Ride 57**

N

0 — 1
Miles

# RIDE 58
## Loop of the Gods

**Location:** Gallatin and Hardin counties
**Distance:** 25.1 miles
**Pedaling time:** 2–3 hours
**Surface:** Chip-seal roads
**Terrain:** Hilly
**Sweat factor:** High
**Trailhead:** Observation Trail parking lot, Garden of the Gods

### Shawnee Biking

There is plenty of great bicycling in Shawnee National Forest. Aside from state highways, most roads have low traffic. The many dirt and gravel roads provide plenty of mountain biking opportunities, too. Mountain biking also is permitted on system trails within the forest except in designated wilderness or natural areas (the area around Garden of the Gods is one such wilderness area). The forest is in the process of updating its Land and Resource Management Plan, which may change those rules in the future. The Shawnee Mountain Bike Association is the best resource for trail riding in and around the forest. This group is working with forest personnel and the International Mountain Biking Association to develop and maintain trails and access to them. Visit www.smbatrails.com for more information.

The most famous natural feature in Shawnee National Forest is the Garden of the Gods. Photos of its striking rock formations grace nearly every brochure about the region. As you may expect after driving to the Observation Trail parking lot at Garden of the Gods Recreation Area, this is a very hilly ride, possibly the toughest in this book.

Zero your odometer where the one-way loop returns to the park road and keep right to head out of the park. The River-to-River Trail, which is for equestrians and hikers, crosses the road. Begin climbing your first hill soon after, then climb another hill before you even get out of the park. At the end of the road, turn left on Garden of the Gods Road and climb some more. You are climbing a formation known as Buzzards Point. As you wind around the curves, it kicks up steeper, then finally levels off. This tree-lined road is like a giant rollercoaster, including a long, fast descent at 3.2 miles. At the stop sign, turn right on Barrett Cemetery Road, which is also labeled Gape Hollow Road. This road has fewer trees, and around 6.1 miles you can see a coal mining operation to your left. As you come over a hill at 7 miles, turn right on High Knob Road. Cross Little Eagle Creek, then go uphill to the intersection with Leamington Road at 7.6 miles. Visibility is poor, so approach carefully before turning left. Leamington Road has a few rolling hills, but they are nothing compared to the monsters you've seen. Pass Leamington Church Road on the left, then turn right on Thacker Hollow Road at 9.6 miles. At Burroughs Road, keep left to stay on Thacker Hollow Road. This road is a cyclist's treat—trees, curves, and a few steep but short hills make this a nice place to ride. The road is narrow, but traffic is very light. The Trail's End Restaurant at 11.7 miles has a pop machine outside.

At the end of this enjoyable road, turn right on State Highway 1, which is designated as the Illinois Korean War Veterans Highway. This road has some truck traffic, but you won't be on it for long. After less than a mile, turn right on Pounds Hollow Road toward Karbers Ridge. The motel and restaurant on the corner have a pop machine outside. The big hills return to the mix as you climb for the better part of a mile, get a downhill reprieve, and then do it again. You ride past the popular Rim Rock Trail; you may want to come back later for a hike. The road's name changes to Karbers Ridge Road at the Hardin County line (16.8 miles). The town of Karbers Ridge has no services, but there is a post office at 20.5 miles. After two more miles of rolling hills, turn right on Garden of the Gods Road at 22.3 miles. You climb again, then descend to the bridge over Rose Creek. The next big climb gets steep, but the good news is that you get to turn into Garden of the Gods Recreation Area at 23.7 miles before you reach the top. Of course, you already climbed the rest of the hill near the beginning of the ride anyway. Now you have to climb the descents you enjoyed at the start. The ride finishes with a hill that you swear couldn't have been as steep when you went down it hours ago.

If your legs haven't turned to jelly, hike the Observation Trail to see what all the fuss is about. It's only a quarter of a mile long, but it might take you half an hour with all the ups and downs, not to mention taking time to enjoy the views. For more ambitious hikers, there are many more miles of trails around the Garden of the Gods, along with the River-to-River Trail.

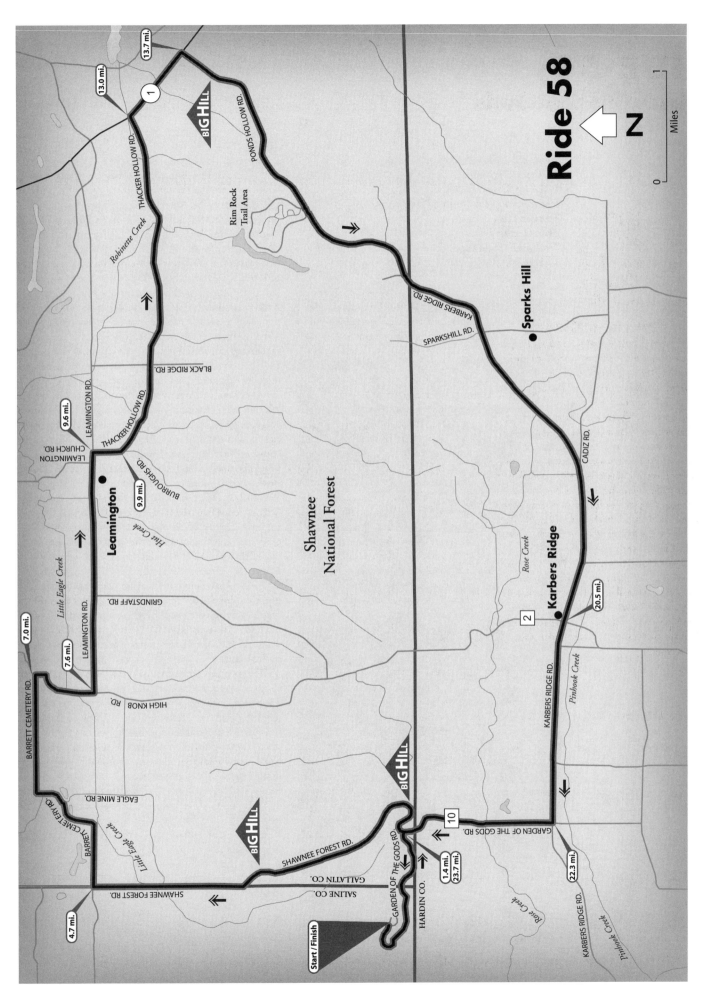

Ride 58

N

Miles

Start / Finish

119

# RIDE 59
## Lucky Horseshoe

**Location:** Alexander County
**Distance:** 12.2 miles
**Pedaling time:** 60–75 minutes
**Surface:** Paved and chip-seal roads
**Terrain:** Flat
**Sweat factor:** Low
**Trailhead:** Corner of State Highway 3 and Railroad Street, Olive Branch

Note: This ride goes through Horseshoe Lake Conservation Area in far southern Illinois. This is not to be confused with Horseshoe Lake State Park, which is 100 miles to the north in the Saint Louis metro area.

**Is this an Illinois lake or a Louisiana bayou?**

The southern tip of Illinois isn't quite the Deep South, but no one told the trees that grow at Horseshoe Lake Conservation Area: tupelo gum, bald cypress, and swamp cottonwood. It looks more like a Louisiana bayou than an Illinois lake. The area has been phenomenally successful as a wintering site for Canada geese. The park started as a Canada goose sanctuary with a thousand birds in 1928. Now up to 150,000 stay here during the colder months, along with other waterfowl and bald eagles. The 2,400-acre lake is maintained at a depth of four feet. This presented a challenge for anglers; they had to invent a new technique to fish the shallow waters. For the cyclist, Horseshoe Lake offers not only great scenery, but unusually easy terrain for southern Illinois. Ride 60, which has the same trailhead, is more typical.

Take State Highway 3 to Olive Branch. Highway 3 has two mini-marts and a grocery store for last-minute supplies, plus a restaurant. Turn north on Railroad Street from Highway 3. There is ample parking at the park on the right, next to Horseshoe Lake Community Center. Begin the ride heading southeast on Highway 3. This is a well-traveled road, but it has a wide, paved shoulder. At 1.9 miles, continue past Refuge Office Road. Turn right on East Side Drive at 3.1 miles and head straight toward the lake. There is a campground ahead to the right, but the road takes a sharp left instead and follows the shoreline of the lake. Here you can get a good look at "Bayou Horseshoe." Along the way, there is a tavern on the left with a pop machine on the right. There are toilets and drinking fountains scattered throughout the campgrounds and picnic areas. Turn right on Promised Land Road where a picnic area with a playground is located. As you pedal over the nearby bridge, you can see the concrete spillway that regulates the lake's depth to your right. Make the next right turn on West Side Drive, which traces the inside of the horseshoe. This narrow road passes a few campgrounds. You can also see several wood piers that extend into the lake. Take a walk out on one to be surrounded by the sounds of birds.

At the west end of the lake, there is a huge mass of wild lotus visible from the road. In June the wild lotus is in full bloom. When this road ends at Miller City Road, turn right. Miller City Road has more traffic than the roads through the conservation area, but it isn't heavy. Island Road goes off to the right at 11 miles. This gravel road leads to a short gravel trail near the lake which is best suited to mountain bikes. As you approach the stop sign at Highway 3 in Olive Branch, veer right on an unmarked road. The ride ends at Highway 3, and Railroad Street is straight ahead.

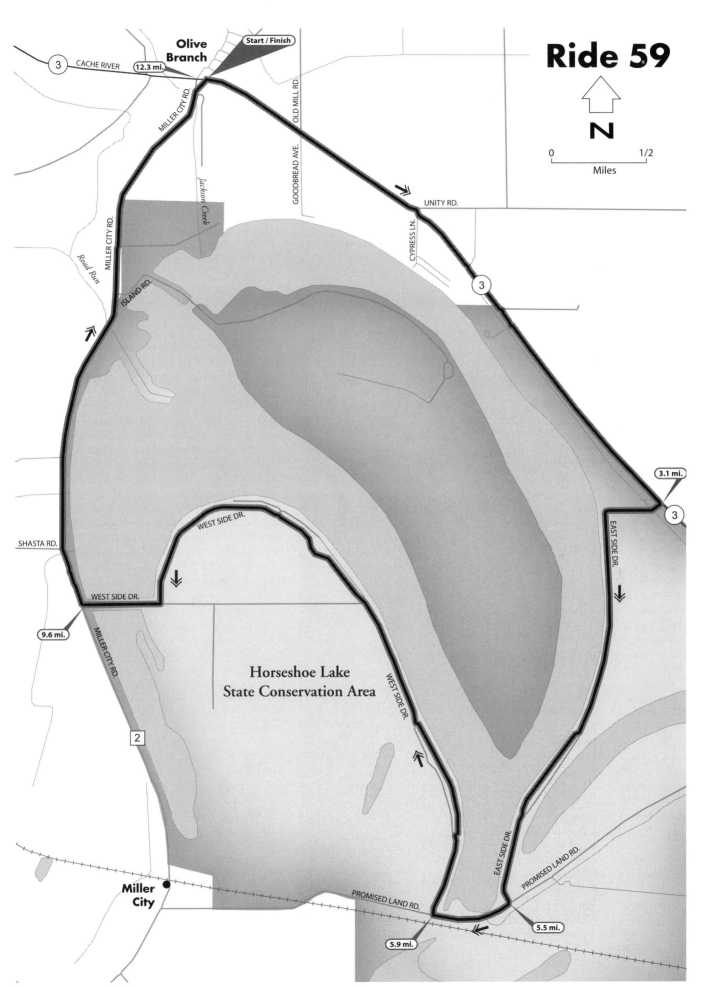

**Ride 59**

N

0        1/2

Miles

Olive Branch

Start / Finish

3  CACHE RIVER  12.3 mi.

MILLER CITY RD.

OLD MILL RD.

GOODBREAD AVE.

Jackson Creek

MILLER CITY RD.

Road Run

ISLAND RD.

UNITY RD.

CYPRESS LN.

3

3.1 mi.

3

SHASTA RD.

WEST SIDE DR.

WEST SIDE DR.

EAST SIDE DR.

9.6 mi.

MILLER CITY RD.

2

Horseshoe Lake
State Conservation Area

WEST SIDE DR.

EAST SIDE DR.

Miller City

PROMISED LAND RD.

PROMISED LAND RD.

5.5 mi.

5.9 mi.

# RIDE 60
## Give Peace a Chance

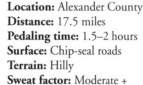

**Location:** Alexander County
**Distance:** 17.5 miles
**Pedaling time:** 1.5–2 hours
**Surface:** Chip-seal roads
**Terrain:** Hilly
**Sweat factor:** Moderate +
**Trailhead:** Corner of State Highway 3 and Railroad Street, Olive Branch

### Shawnee National Forest

Shawnee National Forest is undoubtedly the recreational highlight of Southern Illinois. It stretches from the Ohio River to the Mississippi River. In between, it encompasses such sights as the Garden of the Gods, Lusk Creek Canyon, and the Little Grand Canyon.

One might think that this scenic treasure is a great example of the pioneers' foresight to protect green space for recreation, but the reality is quite the opposite. In fact, almost the entire forest is less than a hundred years old. Early Illinois farmers cleared the existing trees to grow crops, but the land was ill suited for that purpose. By 1930, many farmers had given up, some of them simply abandoning their property. Not only were they unable to make a living, their farming practices were devastating to the land. Erosion was a terrible problem in this hilly region.

In 1933, a national forest was created to acquire and stabilize this land. Actually, two national forest "purchase units" were designated. The area near the Ohio River was the Shawnee Unit, and the area including Alexander County along the Mississippi was called the Illini Unit. The two relatively small forests were combined in 1939. While certainly recreation was an intended use, the primary purposes were erosion prevention, timber production, and demonstration of correct forestry methods.

For more information about Shawnee National Forest, see www.fs.fed.us/r9/forests/shawnee/ or call (800) 699-6637 (office open Monday–Friday from 8 to 4:30).

Although this ride starts in Olive Branch and traverses bucolic farmland and shady forests, it is not entirely peaceful. You will wage war against some steep hills and a few chasing dogs. This ride may begin at the same spot as Ride 59, but it covers very different terrain. There are no services on this ride, so stock up on water and food before you leave Olive Branch.

Head west on busy but wide-shouldered State Highway 3 and turn left on Fayville Road at the Kozy Korner Café. Follow this road out of town. Continue straight at Twente Crossing Road, but turn right at 3.1 miles on Twente School Road. It's been pretty peaceful so far, but the fun begins with a long climb at 3.5 miles. This area is known as the Santa Fe Hills. After a few ups and downs, there is a steep descent around 5 miles. You can coast to the stop sign at Rock Springs Hollow Road, where you turn left. This road starts calmly, then turns mean at 5.8 miles, including an extra kick near the summit. Fortunately, you get a chance to recover from that effort over the next couple of miles. The road skirts the edge of Shawnee National Forest, and sometimes you can see Orchard Creek through the trees to the south. All good things must come to an end, and this pleasant road terminates at Rock Springs Road at 8.5 miles. Turn right and begin a long but gentle and shaded climb. Like other hills on this ride, this one gets steep near the top.

You won't see it as you climb toward the stop sign at 9.8 miles, but this road continues on the other side of Highway 3, its name changing to Bracken Ford Road. Half a mile later, turn right on Brownville Road at the T. This road also parallels a creek. As you approach trees at 11.6 miles, keep right at the Y to stay on Brownville Road. There is another big hill at 13.2 miles. This one also gets steep near the summit as it passes Mount Zion Cemetery. At the top of the hill, turn left on Greg Hollow Road. The reward for your efforts comes at 14.4 miles. You can coast for at least half a mile on this long descent. At 16 miles, go straight onto Pigeon Roost Road. There is one last short, steep climb ahead, followed by a steep descent with a sharp curve to the right at the bottom. Pigeon Roost Road gradually leads back to Highway 3 in Olive Branch at 17.2 miles. Turn left on the highway and finish at Railroad Street.

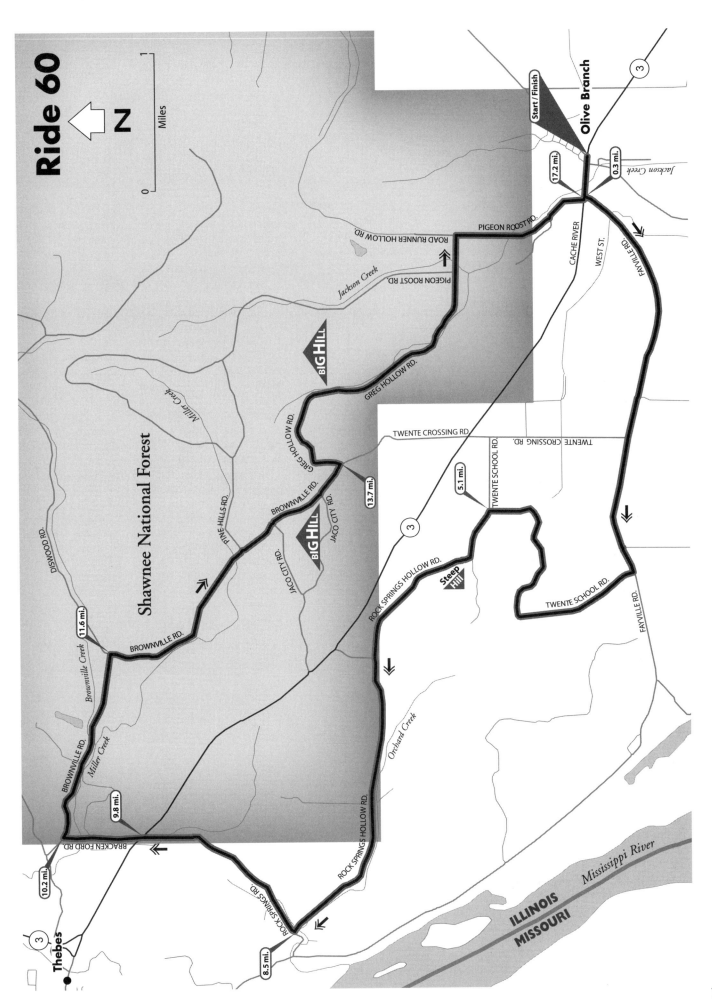

# SHORT INDEX OF RIDES

## State Parks, Trails, and Forests
14. A Gift From the Glaciers
33. Bring Your Quiver to the River
34. Goodbye Norma Jean
37. A Mighty Good Trail
39. Havana
50. Watch for Wild Turkeys
54. Giant City
57. Tunnel Vision

## Rail Trails
3. Jane Addams Trail
5. Long Trail on the Prairie
16. Hangin' on the Elgin Branch
23. The Corn Belt Route
24. Virgil Gilman Trail
25. Great Western Prairie Triangle
32. Ride the Plank
37. A Mighty Good Trail
43. Where's the Bridge?
57. Tunnel Vision

## Rollin' by the River
6. Windmill and Cactus
7. Where the River Runs West
15. Frolic Along the Fox
19. Des Plaines River Trail
26. Take Me to the Zoo
46. Bluffing on the Mississippi
47. Lewis and Clark

## Man-Made Rivers
8. Trail to Tampico
11. Ride the White Elephant
12. End of the I & M
22. Pedaling the Channel
31. Make Like a Mule

## Lakes
27. Cooler by the Lake
28. Museums and Beaches
35. Spoon Lake
50. Watch for Wild Turkeys
59. Lucky Horseshoe

## Forest Preserves
17. Poplar Creek Trail
18. Busse Woods
19. Des Plaines River Trail
20. Going to the Garden
26. Take Me to the Zoo
29. Lap Around the Lab
30. Tinley Creek Trail
40. Short But Sweet

## Who Says Illinois is Flat?
1. Hellacious Hills of Hanover
2. Are You in Shape for Schapville?
13. Hills and Valleys
51. Merry Miles to Maeystown
52. Ava Loop
54. Giant City
55. Climb to the Cross
56. Dongola Churches
58. Loop of the Gods
60. Give Peace a Chance

## Okay, Maybe It's a Little Flat
11. Ride the White Elephant
12. End of the I & M
16. Hangin' on the Elgin Branch
23. The Corn Belt Route
25. Great Western Prairie Triangle
31. Make Like a Mule
44. Ambling Among the Amish
53. Gorham Floodplain
59. Lucky Horseshoe

## Along I-57
30. Tinley Creek Trail
32. Ride the Plank
33. Bring Your Quiver to the River
44. Ambling Among the Amish
50. Watch for Wild Turkeys
56. Dongola Churches

## Historic Highways
21. Sheridan Road
38. Around the Lake and Down Memory Lane
47. Lewis and Clark
49. Greenville

## Cities
4. Ride the Rock
7. Where the River Runs West
27. Cooler by the Lake
28. Museums and Beaches
36. Historic Galesburg

## History Comes Alive
2. Are You in Shape for Schapville?
9. Deere Country
25. Great Western Prairie Triangle
42. Follow in Young Abe's Footsteps
47. Lewis and Clark

# APPENDIX A: FOR MORE INFORMATION

## General Bicycling

Mike's Mega Bicycle Links – This site includes links to shops, clubs, manufacturers, and much, much more: *www.mikebentley.com/bike/index.html*

Mike's Illinois Bicycle Rides – This is the most complete list of event rides in Illinois, including contact information for each one: *www.mikebentley.com/bike/ilrides.htm*

Harris Cyclery – Sheldon Brown's site is packed with useful information about all aspects of bicycles and bicycling: *www.sheldonbrown.com/articles.html*

*www.bikingillinois.com* – This site is dedicated to the book in your hands. Visit for updates, extra photographs, and more.

## Advocacy

League of Illinois Bicyclists – This statewide organization lobbies for cyclists' rights and promotes bicycle access, education, and safety: 2550 Cheshire Drive, Aurora, IL 60504 (630) 978-0583 *www.bikelib.org*

Chicagoland Bicycle Federation – This group works to improve the bicycling environment in northeastern Illinois: 9 W. Hubbard St. Suite 402, Chicago, IL 60610-6545 (312) 427-3325 *www.biketraffic.org*

## State of Illinois

Illinois Department of Natural Resources – For information about state parks, forests, trails, wildlife refuges, etc.: One Natural Resource Way, Springfield, Il 62702-1271 (217) 782-7454. *www.dnr.state.il.us*

For an alphabetical list of trails, parks and forests, see *www.dnr.state.il.us/lands/landmgt/parks/ilstate.htm*

Illinois Bureau of Tourism: (800) 2CONNECT *www.enjoyillinois.com*

# MORE
# GREAT TITLES
## FROM TRAILS BOOKS & PRAIRIE OAK PRESS

## Activity Guides

**Biking Wisconsin: 50 Great Road and Trail Rides,** Steve Johnson
**Biking Iowa,** Bob Morgan
**Great Cross-Country Ski Trails: Wisconsin, Minnesota, Michigan & Ontario,**
Wm. Chad McGrath
**Great Iowa Walks: 50 Strolls, Rambles, Hikes, and Treks,** Lynn L. Walters
**Great Midwest Country Escapes,** Nina Gadowski
**Great Minnesota Walks: 49 Strolls, Rambles, Hikes, and Treks,** Wm. Chad McGrath
**Great Wisconsin Walks: 45 Strolls, Rambles, Hikes, and Treks,** Wm. Chad McGrath
**Horsing Around in Wisconsin,** Anne M. Connor
**Iowa Underground,** Greg A. Brick
**Minnesota Underground & the Best of the Black Hills,** Doris Green
**Paddling Illinois: 64 Great Trips by Canoe and Kayak,** Mike Svob
**Paddling Iowa: 96 Great Trips by Canoe and Kayak,** Nate Hoogeveen
**Paddling Northern Minnesota: 86 Great Trips by Canoe and Kayak,**
Lynne Smith Diebel
**Paddling Northern Wisconsin: 82 Great Trips by Canoe and Kayak,** Mike Svob
**Paddling Southern Wisconsin: 82 Great Trips by Canoe and Kayak,** Mike Svob
**Walking Tours of Wisconsin's Historic Towns,**
Lucy Rhodes, Elizabeth McBride, Anita Matcha
**Wisconsin's Outdoor Treasures: A Guide to 150 Natural Destinations,** Tim Bewer
**Wisconsin Underground,** Doris Green

## Travel Guides

**Classic Wisconsin Weekends,** Michael Bie
**County Parks of Minnesota,** Timothy J. Engrav
**Great Indiana Weekend Adventures,** Sally McKinney
**Great Iowa Weekend Adventures,** Mike Whye
**Great Little Museums of the Midwest,** Christine des Garennes
**Great Minnesota Taverns,** David K. Wright & Monica G. Wright
**Great Minnesota Weekend Adventures,** Beth Gauper
**Great Weekend Adventures,** the Editors of Wisconsin Trails
**Great Wisconsin Romantic Weekends,** Christine des Garennes
**Great Wisconsin Taverns: 101 Distinctive Badger Bars,** Dennis Boyer
**Iowa's Hometown Flavors,** Donna Tabbert Long
**Sacred Sites of Minnesota,** John-Brian Paprock & Teresa Peneguy Paprock
**Sacred Sites of Wisconsin,** John-Brian Paprock & Teresa Peneguy Paprock
**Tastes of Minnesota: A Food Lover's Tour,** Donna Tabbert Long
**Twin Cities Restaurant Guide,** Carla Waldemar
**The Great Indiana Touring Book: 20 Spectacular Auto Trips,** Thomas Huhti
**The Great Iowa Touring Book: 27 Spectacular Auto Trips,** Mike Whye
**The Great Minnesota Touring Book: 30 Spectacular Auto Trips,** Thomas Huhti
**The Great Wisconsin Touring Book: 30 Spectacular Auto Tours,** Gary Knowles
**Wisconsin Family Weekends: 20 Fun Trips for You and the Kids,**
Susan Lampert Smith
**Wisconsin Golf Getaways,** Jeff Mayers and Jerry Poling

Wisconsin Lighthouses: A Photographic and Historical Guide,
Ken and Barb Wardius
Wisconsin's Hometown Flavors, Terese Allen
Wisconsin Waterfalls, Patrick Lisi
Up North Wisconsin: A Region for All Seasons, Sharyn Alden

## Home & Garden

Codfather 2, Jeff Hagen
Creating a Perennial Garden in the Midwest, Joan Severa
Eating Well in Wisconsin, Jerry Minnich
Foods That Made Wisconsin Famous: 150 Great Recipes, Richard J. Baumann
Midwest Cottage Gardening, Frances Manos
North Woods Cottage Cookbook, Jerry Minnich
Wisconsing Almanac, Jerry Minnich
Wisconsin Country Gourmet, Marge Snyder & Suzanne Breckenridge
Wisconsin Garden Guide, Jerry Minnich
Wisconsin Wildfoods: 100 Recipes for Badger State Bounties, John Motouiloff

## Historical Books

Duck Hunting on the Fox: Hunting and Decoy-Carving Traditions,
Stephen M. Miller
Grand Army of the Republic: Department of Wisconsin, Thomas J. McCrory
Prairie Whistles: Tales of Midwest Railroading, Dennis Boyer
Shipwrecks of Lake Michigan, Benjamin J. Shelak
Wisconsin At War: 20th Century Conflicts Through the Eyes of Veterans,
Dr. James F. McIntosh, M.D.
Wisconsin's Historic Houses & Living History Museums, Krista Finstad Hanso

## Gift Books

Celebrating Door County's Wild Places, The Ridges Sanctuary
Madison, Photography by Brent Nicastro
Milwaukee, Photography by Todd Dacquisto
Spirit of the North: A Photographic Journey Through Northern Wisconsin,
Richard Hamilton Smith
The Spirit of Door County: A Photographic Essay, Darryl R. Beers

## Legends and Lore

Driftless Spirits: Ghosts of Southwest Wisconsin, Dennis Boyer
Haunted Wisconsin, Michael Norman and Beth Scott
Hunting the American Werewolf, Linda S. Godfrey
The Beast of Bray Road: Tailing Wisconsin's Werewolf, Linda S. Godfrey
The Eagle's Voice: Tales Told by Indian Effigy Mounds, Gary J. Maier, M.D.
The Poison Widow: A True Story of Sin, Strychnine, & Murder, Linda S. Godfrey
The W-Files: True Reports of Wisconsin's Unexplained Phenomena, Jay Rath

## Young Readers

**ABCs Naturally,** Lynne Smith Diebel & Jann Faust Kalscheur
**ABCs of Wisconsin,** Dori Hillestad Butler, Illustrated by Alison Relyea
**H is for Hawkeye,** Jay Wagner, Illustrated by Eileen Potts Dawson
**H is for Hoosier,** Dori Hillestad Butler, Illustrated by Eileen Potts Dawson
**Wisconsin Portraits,** Martin Hintz
**Wisconsin Sports Heroes,** Martin Hintz
**W is for Wisconsin,** Dori Hillestad Butler, Illustrated by Eileen Potts Dawson

## Sports

**Always a Badger: The Pat Richter Story,** Vince Sweeney
**Baseball in Beertown: America's Pastime in Milwaukee,** Todd Mishler
**Before They Were the Packers: Green Bay's Town Team Days,**
Denis J. Gullickson & Carl Hanson
**Cold Wars: 40+ Years of Packer-Viking Rivalry,** Todd Mishler
**Great Moments in Wisconsin Sports,** Todd Mishler
**Green Bay Packers Titletown Trivia Teasers,** Don Davenport
**Mean on Sunday: The Autobiography of Ray Nitschke,** Robert W. Wells
**Mudbaths and Bloodbaths: The Inside Story of the Bears-Packers Rivalry,**
Gary D'Amato & Cliff Christl
**Packers By the Numbers: Jersey Numbers and the Players Who Wore Them,**
John Maxymuk

**For a free catalog, phone, write, or visit us online.**

## Trails Books
a division of Big Earth Publishing
923 Williamson Street
Madison, WI 53703
www.trailsbooks.com